D1123742

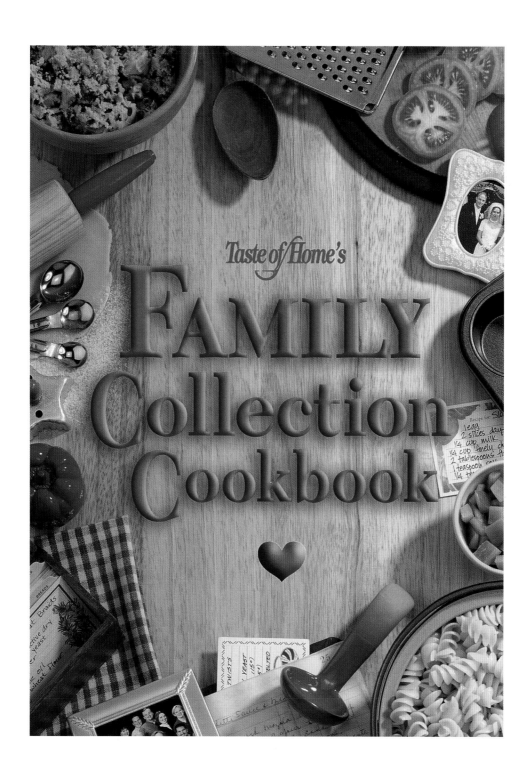

Taste of Home's

FAMILY
Collection
Cookbook

Reader's
Digest

The Reader's Digest Association, Inc.
Pleasantville, New York/Montreal

A READER'S DIGEST BOOK

Taste of Home Books
© 2006 Reiman Media Group, Inc.
5400 S. 60th Street, Greendale, WI 53129

Editor: Michelle Bretl
Art Director: Maribeth Greinke
Executive Editor, Books: Heidi Lloyd
Associate Editor: Beth Wittlinger
Associate Art Director: Lori Arndt
Cover Design: George McKeon
Graphic Art Associates: Ellen Lloyd, Catherine Fletcher
Editorial Assistant: Barb Czysz

Food Editor: Janaan Cunningham
Associate Food Editors: Coleen Martin, Diane Werner
Senior Recipe Editor: Sue A. Jurack
Recipe Editors: Janet Briggs, Mary King
Test Kitchen Director: Mark Morgan
Test Kitchen Home Economists: Peggy Fleming,
Nancy Fridirici, Tina Johnson, Ann Liebergen, Pat Schmeling,
Wendy Stenman, Amy Welk-Thieding, Karen Wright
Test Kitchen Assistants: Suzanne Kern, Rita Krajcir,
Kris Lehman, Sue Megonigle, Megan Taylor

Food Photograpers: Rob Hagen, Dan Roberts
Set Stylists: Julie Ferron, Stephanie Marchese,
Sue Myers, Jennifer Bradley Vent
Food Stylists: Kristin Arnett,
Sarah Thompson, Joylyn Trickel
Photographers Assistant: Lori Foy

Senior Vice President, Editor in Chief:
Catherine Cassidy
President: Barbara Newton
Chairman and Founder: Roy Reiman

International Standard Book Number: 0-89821-448-3
Library of Congress Control Number: 2005901780

For more Reader's Digest products and information,
visit our website at www.rd.com

Printed in China

3 5 7 9 10 8 6 4

Table of Contents

Here's Your Chance to Peek Inside The Recipe Collections of Families From Across the Country

EVERY FAMILY has its favorite recipes…from best-loved treasures made by Grandma that have been passed down through the generations to newfound dishes recently added to a family's files.

These recipes may be handwritten in a dog-eared notebook, recorded on recipe cards in a well-worn box or even published as a family's own cookbook. However they're preserved, they form enduring collections as unique and varied as each family itself.

Ever wish you could peek inside some of these one-of-a-kind compilations? Now you can! In this exciting new book from the editors at *Taste of Home* magazine, cooks from across the country have shared favorite recipes—438 of them—straight from their own special family collections.

The Recipes Families Love

Hundreds of cooks have revealed their very best dishes in this heirloom-quality book. You'll discover long-kept secret family recipes, traditional "must-have" Christmas treats, crowd-pleasing picnic and party fare and plenty of old-fashioned gems just like Mom used to make.

Page through, and you'll also find regional specialties that showcase local flavor…signature dishes created by talented family cooks…and delicious twists on recipes that are time-tested standbys.

Twelve big chapters give you home-style main dishes, breads, soups, appetizers, side dishes, desserts and much more. No matter what kind of recipe you're looking for, you'll find something special in this time-honored treasury.

Because every single recipe in this classic cookbook has been tested by the home economists in the *Taste of Home* Test Kitchen, you're guaranteed to have successful results no matter what fare you fix.

A Colorful, Practical Cookbook

Many of the recipes have gorgeous full-color photos of the prepared dish, showing exactly what it'll look like on your table. You'll want to page through each chapter just to see the wide variety of prized recipes that have been shared from coast to coast.

To help you locate a specific dish you may need, we've included two indexes at the back of the book. The General Index lists recipes by course, ingredient and cooking method, while the Alphabetical Index lists each recipe by name.

In this jam-packed book, you'll also find tried-and-true kitchen tips, plus amusing and thought-provoking quotes that celebrate the very meaning of the word "family."

Make *Taste of Home's Family Collection Cookbook* a cherished part of your own family recipe collection…and start all-new mealtime traditions your loved ones are sure to enjoy for generations to come.

family

Chapter one

Christmas celebrations…family reunions…

annual parties…they're all extra-special when you

start them off with appetizing bites and refreshing

beverages. Look here to find super snacks and

thirst-quenchers that have been tasty traditions

at family events for years. These favorites are

sure to please your loved ones, too.

Cheddar-Bacon Dip (Recipe on page 8)

♥ Appetizers & Beverages

LINDA'S BLT SPREAD

(Pictured above)

This spread is a different way to enjoy the winning combination of bacon, lettuce and tomato. It's especially flavorful using garden tomatoes.
—Linda Nilsen, Anoka, Minnesota

1/2 cup sour cream
1/2 cup mayonnaise
1/2 pound bacon, cooked and crumbled
  1 small tomato, diced
Small lettuce leaves
Toasted snack bread *or* crackers
Assorted fresh vegetables

In a bowl, combine sour cream, mayonnaise and bacon; mix well. Stir in tomato. Serve with lettuce, bread, crackers and fresh vegetables. **Yield:** 1-1/2 cups.

CHEDDAR-BACON DIP

(Pictured on page 7)

Both children and adults enjoy this dip. I make it for special occasions like birthdays or holiday parties.
—Carol Werkman, Neerlandia, Alberta

1 package (8 ounces) cream cheese, softened
1 cup (8 ounces) sour cream
5 green onions, thinly sliced
4 medium tomatoes, chopped
1 large green pepper, chopped
1 jar (16 ounces) taco sauce
2 cups (8 ounces) shredded cheddar cheese
1 pound sliced bacon, cooked and crumbled
Tortilla *or* taco chips

In a mixing bowl, beat cream cheese and sour cream. Spread in an ungreased 13-in. x 9-in. x 2-in. dish or on a 12-in. plate. Combine onions, tomatoes and green pepper; sprinkle over the cream cheese layer. Pour taco sauce over the vegetables. Sprinkle with cheddar cheese. Refrigerate. Just before serving, sprinkle with bacon. Serve with tortilla or taco chips. **Yield:** 10-12 servings.

Family-Tested Tips

Save and freeze little bits and pieces of leftover bacon from breakfast—they can quickly be added to spreads and dips. Or, use the bacon bits as a fast flavor-enhancer for casseroles and other dishes.
—Lucy Mohlman, Crete, Nebraska

Before grating cheese, spray the grater with non-stick cooking spray. The cheese will fall off without sticking, and the grater will be easier to clean, too.
—Christine Arter, Crestline, Ohio

Use your favorite ranch salad dressing as a no-fuss dip for fresh vegetables and pretzels. Choose a low-fat dressing if you want a snack that's lighter.
—Sue Call, Beech Grove, Indiana

SPICY TOMATO JUICE

(Pictured below)

Drink this juice plain or use it in most any recipe, such as chili, that calls for vegetable juice as an ingredient.
—Kathleen Gill, Butte, Montana

13 pounds ripe tomatoes (about 40 medium)
 2 celery ribs, coarsely chopped
 3 medium onions, coarsely chopped
 1 medium green pepper, coarsely chopped
1-1/2 cups chopped fresh parsley
 1/2 cup sugar
 1 tablespoon Worcestershire sauce
 4 teaspoons salt
 1/4 teaspoon hot pepper sauce
 1/4 teaspoon cayenne pepper
 1/4 teaspoon pepper

Quarter tomatoes; place in a 6-qt. kettle. Add the celery, onions, green pepper and parsley. Simmer, uncovered, until vegetables are tender, about 45 minutes, stirring occasionally.

Cool slightly; put through a sieve or food mill. Return to kettle. Add remaining ingredients; mix well. Bring to a boil. Remove from the heat; cool. Pour into freezer containers, leaving 1/2-in. headspace. Freeze for up to 12 months. **Yield:** about 5 quarts.

ITALIAN SNACK BREAD

This snack bread's very versatile—I've served it with spaghetti, as an appetizer and as a main dish. Because it stays so moist, I often bake it a day before.
—Joan Nowacki, Pewaukee, Wisconsin

2-1/2 cups all-purpose flour, *divided*
 1 package (1/4 ounce) active dry yeast
2-1/2 teaspoons dried oregano
 1/2 teaspoon salt
 1 cup warm water (120° to 130°)
 2 tablespoons olive oil
 1 egg, beaten
TOPPING:
1-1/2 cups thinly sliced onion
 1/4 cup olive oil
 1 teaspoon dried rosemary, crushed
 1 teaspoon coarse salt, optional

In a large bowl, combine 1-1/2 cups flour, yeast, oregano and salt. Stir in water, oil and egg; mix well. Stir in enough remaining flour to form a soft dough. Cover and let rest 10 minutes. Pat into a greased 13-in. x 9-in. x 2-in. baking pan; set aside.

In a skillet, saute onion in oil until tender. Spoon evenly over dough. Sprinkle with rosemary and salt if desired. Cover and let rise in warm place until doubled, about 30 minutes. Bake at 400° for 25-30 minutes or until lightly browned. Cut into small squares. Serve warm or at room temperature. **Yield:** about 8 servings.

LEMON-LIME PUNCH

This festive-looking green punch has starred at many holiday parties and other events. The recipe comes from a cookbook I received when I was a child. The cover is lost now, and the pages are yellowing...but the recipes are as wonderful as ever.
—Karen Engstrand, Alma, Wisconsin

1   **envelope (.13 ounce) unsweetened lemon-lime drink mix**
1   **quart pineapple juice, chilled**
1   **quart lime sherbet**
2   **quarts ginger ale, chilled**

Pour drink mix into a punch bowl. Stir in pineapple juice. Spoon sherbet into bowl; add ginger ale and stir gently. Serve immediately. **Yield:** about 3-1/2 quarts.

BLACKBERRY FIZZ

For a refreshing beverage with a distinctive berry flavor and a hint of spice, try this recipe. We save it for holidays and special times with family and friends. It's a delightful drink people will remember.
—Andrea Eberly, Sarasota, Florida

3   **quarts fresh *or* frozen blackberries**
4   **cups water**
3   **cups sugar**
1   **tablespoon whole cloves**
1   **tablespoon whole allspice**
2   **cinnamon sticks (4 inches), broken**
Lemon-lime *or* white soda

Crush the blackberries in a large kettle. Add water and bring to a boil. Reduce heat to medium and cook for 10 minutes. Strain through a jelly bag, reserving juice and discarding pulp.

Add water to juice if necessary to equal 2 qts.; pour into a large kettle. Slowly stir in sugar until dissolved. Place spices in a cheesecloth bag; add to juice. Simmer, uncovered, for 30 minutes. Bring to a boil; remove the spice bag and discard.

Pour hot into hot jars, leaving 1/4-in. headspace. Adjust caps. Process for 15 minutes in a boiling-water bath. To serve, mix about one-third concentrate with two-thirds soda. **Yield:** about 4 pints concentrate.

PEANUT BUTTER APPLE DIP

At our family gatherings, I'm "required" to serve this creamy dip—so I'm thankful it mixes up so quickly! It's especially attractive served with red and green apple wedges.
—Kim Marie Van Rheenen, Mendota, Illinois

1   **package (8 ounces) cream cheese, softened**
1   **cup peanut butter**
1   **cup packed brown sugar**
1/4   **cup milk**
3   **to 4 apples, cut into wedges**

In a mixing bowl, combine the first four ingredients; mix well. Serve with apples. Store in the refrigerator. **Yield:** 2-2/3 cups.

"In every conceivable manner, the family is link to our past, bridge to our future."
—Alex Haley

SPICY CHICKEN WINGS

(Pictured above)

This area is known for its delicious chicken wings, and these are the best I've ever tasted. They're always popular served alongside carrots, celery sticks and blue cheese dressing.
—Varina Caton, Appleton, New York

16 to 18 chicken wings (about 4 pounds)
Vegetable oil
1/2 cup butter, melted
1/2 cup hot pepper sauce
2 tablespoons cider vinegar
Carrots and celery sticks
Blue cheese dressing

Cut wings into three pieces; discard the wing tips. Fry chicken in hot oil until crisp and juices run clear (5-7 minutes for the small part, 6-8 minutes for drumettes). Combine butter, hot pepper sauce and vinegar in a bowl; add chicken and toss to coat. Drain. Serve with carrots, celery and dressing. **Yield:** about 3 dozen.

HOT PIZZA DIP

(Pictured below)

*I love this cheesy pizza-flavored recipe because it's easy to prepare in advance
and keep refrigerated. Put it in the oven when guests arrive, and by the time you've poured beverages,
the dip is ready to serve. If you like, add bits of pepperoni or chopped onion.*
—Karen Riordan, Fern Creek, Kentucky

1 package (8 ounces) cream cheese,
   softened
1 teaspoon Italian seasoning
1/4 teaspoon garlic powder
2 cups (8 ounces) shredded mozzarella
   cheese
1 cup (4 ounces) shredded cheddar cheese
1/2 cup pizza sauce
1/2 cup finely chopped green pepper
1/2 cup finely chopped sweet red pepper
Tortilla chips *or* breadsticks

In a bowl, combine cream cheese, Italian seasoning and garlic powder; spread on the bottom of a greased 9-in. pie plate. Combine cheeses; sprinkle half over the cream cheese layer. Top with the pizza sauce and peppers. Sprinkle with the remaining cheeses. Bake at 350° for 20 minutes. Serve warm with tortilla chips or breadsticks. **Yield:** about 3-1/2 cups.

HEARTY CHEESE SPREAD

(Pictured at right)

I use the red wax covering from gouda cheese to make a "poinsettia" bowl in which to serve this treat.
—Ferne Nicolaisen, Cherokee, Iowa

- 1 **gouda cheese round in red wax covering (7 ounces), room temperature**
- 1 **package (2-1/2 ounces) smoked sliced beef, finely chopped**
- 1/4 **cup sour cream**
- 2 **tablespoons sweet pickle relish**
- 2 **teaspoons prepared horseradish**

Apple slices *or* crackers

Carefully slice through wax and cheese to within 1 in. of the bottom, forming eight pie-shaped wedges. Carefully fold wax back to expose cheese; remove cheese.

In a mixing bowl, beat the cheese until creamy. Add the beef, sour cream, relish and horseradish; mix well. Spoon into wax shell. Chill. Serve with apple slices or crackers. **Yield:** 1-1/2 cups.

FRIED ONION RINGS

Try these as an accompaniment to hamburgers or fried fish, or with steaks on the grill. The recipe's from my mom, and it's one of her most popular.
—Marsha Moore, Poplar Bluff, Missouri

- 2 **large sweet onions**
- 1 **egg, lightly beaten**
- 2/3 **cup water**
- 1 **tablespoon vegetable oil**
- 1 **teaspoon lemon juice**
- 1 **cup all-purpose flour**
- 1-1/2 **teaspoons baking powder**
- 1 **to 1-1/4 teaspoons salt**
- 1/8 **to 1/4 teaspoon cayenne pepper**

Vegetable oil for deep-fat frying

Cut onions into 1/2-in. slices; separate into rings. Place in a bowl; cover with ice water and soak for 30 minutes. Meanwhile, combine egg, water, oil and lemon juice in a bowl; mix well. Combine flour, baking powder, salt and cayenne; stir into egg mixture until smooth.

Drain onion rings; dip into batter. In an electric skillet or deep-fat fryer, heat 1 in. of oil to 375°. Fry onion rings, a few at a time, for 1 to 1-1/2 minutes per side or until golden brown. Drain on paper towels. **Yield:** 4-6 servings.

Editor's Note: Onion rings may be kept warm in a 300° oven while frying remainder of batch.

NEW YEAR'S PUNCH

It's tradition for our family to ring in the New Year with this sparkling beverage. The punch is so quick to stir together, I've also prepared it for springtime luncheons and bridal showers.
—Audrey Thibodeau, Mesa, Arizona

- 1 **can (46 ounces) pineapple juice**
- 4 **cups brewed tea**
- 3 **cups apple juice**
- 1/2 **cup lemon juice**
- 2 **cups ginger ale**

In a gallon container, combine pineapple juice, tea, apple juice and lemon juice; mix well. Store in the refrigerator. Add the ginger ale just before serving. **Yield:** about 30 servings.

HAM ROLL-UPS

(Pictured at right)

*Green onions and ripe olives give lively flavor
to these bite-size appetizers. They're quick to assemble
and can be made the day before they're needed.
My family and friends just love them.*
—Kathleen Green, Republic, Missouri

1 package (8 ounces) cream cheese,
  softened
1 can (2-1/4 ounces) chopped ripe olives,
  drained
1/3 cup thinly sliced green onions
8 to 10 thin slices fully cooked ham

In a mixing bowl, beat cream cheese until smooth;
stir in the olives and onions. Spread over ham
slices. Roll up, jelly-roll style, starting with a short
side. Chill for at least 1 hour. Just before serving,
cut into 1-in. pieces. **Yield:** 40 appetizers.

TURKEY MEATBALLS

(Pictured at right)

*I don't like to spend a lot of time in the kitchen, so I
always turn to fast and easy recipes like this one. A sweet
sauce coats these firm meatballs that are made with
ground turkey for a nice change of pace.*
—Hazel Bates, Clinton, Oklahoma

1 pound ground turkey
1/4 cup oat bran cereal
1 bottle (14 ounces) ketchup
1 cup grape jelly
3 to 4 tablespoons lemon juice

In a bowl, combine turkey and cereal; mix well.
Shape into 1-in. balls. In a Dutch oven, combine
ketchup, jelly and lemon juice; bring to a boil. Add
meatballs. Reduce heat; simmer, uncovered, for 30-
35 minutes or until meat is no longer pink, stirring
several times. **Yield:** 4-1/2 dozen.

SAUSAGE BISCUIT BITES

(Pictured at right)

*I sometimes bake these little morsels the night before,
refrigerate them, then put them in the slow cooker in the
morning so my husband can share them with his
co-workers. These bites are always gone in a hurry.*
—Audrey Marler, Kokomo, Indiana

1 tube (7-1/2 ounces) refrigerated
  buttermilk biscuits
1 tablespoon butter, melted
4-1/2 teaspoons grated Parmesan cheese
1 teaspoon dried oregano
1 package (8 ounces) brown-and-serve
  sausage links

On a lightly floured surface, roll out each biscuit
into a 4-in. circle; brush with butter. Combine
Parmesan cheese and oregano; sprinkle over butter. Place a sausage link in the center of each; roll
up. Cut each widthwise into four pieces; insert a
toothpick into each. Place on an ungreased baking sheet. Bake at 375° for 8-10 minutes or until
golden brown. **Yield:** 40 appetizers.

FRUITY SHERBET PUNCH

(Pictured at right)

*Everybody loves glasses of this sweet fruit punch. When
entertaining, I start with a quart of sherbet, then add
more later so it all doesn't melt right away.*
—Betty Eberly, Palmyra, Pennsylvania

4 cups *each* apple, pineapple and orange
  juice, chilled
2 liters ginger ale, chilled
1 to 2 quarts orange *or* pineapple sherbet

Combine juices in a punch bowl. Stir in ginger
ale. Top with sherbet. Serve immediately. **Yield:** 15-
20 servings (about 5 quarts).

MUSHROOM BACON BITES

This is the perfect appetizer for most any occasion. The saucy grilled bites are easy to assemble.
—Gina Roesner, Ashland, Missouri

24 **medium fresh mushrooms**
12 **bacon strips, halved**
1 **cup barbecue sauce**

Wrap each mushroom with a piece of bacon; secure with a toothpick. Thread onto metal or soaked bamboo skewers; brush with barbecue sauce. Grill, uncovered, over indirect medium heat for 10-15 minutes or until the bacon is crisp and the mushrooms are tender, turning and basting occasionally with remaining barbecue sauce. **Yield:** 2 dozen.

MOZZARELLA PUFFS

(Pictured above)

These savory cheese biscuits go over great at my house. Since they're so quick to make, I can whip up a batch whenever my family asks for them.
—Joan Mousley Dziuba, Waupaca, Wisconsin

1 **tube (7-1/2 ounces) refrigerated buttermilk biscuits**
1 **teaspoon dried oregano**
1 **block (2 to 3 ounces) mozzarella cheese**
2 **tablespoons pizza sauce**

Make an indentation in the center of each biscuit; sprinkle with oregano. Cut the mozzarella into 10 cubes, 3/4 in. each; place a cube in the center of each biscuit. Pinch dough tightly around cheese to seal. Place seam side down on an ungreased baking sheet. Spread pizza sauce over tops. Bake at 375° for 10-12 minutes or until golden brown. **Yield:** 10 servings.

ICED STRAWBERRY TEA

Strawberry season here coincides with the herald of summer and the conclusion of our school year. We take advantage of that popular fruit in recipes like this quencher.
—Laurie Andrews, Milton, Ontario

1 **pint fresh strawberries**
4 **cups cold tea**
1/3 **to 1/2 cup sugar**
1/4 **cup fresh lemon juice**

Set aside five whole strawberries. Cover and puree the rest in a blender; strain into a pitcher. Stir in tea, sugar and lemon juice until sugar dissolves. Chill. Serve over ice; garnish with berries. **Yield:** 5 cups.

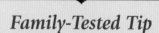

Family-Tested Tip

For an easy appetizer, use 2 pounds of cocktail wieners and 1 pound each of bacon and brown sugar. Just wrap a bacon slice around each wiener, secure them with a toothpick and place them in a slow cooker. Add the sugar on top of the wrapped wieners and heat them on low for 6-8 hours.
—Deborah Loney, Central City, Kentucky

BACON BISCUIT WREATH

(Pictured below)

As a Girl Scout leader, I showed my troop how to make this pretty golden wreath. The girls (and even some of their parents) enjoyed making and sampling the cheesy appetizer. It's a snap to prepare with cheese spread and convenient refrigerated biscuits.
—Kathy Kirkland, Denham Springs, Louisiana

1 jar (5 ounces) sharp American cheese spread
3 tablespoons butter-flavored shortening
1 tube (12 ounces) flaky biscuits
4 bacon strips, cooked and crumbled
2 tablespoons minced fresh parsley

In a small saucepan, melt the cheese spread and shortening; stir until blended. Pour into a well-greased 6-cup ovenproof ring mold or 9-in. fluted tube pan. Cut each biscuit into quarters and place over cheese mixture. Bake at 400° for 12-14 minutes or until golden brown. Immediately invert pan onto a serving platter and remove. Sprinkle with bacon and parsley. Serve warm. **Yield:** 10 servings.

MEXICAN DEVILED EGGS

(Pictured below)

I adapted this recipe to suit our tastes. Folks who are expecting the same old deviled eggs are surprised when they try this delightful tangy variation featuring salsa and cheddar cheese.
—Susan Klemm, Rhinelander, Wisconsin

Family-Tested Tip

To easily fill deviled eggs, put the cooked yolks and other ingredients for the filling in a large resealable plastic bag. Seal it and knead everything together by hand. With a scissors, snip off one corner of the bag and use it like a pastry bag to squeeze the mixture into the egg white halves. When you finish, cleanup is a snap—simply throw away the bag.
—Julie Bishop, Bluff Dale, Texas

8 hard-cooked eggs
1/2 cup shredded cheddar cheese
1/4 cup mayonnaise
1/4 cup salsa
2 tablespoons sliced green onions
1 tablespoon sour cream
Salt to taste

Slice the eggs in half lengthwise; remove yolks and set whites aside. In a small bowl, mash yolks with cheese, mayonnaise, salsa, onions, sour cream and salt. Stuff or pipe into egg whites. Refrigerate until serving. **Yield:** 16 servings.

CINNAMON CANDY POPCORN

This crisp, bright-colored snack is more festive than traditional caramel corn. My family just loves it! Set out in eye-catching bowls, the popcorn makes a tasty table decoration. I also put it in sandwich bags for a children's party treat.
—Kaye Kemper, Windfall, Indiana

8 quarts popped popcorn
1 cup butter
1/2 cup light corn syrup
1 package (9 ounces) red-hot candies

Place popcorn in a large bowl and set aside. In a saucepan, combine butter, corn syrup and candies; bring to a boil over medium heat, stirring constantly. Boil for 5 minutes, stirring occasionally. Pour over popcorn and mix thoroughly.

Turn into two greased 15-in. x 10-in. x 1-in. baking pans. Bake at 250° for 1 hour, stirring every 15 minutes. Remove from pans and place on waxed paper to cool. Break apart; store in airtight containers. **Yield:** 8 quarts.

VEGGIE CHRISTMAS TREE

(Pictured above)

Whenever I bring this fun Christmas appetizer to a party, everyone comments on how pretty it is. I especially like the fact that it's so easy to prepare. If you prefer, use pieces of red and yellow peppers instead of the tomatoes and carrots for the tree ornaments.
—Leola Seltmann, Wichita, Kansas

1 bottle (8 ounces) ranch salad dressing
4 cups fresh broccoli florets
1 broccoli stem
3 to 4 cups cauliflowerets
4 to 5 cherry tomatoes, quartered
1 medium carrot, sliced

Cover the bottom of a 13-in. x 9-in. x 2-in. glass dish with dressing. Arrange broccoli in a tree shape, using the stem as the trunk. Place cauliflower around tree. Add tomatoes and carrot slices as ornaments. **Yield:** 20 servings.

ANGEL FROST

I've been serving this refreshing, creamy beverage for holiday breakfasts and brunches for more than 20 years. No one can stop with just one sip.
—Susan O'Brien, Scottsbluff, Nebraska

3/4 cup pink lemonade concentrate
1 cup milk
1 package (10 ounces) frozen strawberries in syrup, partially thawed
1 pint vanilla ice cream
Fresh strawberries, optional

In a blender, combine the lemonade concentrate, milk, strawberries and ice cream; cover and process until smooth. Pour into glasses. Garnish with fresh strawberries if desired. **Yield:** 4-6 servings (about 1 quart).

HOLIDAY WASSAIL

(Pictured above)

Apricots lend golden color and goodness to this fruity beverage. It's so delicious you'll want to make it year-round.
—Ruth Seitz, Columbus Junction, Iowa

  1 **can (16 ounces) apricot halves,
       undrained**
  4 **cups unsweetened pineapple juice**
  2 **cups apple cider**
  1 **cup orange juice**
18 **whole cloves**
  6 **cinnamon sticks (3-1/2 inches), broken**
Additional cinnamon sticks, optional

In a blender or food processor, blend apricots and liquid until smooth. Pour into a large saucepan. Add pineapple juice, cider and orange juice. Place the cloves and cinnamon sticks in a double thickness of cheesecloth; bring up corners of cloth and tie with a string to form a bag. Add to saucepan. (Or place loose spices directly in the saucepan and strain before serving.)

Bring to a boil. Reduce heat; cover and simmer for 15-20 minutes. Serve hot in mugs. Garnish each with a cinnamon stick if desired. **Yield:** 2 quarts.

Appetizers & Beverages

PERCOLATOR PUNCH

(Pictured at left)

I serve this simple punch for family and club activities. Because it calls for just two ingredients and is "brewed" in a coffeepot, it couldn't be easier!
—Margaret Allen, Abingdon, Virginia

> 9 **cups apple cider**
> 1/2 **cup cinnamon red-hot candies**

Pour apple cider into percolator; place candies in percolator basket. Cover and begin the perking cycle. When cycle is complete, remove the basket and leave punch in the pot to keep warm. **Yield:** 2-1/4 quarts.

HOMEMADE EGGNOG

(Pictured at left)

This holiday treat is well worth the time it takes to make it. After just one taste, folks will know it's homemade and not a store-bought variety.
—Pat Waymire, Yellow Springs, Ohio

> 12 **eggs**
> 1-1/2 **cups sugar**
> 1/2 **teaspoon salt**
> 2 **quarts milk,** *divided*
> 2 **tablespoons vanilla extract**
> 1 **teaspoon ground nutmeg**
> 2 **cups heavy whipping cream**
> **Additional nutmeg, optional**

In a heavy 4-qt. saucepan, whisk together eggs, sugar and salt. Gradually add 1 qt. of milk. Cook and stir over low heat until a thermometer reads 160°-170°, about 30-35 minutes. Pour into a large heatproof bowl; stir in the vanilla, nutmeg and remaining milk.

Place the bowl in an ice-water bath, stirring frequently until mixture is cool. If the mixture separates, process in a blender until smooth. Cover and refrigerate for at least 3 hours. When ready to serve, beat the cream in a mixing bowl on high until soft peaks form; whisk gently into the cooled milk mixture. Pour into a chilled 5-qt. punch bowl. Sprinkle with nutmeg if desired. **Yield:** 3-1/2 quarts.

Editor's Note: Eggnog may be stored, covered, in the refrigerator for several days. Whisk before serving.

ICED ALMONDS

(Pictured below)

My mother-in-law gave me this recipe some 15 years ago. I've made well over 100 batches since then!
—Susan Marie Taccone, Erie, Pennsylvania

> 1/4 **cup butter**
> 2-1/2 **cups whole unblanched almonds**
> 1 **cup sugar**
> 1 **teaspoon vanilla extract**

In a heavy saucepan, melt butter over medium-high heat. Add almonds and sugar. Cook and stir constantly for 7-8 minutes or until syrup is golden brown. Remove from the heat; stir in vanilla. Immediately drop by clusters or separate almonds on a greased baking pan. Cool. Store in an airtight container. **Yield:** 4 cups.

SPARKLING GRAPE PUNCH

I rely on this lovely mauve-colored punch for quenching the thirst of my weekend brunch guests.
—Arlyn Kramer, Dumas, Arkansas

2 cups water
1 cup sugar
2 cups grape juice, chilled
1 cup orange juice, chilled
2 liters ginger ale, chilled

In a saucepan, combine water and sugar. Bring to a boil; boil for 3 minutes. Cool. Transfer to a punch bowl. Add juices and mix well. Stir in ginger ale just before serving. **Yield:** about 5-1/2 quarts.

CREAMY THYME SPREAD

This make-ahead cracker spread showcases thyme and garlic. I like that the recipe is easy to prepare.
—Mary Steiner, West Bend, Wisconsin

1 package (8 ounces) cream cheese, softened
1 tablespoon minced fresh thyme *or* 1 teaspoon dried thyme
1 tablespoon minced fresh parsley *or* 1 teaspoon dried parsley flakes
1 garlic clove, minced
Assorted crackers

In a bowl, combine the cream cheese, thyme, parsley and garlic; mix well. Cover and refrigerate until serving. Serve with assorted crackers. **Yield:** about 1 cup.

FLUFFY HOT CHOCOLATE

(Pictured above)

Melted marshmallows provide the frothy texture that your family will savor in this sweet and speedy homemade beverage. Chocolaty and comforting, it's our daughter's favorite hot cocoa drink.
—Jo Ann Schimcek, Weimar, Texas

8 teaspoons sugar
4 teaspoons baking cocoa
4 cups milk
1-1/2 cups miniature marshmallows
1 teaspoon vanilla extract

In a saucepan, combine the first four ingredients. Cook and stir over medium heat until the marshmallows are melted, about 8 minutes. Remove from the heat; stir in vanilla. Ladle into mugs. **Yield:** 4 servings.

"A family is a place where minds come in contact with one another."
—Buddha

Hot Kielbasa Dip

(Pictured at right)

My husband and I are retired, and I appreciate recipes that are simple and speedy. This thick cheesy dip, with the unusual addition of sausage, goes together in a jiffy. Accompanied by crackers or fresh veggies, it's a hearty appetizer for a football party or family gathering.
—Mary Bondegard, Brooksville, Florida

  1 package (8 ounces) cream cheese
1/2 cup sour cream
1/3 cup milk
  1 tablespoon mayonnaise
1/2 teaspoon Worcestershire sauce
  8 ounces fully cooked kielbasa *or* Polish sausage, finely chopped
1/2 cup sliced green onions, *divided*
1/4 cup grated Parmesan cheese
Assorted crackers *or* raw vegetables

In a 1-1/2-qt. microwave-safe bowl, heat cream cheese, uncovered, on high for 1 minute. Stir in the sour cream, milk, mayonnaise and Worcestershire sauce. Add the kielbasa, 1/4 cup of onions and Parmesan cheese; mix well.

Microwave, uncovered, on high for 3-4 minutes or until heated through, stirring once. Sprinkle with remaining onions. Serve with crackers or vegetables. Store in refrigerator. **Yield:** about 3 cups.

Fresh Salsa

The addition of ripe olives makes this easy homemade salsa a little different from other varieties. You can seed the jalapeno peppers if desired. But if your family likes salsa that has some "heat" to it, leave them in.
—Sharon Lucas, Raymore, Missouri

  8 medium tomatoes, chopped
3/4 cup sliced green onions
1/3 cup finely chopped fresh cilantro
1/3 cup chopped onion
  2 small jalapeno peppers, finely chopped (seeded if desired)
  1 can (2-1/4 ounces) sliced ripe olives, drained
3-1/2 teaspoons fresh lime juice
  1 tablespoon cider vinegar
  1 tablespoon vegetable oil
  1 to 2 teaspoons chili powder
  1 to 2 teaspoons ground cumin
  1 teaspoon garlic powder
  1 teaspoon dried oregano
1/4 teaspoon salt

Combine all of the ingredients in a large bowl. Cover and refrigerate overnight. Keeps up to 1 week. **Yield:** 8 cups.

Editor's Note: When cutting or seeding hot peppers, use rubber or plastic gloves to protect your hands. Avoid touching your face.

Chapter two

What better way for families to begin the day

than with best-loved dishes for breakfast or

brunch? You'll tempt early risers and late sleepers

alike when you serve stacks of fluffy pancakes,

hearty egg bakes, fruit medleys or any of the

other unforgettable recipes here.

Blueberry Sour Cream Pancakes
(Recipe on page 29)

♥ Breakfast & Brunch

CHOCOLATE CHIP COFFEE RING

(Pictured at right)

When I was a girl, my mother served this only once a year—for Christmas-morning brunch. But it could easily be served as dessert or as a snack packed in a lunch. It travels very well.
—Laura Hertel, Columbia, Missouri

1/2 **cup butter, softened**
  1 **cup sugar**
  2 **eggs**
  1 **cup (8 ounces) sour cream**
  1 **teaspoon vanilla extract**
  2 **cups all-purpose flour**
  1 **teaspoon baking powder**
  1 **teaspoon baking soda**
1/2 **teaspoon salt**
3/4 **cup semisweet chocolate chips**
TOPPING:
1/2 **cup all-purpose flour**
1/2 **cup packed brown sugar**
1-1/2 **teaspoons baking cocoa**
1/4 **cup cold butter**
1/2 **cup chopped pecans**
1/4 **cup semisweet chocolate chips**

In a mixing bowl, cream butter and sugar until fluffy. Beat in eggs. Add sour cream and vanilla; mix just until combined. Set aside. Combine flour, baking powder, baking soda and salt; add to creamed mixture. Stir in the chocolate chips. Pour into a greased 8-cup fluted tube pan.

For topping, combine flour, sugar and cocoa; cut in butter until mixture resembles coarse crumbs. Stir in pecans and chocolate chips. Sprinkle over batter. Bake at 350° for 55-60 minutes or until a toothpick inserted in cake comes out clean. Cool in pan 20 minutes before removing to a wire rack to cool completely. **Yield:** 8-10 servings.

Editor's Note: A greased 9-in. square baking pan can be used instead of the tube pan; bake for 45-50 minutes.

HAM 'N' CHEESE POTATO BAKE

This hearty ham and hash brown casserole is frequently requested at family gatherings. I include it in my brunch buffets and sometimes serve it as a meal in itself along with juice and toast. It offers fix-and-forget-it ease.
—Barbara Larson, Rosemount, Minnesota

  1 **package (24 ounces) frozen O'Brien hash brown potatoes**
  2 **cups cubed fully cooked ham**
3/4 **cup shredded cheddar cheese, *divided***
  1 **small onion, chopped**
  2 **cups (16 ounces) sour cream**
  1 **can (10-3/4 ounces) condensed cheddar cheese soup, undiluted**
  1 **can (10-3/4 ounces) condensed cream of potato soup, undiluted**
1/4 **teaspoon pepper**

In a large bowl, combine potatoes, ham, 1/2 cup cheese and onion. In another bowl, combine sour cream, soups and pepper; add to potato mixture and mix well. Transfer to a greased 3-qt. baking dish. Sprinkle with remaining cheese.

Bake, uncovered, at 350° for 60-65 minutes or until bubbly and potatoes are tender. Let casserole stand for 10 minutes before serving. **Yield:** 10-12 servings.

CRUSTLESS SWISS QUICHE

(Pictured below)

I received this recipe from my mother-in-law, an all-around great cook. It makes two rich cheese quiches that skip the crust but don't skimp on flavor. Every time I serve them to family or friends, I hear raves.
—*Marlene Kole, Highland Heights, Ohio*

1/2	cup butter
1/2	cup all-purpose flour
1-1/2	cups milk
2-1/2	cups cottage cheese
1	teaspoon baking powder
1	teaspoon salt
1	teaspoon Dijon mustard
9	eggs
2	packages (one 8 ounces, one 3 ounces) cream cheese, softened
3	cups (12 ounces) shredded Swiss cheese
1/3	cup grated Parmesan cheese

Melt butter in a medium saucepan. Stir in flour; cook and stir until bubbly. Gradually add milk; cook over medium heat, stirring occasionally, until sauce thickens. Remove from the heat; set aside to cool, about 15-20 minutes. Meanwhile, combine cottage cheese, baking powder, salt and mustard; set aside.

In a large mixing bowl, beat the eggs. Slowly add cream cheese, cottage cheese mixture and cream sauce. Fold in Swiss and Parmesan cheeses. Pour into two greased 10-in. pie plates. Bake at 350° for 40 minutes or until a knife inserted near the center comes out clean. Serve immediately. **Yield:** 16-20 servings.

LEMON BUTTER SPREAD

(Pictured above)

My grandmother, who was a great cook, brought this versatile spread recipe with her from England.
—Gloria Costes, West Hills, California

1 cup butter
2 cups sugar
3 eggs, lightly beaten
1/2 cup lemon juice
1 tablespoon grated lemon peel

In the top of a double boiler over boiling water, melt butter. Stir in sugar, eggs, lemon juice and peel. Cook over simmering water for 1 hour or until mixture is thickened and coats the back of a spoon. Pour into containers. Store in the refrigerator. Use over cake or spread on toast or muffins. **Yield:** 3 cups.

SUNDAY SAUSAGE BREAKFAST

This delicious, meaty dish looks as appealing as it is tasty. With eggs and cheese, it makes a complete breakfast.
—Bill Schultz, Walden, New York

1 pound bulk pork sausage
1 package (6 ounces) onion and garlic croutons

2 cups cubed mild cheddar cheese
2 cups cubed Monterey Jack cheese
1 dozen eggs, beaten
1/2 cup milk
1/2 teaspoon dried basil
1/4 teaspoon salt
1/4 teaspoon pepper

In a skillet, cook sausage over medium heat until no longer pink; drain. In a greased 13-in. x 9-in. x 2-in. baking dish, layer the croutons, sausage and cheese. Combine eggs and milk; mix well. Pour over cheese; sprinkle with basil, salt and pepper.

Bake, uncovered, at 350° for 40-45 minutes or until the top is lightly browned and a knife inserted near the center comes out clean. Serve immediately. **Yield:** 6-8 servings.

SOUTHWESTERN OMELET

Flavors of another region spark the eggs in this recipe. Hearty home-style food is popular in our small farming and timber community.
—Patricia Collins, Imbler, Oregon

1/2 cup chopped onion
1 jalapeno pepper, minced
1 tablespoon vegetable oil
6 eggs, beaten
6 bacon strips, cooked and crumbled
1 small tomato, chopped
1 ripe avocado, cut into 1-inch slices
1 cup (4 ounces) shredded Monterey Jack cheese, *divided*
Salt and pepper to taste
Salsa, optional

In a skillet, saute onion and jalapeno in oil until tender; remove with a slotted spoon and set aside. Pour eggs into the same skillet; cover and cook over low heat for 3-4 minutes.

Sprinkle with onion, jalapeno, bacon, tomato, avocado and 1/2 cup cheese. Season with salt and pepper. Fold omelet in half over filling. Cover and cook for 3-4 minutes or until eggs are set. Sprinkle with remaining cheese. Serve with salsa if de-

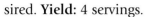

sired. **Yield:** 4 servings.

Editor's Note: When cutting or seeding hot peppers, use rubber or plastic gloves to protect your hands. Avoid touching your face.

BLUEBERRY SOUR CREAM PANCAKES

(Pictured on page 25)

When our large family goes blueberry picking, we have a bounty of blueberries in no time. They're wonderful in these melt-in-your-mouth pancakes.
—*Paula Hadley, Forest Hill, Louisiana*

1/2 cup sugar
2 tablespoons cornstarch
1 cup water
4 cups fresh *or* frozen blueberries
PANCAKES:
2 cups all-purpose flour
1/4 cup sugar
4 teaspoons baking powder
1/2 teaspoon salt
2 eggs
1-1/2 cups milk
1 cup (8 ounces) sour cream
1/3 cup butter, melted
1 cup fresh *or* frozen blueberries

In a medium saucepan, combine sugar and cornstarch. Gradually stir in water. Add blueberries; bring to a boil over medium heat. Boil for 2 minutes, stirring constantly. Remove from the heat; cover and keep warm.

For pancakes, combine dry ingredients in a bowl. In another bowl, beat the eggs. Add milk, sour cream and butter; mix well. Stir into the dry ingredients just until blended. Fold in the blueberries.

Pour batter by 1/4 cupfuls onto a greased hot griddle; turn when bubbles form on top of pancakes. Cook until the second side is golden brown. Serve with blueberry topping. **Yield:** about 20 pancakes (3-1/2 cups topping).

SUNSHINE SALAD

(Pictured above)

This refreshing medley of fruit and lemon pudding is just as delightful late in the day as it is for breakfast or brunch. When I prepare the recipe for an evening meal, I change the name…I refer to it as "Sunset Salad" instead!
—*Margaret Ulrich, Braidwood, Illinois*

1 can (20 ounces) pineapple tidbits
1 can (11 ounces) mandarin oranges
1 package (3.4 ounces) instant lemon pudding
1 cup quartered strawberries
1 cup sliced ripe bananas

Drain pineapple and oranges, reserving liquid. In a large bowl, combine pudding mix with reserved fruit juices. Fold in pineapple, oranges and strawberries; chill for at least 2 hours. Add bananas just before serving. **Yield:** 8-10 servings.

CRANBERRY CRUMBLE COFFEE CAKE

(Pictured below)

People are delighted when they see the ruby-red cranberry sauce swirled inside this tempting breakfast treat. With the crumble topping, moist texture and tangy filling, this coffee cake tastes special and never lasts long.
—Jeani Robinson, Weirton, West Virginia

1/4 cup chopped almonds
1 cup sugar
1/2 cup butter, softened
1 teaspoon vanilla extract
2 eggs
2 cups all-purpose flour
1-1/4 teaspoons baking powder
1/2 teaspoon baking soda
1/4 teaspoon salt
1 cup (8 ounces) sour cream
1 cup whole-berry cranberry sauce
TOPPING:
1/4 cup all-purpose flour
1/4 cup sugar
1/4 cup chopped almonds
1/4 teaspoon vanilla extract
2 tablespoons cold butter

Sprinkle almonds over the bottom of a greased 9-in. springform pan; set aside. In a mixing bowl, cream the sugar, butter and vanilla; beat on medium for 1-2 minutes. Add eggs, one at a time, beating well after each addition.

Combine dry ingredients; add to batter alternately with sour cream. Mix well. Spread 3 cups over almonds. Spoon cranberry sauce over batter. Top with remaining batter.

For topping, combine flour, sugar, almonds and vanilla; cut in butter until crumbly. Sprinkle over batter.

Bake at 350° for 70-75 minutes or until a toothpick inserted near the center comes out clean. Cool in pan on a wire rack for 15 minutes; remove sides of pan. Serve warm. **Yield:** 12 servings.

CREAMY FRUIT BOWL

Sweetened with whipped cream and mini marshmallows, this fluffy medley also makes a delightful dessert.
—*Gretchen Baudhuin, Palm Coast, Florida*

> 1 **can (20 ounces) pineapple tidbits, undrained**
> 3 **egg yolks, beaten**
> 2 **tablespoons sugar**
> 2 **tablespoons vinegar**
> 1 **tablespoon butter**

Dash salt

> 4 **oranges, sectioned, *divided***
> 3 **cups seedless grapes, *divided***
> 2 **cups miniature marshmallows**
> 1 **cup heavy whipping cream, whipped**

Fresh mint, optional

Drain the pineapple, reserving 2 tablespoons juice; set pineapple aside. Pour the juice into the top of a double boiler; add egg yolks, sugar, vinegar, butter and salt. Cook and stir over medium-low heat until mixture thickens and a thermometer reads at least 160°. Cool.

Stir in pineapple, three oranges, 2-1/2 cups grapes and marshmallows. Cover and chill for at least 12 hours. Fold in whipped cream just before serving. Top with remaining oranges and grapes. Garnish with mint if desired. **Yield:** 10-12 servings.

"The family is one of nature's masterpieces."
—George Santayana

NO-TURN OMELET

(Pictured above)

With ingredients such as sausage, eggs, cheese and peppers, this colorful casserole tastes like a strata.
—*Helen Clem, Creston, Iowa*

> 8 **eggs, beaten**
> 2 **cups cooked crumbled sausage *or* cubed fully cooked ham**
> 2 **cups cubed process cheese (Velveeta)**
> 2 **cups milk**
> 1 **cup crushed saltines (about 24 crackers)**
> 1/4 **cup chopped onion**
> 1/4 **cup chopped green pepper**
> 1/4 **cup chopped sweet red pepper**
> 1/2 **to 1 teaspoon salt**

Combine all ingredients in a large bowl; pour into a greased shallow 3-qt. or 13-in. x 9-in. x 2-in. baking dish. Bake, uncovered, at 350° for 45 minutes or until a knife inserted near the center comes out clean. Let stand for 5 minutes before serving. **Yield:** 8-10 servings.

Editor's Note: This dish may be prepared in advance, covered and refrigerated overnight. Remove from refrigerator 30 minutes before baking.

Breakfast Cookies

This recipe came in handy when I was a 4-H leader. Before morning chores, the young members would grab a glass of milk or juice and a handful of these crisp cookies. Chock-full of bacon, cornflakes and raisins, they're a great breakfast on the go.
—Louise Gangwish, Shelton, Nebraska

- 1/2 cup butter, softened
- 3/4 cup sugar
-    1 egg
-    1 cup all-purpose flour
- 1/4 teaspoon baking soda
-   10 bacon strips, cooked and crumbled
-    2 cups cornflakes
- 1/2 cup raisins

In a mixing bowl, cream butter and sugar. Beat in egg. Add flour and baking soda; mix well. Stir in bacon, cornflakes and raisins. Drop by rounded tablespoonfuls 2 in. apart onto ungreased baking sheets.

Bake at 350° for 15-18 minutes or until lightly browned. Cool for 2 minutes before removing to wire racks. Store in the refrigerator. **Yield:** 2 dozen.

Maple-Bacon Oven Pancake

For years, my mother has served this tasty baked pancake for dinner. But it's so quick and easy, I like to make it for breakfast, too. Leftovers taste just as good the next day warmed up in the microwave.
—Kari Caven, Moscow, Idaho

- 1-1/2 cups biscuit/baking mix
-      1 tablespoon sugar
-   3/4 cup milk
-      2 eggs
-   1/4 cup maple syrup
- 1-1/2 cups (6 ounces) shredded cheddar cheese, *divided*

- 1/2 pound sliced bacon, cooked and crumbled
- **Additional syrup, optional**

In a mixing bowl, combine biscuit mix, sugar, milk, eggs, syrup and 1/2 cup cheese; mix well. Pour into a greased 13-in. x 9-in. x 2-in. baking dish.

Bake, uncovered, at 425° for 10-15 minutes or until a toothpick inserted near the center comes out clean. Sprinkle with bacon and remaining cheese. Bake 3-5 minutes longer or until the cheese is melted. Serve with syrup if desired. **Yield:** 12 servings.

Egg Biscuit Bake

(Pictured at right)

Convenient refrigerated biscuits create a golden border around this all-in-one brunch dish. It's a variation of a simple egg-cheese recipe my mother used to make.
—Alice Le Duc, Cedarburg, Wisconsin

-    1 can (5 ounces) evaporated milk
-    8 ounces process cheese (Velveeta), cubed
-    1 teaspoon prepared mustard
- 3/4 cup cubed fully cooked ham
- 1/2 cup frozen peas
-    2 tablespoons butter
-   10 eggs, beaten
-    1 tube (12 ounces) refrigerated buttermilk biscuits

In a saucepan, combine the milk, cheese and mustard; cook over low heat until smooth, stirring constantly. Stir in ham and peas. Melt butter in a large skillet; add eggs. Cook and stir over medium heat until the eggs are set. Add cheese sauce and stir gently.

Spoon into an ungreased shallow 2-qt. baking dish. Separate the biscuits and cut in half. Place with cut side down around outer edge of dish.

Bake, uncovered, at 375° for 15-20 minutes or until biscuits are golden brown. **Yield:** 4-6 servings.

NUTTY FRENCH TOAST

(Pictured above)

This sweet breakfast treat is a cross of caramel rolls and French toast. It's easy to begin the night before.
—*Mavis Diment, Marcus, Iowa*

12 slices French bread (1 inch thick)
8 eggs
2 cups milk
2 teaspoons vanilla extract
1/2 teaspoon ground cinnamon
3/4 cup butter, softened
1-1/3 cups packed brown sugar
3 tablespoons dark corn syrup
1 cup chopped walnuts

Place bread in a greased 13-in. x 9-in. x 2-in. baking dish. In a large bowl, beat eggs, milk, vanilla and cinnamon; pour over the bread. Cover and refrigerate overnight. Remove from the refrigerator 30 minutes before baking.

Meanwhile, in a mixing bowl, cream butter, sugar and syrup until smooth; spread over bread. Sprinkle with nuts. Bake, uncovered, at 350° for 1 hour or until golden brown. **Yield:** 6-8 servings.

BACON AND CHEESE WAFFLES

(Pictured at right)

Pancake mix gives a jump-start to this hearty hurry-up breakfast. Including bacon and cheese in the waffle batter creates an all-in-one breakfast flavor. Freeze extras to reheat another day.
—MarGenne Rowley, Oasis, Utah

1   egg
1   cup milk
1   cup (8 ounces) sour cream
1   tablespoon butter, melted
2   cups pancake *or* biscuit/baking mix
6   to 8 bacon strips, cooked and crumbled
1   cup (4 ounces) shredded cheddar cheese

In a medium bowl, beat egg; add milk, sour cream and butter. Stir in pancake mix; mix well. Fold in bacon and cheese. Bake in a preheated waffle iron according to the manufacturer's directions until golden brown. **Yield:** 12 waffles (4-inch square).

COUNTRY BRUNCH SKILLET

(Pictured at right)

Frozen hash browns and packaged shredded cheese shave minutes off preparation of this skillet breakfast. It's an appealing meal-in-one that you can make in about half an hour.
—Elvira Brunnquell, Port Washington, Wisconsin

6   bacon strips
6   cups frozen cubed hash brown potatoes
3/4 cup chopped green pepper
1/2 cup chopped onion
1   teaspoon salt
1/4 teaspoon pepper
6   eggs
1/2 cup shredded cheddar cheese

In a large skillet over medium heat, cook bacon until crisp. Remove bacon; crumble and set aside. Drain, reserving 2 tablespoons of drippings. Add

potatoes, green pepper, onion, salt and pepper to drippings; cook and stir for 2 minutes. Cover and cook, stirring occasionally, until potatoes are browned and tender, about 15 minutes. Make six wells in the potato mixture; break one egg into each well. Cover and cook on low heat for 8-10 minutes or until the eggs are completely set. Sprinkle with cheese and bacon. **Yield:** 6 servings.

FROTHY ORANGE DRINK

(Pictured at left)

This sunny slush is sure to put a little "zip" in your day! You can serve up glasses of this thick orange beverage in just a few moments.
—Sue Ellen Bumpus, Lampasas, Texas

1 can (6 ounces) frozen orange juice concentrate, unthawed
1 cup water
1 cup milk
1/2 cup sugar
1 teaspoon vanilla extract
8 to 10 ice cubes

Combine all ingredients in a blender; cover and process until thick and slushy. **Yield:** 4 cups.

FRENCH TOAST CUSTARD

(Pictured at right)

I usually prepare this dish for brunch, but it's also wonderful for breakfast or even dinner. This special French toast offers make-ahead convenience for busy days. Everyone says it just melts in your mouth.
—Pamela Hamp, Arroyo Grande, California

8 to 10 slices day-old French bread (1 inch thick)
5 tablespoons butter, melted
4 eggs
2 egg yolks
3 cups milk
1 cup heavy whipping cream
1/2 cup sugar
1 tablespoon vanilla extract
1/4 teaspoon ground nutmeg
Confectioners' sugar, optional

Brush both sides of the bread slices with butter; place in a greased 13-in. x 9-in. x 2-in. baking dish. In a large bowl, beat eggs and yolks. Add the milk,

cream, sugar, vanilla and nutmeg; mix well. Pour over the bread slices. Cover and chill overnight. Remove from the refrigerator 30 minutes before baking.

Bake, uncovered, at 350° for 55-60 minutes or until a knife inserted near the center comes out clean. Cool 10 minutes before serving. Dust with confectioners' sugar if desired. **Yield:** 8-10 servings.

COCONUT TOAST

(Pictured at left)

This toasty bread has a wonderfully sweet and buttery coconut topping that's simply scrumptious. It's easy to make, too. Enjoy slices with a cup of coffee at breakfast or for a snack any time of day.
—Betty Checkett, St. Louis, Missouri

- 1 cup flaked coconut
- 1 cup sugar
- 1/2 cup butter, melted
- 1 egg, beaten
- 1 teaspoon vanilla extract
- 11 to 12 slices white bread

In a bowl, combine the coconut, sugar, butter, egg and vanilla; mix well. Spread over each slice of bread; place on ungreased baking sheets. Bake at 350° for 15-20 minutes or until lightly browned. **Yield:** 11-12 servings.

MAPLE-GLAZED SAUSAGES

(Pictured at left)

I love to simmer up this cinnamony syrup that nicely coats a skillet full of breakfast sausages. They're my first choice when I want to round out a morning menu of French toast and fruit compote.
—Trudie Hagen, Roggen, Colorado

- 2 packages (8 ounces *each*) brown-and-serve sausage links
- 1 cup maple syrup
- 1/2 cup packed brown sugar
- 1 teaspoon ground cinnamon

In a large skillet, cook sausage links until browned; drain. Combine syrup, brown sugar and cinnamon; stir into skillet. Bring to a boil; cook and stir until sausages are glazed. **Yield:** 6-8 servings.

Family-Tested Tip

Does your pie pastry shrink down into the pan when you're prebaking for a quiche? Place the unbaked pastry in a pie plate and flute the edges. Take the same-size disposable foil pie pan and punch holes in the bottom with a sharp object (such as a clean nail). Turn up the edge of the foil pan so it won't ruin the edge of your pastry. Place the foil pan over the pastry, press firmly and bake as usual.
—Faye Peachey, Bay Tree, Alberta

CURRIED CRAB QUICHE

(Pictured at left)

Curry and crab complement each other perfectly in this fuss-free quiche. With a sunny color and a rich taste, it's special enough for a holiday breakfast or brunch.
—Kathy Kittell, Lenexa, Kansas

- 1 unbaked pastry shell (9 inches)
- 6 to 8 ounces canned *or* frozen crabmeat, thawed, drained and cartilage removed
- 3/4 cup shredded Swiss cheese
- 3 eggs
- 1-1/2 cups heavy whipping cream
- 1/2 to 1 teaspoon curry powder
- 1/2 teaspoon salt

Dash pepper

Line unpricked pastry shell with a double thickness of heavy-duty foil. Bake at 450° for 5 minutes. Remove foil; bake 5 minutes longer. Remove from the oven; reduce heat to 375°. Sprinkle crab and cheese into shell.

In a bowl, beat eggs. Add cream, curry, salt and pepper; pour over cheese. Cover edges of pastry with foil; bake for 30-35 minutes or until a knife inserted near the center comes out clean. **Yield:** 6-8 servings.

HASH BROWN BAKE

Every time I prepare this creamy and cheesy potato dish for breakfast, it receives rave reviews.
—Dorothy Byrom, Overland Park, Kansas

 7 cups water
 2 packages (32 ounces *each*) frozen cubed Southern-style hash brown potatoes
 2 packages (8 ounces *each*) cream cheese, softened
 4 eggs
 2 teaspoons minced chives
1-1/4 teaspoons salt
 1/2 teaspoon pepper
 1/4 cup dry bread crumbs
 1/4 cup grated Parmesan cheese
 3 tablespoons butter, melted

In a Dutch oven, bring water and potatoes to a boil. Reduce heat; cover and simmer until potatoes are tender, about 12 minutes. Drain. Place potatoes in a mixing bowl; beat on low just until mashed. Add cream cheese, eggs, chives, salt and pepper; mix well.

Divide potato mixture between two greased 2-qt. baking dishes. Combine the bread crumbs, Parmesan cheese and butter; sprinkle over potatoes. Cover and refrigerate overnight.

Remove from the refrigerator 30 minutes before baking. Bake, uncovered, at 350° for 50-60 minutes or until top is browned and potatoes are heated through. **Yield:** 24 servings.

AMISH BAKED OATMEAL

(Pictured above)

The first time I had this warm, wonderful treat, I thought it tasted just like a big fresh-from-the-oven oatmeal cookie!
—Colleen Butler, Inwood, West Virginia

1-1/2 cups quick-cooking oats
 1/2 cup sugar
 1/2 cup milk
 1/4 cup butter, melted
 1 egg
 1 teaspoon baking powder
 3/4 teaspoon salt
 1 teaspoon vanilla extract
Warm milk
Fresh fruit *and/or* brown sugar, optional

Combine the first eight ingredients; mix well. Spread evenly in a greased 13-in. x 9-in. x 2-in. baking pan. Bake at 350° for 25-30 minutes or until edges are golden brown. Immediately spoon into bowls; add milk. Top with fruit and/or brown sugar if desired. **Yield:** 6 servings.

"A happy family is but an earlier heaven."
—John Bowring

PECAN WAFFLES

(Pictured below)

I tried for years to duplicate a delicious waffle I sampled at a restaurant here in the South. This crisp and nutty version is what I came up with. Butter and maple syrup are my family's favorite toppings.
—Susan Jansen, Smyrna, Georgia

1-3/4 **cups all-purpose flour**
1 **tablespoon baking powder**
1/2 **teaspoon salt**
2 **eggs,** *separated*
1-3/4 **cups milk**
1/2 **cup vegetable oil**
1 **cup chopped pecans**
Maple syrup

In a bowl, combine the flour, baking powder and salt. Combine the egg yolks, milk and oil; stir into dry ingredients. Beat egg whites until stiff; fold into batter.

Sprinkle hot waffle iron with 2 tablespoons pecans. Pour 1/4 to 1/3 cup of batter over pecans and bake according to manufacturer's directions until golden brown. Repeat with remaining pecans and batter. Serve with syrup. **Yield:** 8-10 waffles (4-1/2 inches).

1 can (8 ounces) crushed pineapple
18 clear plastic cups (9 ounces)

In a large bowl, prepare pineapple juice concentrate according to package directions. Add orange juice concentrate, water, sugar, lemon juice and fruit. Spoon 3/4 cupful into each plastic cup. Place cups in a pan and freeze. Remove from the freezer 40-50 minutes before serving. **Yield:** 18 servings.

CHILLED FRUIT CUPS

(Pictured above)

This refreshing frozen salad is easy to assemble ahead and serve to a group at breakfast—or any time of day.
—Andrea Hawthorne, Bozeman, Montana

1 can (12 ounces) frozen pineapple juice concentrate, thawed
1 can (6 ounces) frozen orange juice concentrate, thawed
1 cup water
1 cup sugar
2 tablespoons lemon juice
3 medium firm bananas, sliced
1 package (16 ounces) frozen unsweetened strawberries
1 can (15 ounces) mandarin oranges, drained

Family-Tested Tip

Fruit juice, such as cran-raspberry juice, can give a taste boost to morning oatmeal. Simply cook the oatmeal as usual using the juice in place of water.
—Wini Long, Julian, California

UPSIDE-DOWN ORANGE BISCUITS

I guarantee that the aroma of these biscuits baking is enough to get even the soundest sleeper out of bed!
—Kim Marie Van Rheenen, Mendota, Illinois

2 cups all-purpose flour
1 tablespoon baking powder
1/2 teaspoon salt
3 tablespoons shortening
3/4 cup milk
2 tablespoons butter, softened
1/4 cup sugar
1 teaspoon ground cinnamon
TOPPING:
1/2 cup sugar
1/2 cup orange juice
3 tablespoons butter, melted
2 teaspoons grated orange peel

In a large bowl, combine flour, baking powder and salt; cut in shortening until mixture resembles coarse crumbs. Stir in milk just until moistened. Turn onto a lightly floured surface; knead gently 10-12 times.

Roll into a 15-in. x 12-in. rectangle. Spread with butter. Combine sugar and cinnamon; sprinkle over butter. Roll up jelly-roll style, starting from the short side. Cut into 12 equal slices. Place, cut side down, in a greased 9-in. round baking pan.

Combine topping ingredients; pour over biscuits. Bake at 450° for 20-25 minutes or until lightly browned. Cool in pan 5 minutes; invert onto a platter and serve warm. **Yield:** 1 dozen.

HEARTY BRUNCH POTATOES

(Pictured below)

Our family has long enjoyed this meaty dish with eggs and toast for breakfast. The popular potatoes are also delicious with salad or green beans and crusty bread for lunch or supper.
—Madonna McCollough, Harrison, Arkansas

 7 medium potatoes, peeled and cut into 1/2-inch cubes
1/2 cup chopped green pepper
1/2 cup chopped sweet red pepper
1/2 cup fresh *or* frozen corn
 1 small onion, chopped
 1 to 2 garlic cloves, minced
1/2 pound smoked turkey sausage links
 2 tablespoons olive oil
1/4 teaspoon pepper

Place potatoes in a saucepan and cover with water. Bring to a boil; reduce heat. Cook, uncovered, just until tender, about 10 minutes.

Meanwhile, in a skillet coated with nonstick cooking spray, saute the peppers, corn, onion and garlic until tender. Cut sausage into small chunks; add to the vegetable mixture. Cook, uncovered, for 6-8 minutes or until heated through.

Drain potatoes; add to the vegetable mixture. Add oil and pepper; mix well. Transfer to an ungreased 13-in. x 9-in. x 2-in. baking dish. Bake, uncovered, at 350° for 35 minutes or until heated through. **Yield:** 12 servings.

SCRAMBLED EGG MUFFINS

After sampling scrambled egg muffins at a local restaurant, I came up with this no-fuss version that my husband likes even better. They're pretty, satisfying and fun to serve guests, too.
—Cathy Larkins, Marshfield, Missouri

1/2 pound bulk pork sausage
 12 eggs
1/2 cup chopped onion
1/4 cup chopped green pepper
1/2 teaspoon salt
1/4 teaspoon pepper
1/4 teaspoon garlic powder
1/2 cup shredded cheddar cheese

In a skillet, cook the sausage over medium heat until no longer pink; drain. In a bowl, beat the eggs. Add onion, green pepper, salt, pepper and garlic powder. Stir in sausage and cheese. Spoon by 1/3 cupfuls into greased muffin cups.

Bake at 350° for 20-25 minutes or until a knife inserted near the center comes out clean. **Yield:** 1 dozen.

Chapter three

Sometimes special family meals can be as simple as

sharing steaming bowls of home-style soup, chock-full

salads and satisfying sandwiches. When the time's right

for these ever-popular entree and side-dish options,

just turn to the rave-winning recipes in this chapter.

You'll serve up a lunch or supper to remember.

Sandwich for 12
(Recipe on page 44)

42

❤ Soups, Salads & Sandwiches

FRENCH ONION SOUP

(Pictured below)

Our daughter and I enjoy spending time together cooking, but our days are busy, so we appreciate quick and tasty recipes like this one. Hot and delicious, this soup hits the spot for lunch or dinner.
—*Sandra Chambers, Carthage, Mississippi*

  4   cups thinly sliced onions
  1   garlic clove, minced
1/4   cup butter
  6   cups water
  8   beef bouillon cubes
  1   teaspoon Worcestershire sauce
  6   slices French bread (3/4 inch thick),
        buttered and toasted
  6   slices Swiss cheese

In a large covered saucepan, cook onions and garlic in butter over medium-low heat for 8-10 minutes or until tender and golden, stirring occasionally. Add water, bouillon and Worcestershire sauce; bring to a boil. Reduce heat; cover and simmer for 30 minutes. Ladle hot soup into six ovenproof bowls. Top each with a piece of French bread. Cut each slice of cheese in half and place over the bread. Broil until cheese is melted. Serve immediately. **Yield:** 6 servings.

SANDWICH FOR 12

(Pictured on page 43)

Cut into wedges, this big round sandwich is a great way to feed a bunch. It's versatile, too—feel free to add your family's favorite filling ingredients.
—*Melissa Collier, Wichita Falls, Texas*

1/2   cup old-fashioned oats
1/2   cup boiling water
  2   tablespoons butter
  1   package (16 ounces) hot roll mix
3/4   cup warm water (110° to 115°)
  2   eggs, beaten
  1   tablespoon dried minced onion
TOPPING:
  1   egg
  1   teaspoon garlic salt
  1   tablespoon dried minced onion
  1   tablespoon sesame seeds
FILLING:
1/2   cup mayonnaise
  4   teaspoons prepared mustard
1/2   teaspoon prepared horseradish
Lettuce leaves
  8   ounces thinly sliced fully cooked ham
  8   ounces thinly sliced cooked turkey
  1   medium green pepper, thinly sliced
  1   medium onion, thinly sliced
  6   ounces thinly sliced Swiss cheese
  2   large tomatoes, thinly sliced

In a large bowl, combine oats, boiling water and butter; let stand for 5 minutes. Meanwhile, dissolve yeast from hot roll mix in warm water. Add to the oat mixture with eggs and onion. Add flour mixture from hot roll mix; stir well (do not knead).

Spread dough into a 10-in. circle on a well-greased pizza pan. Cover with plastic wrap coated with nonstick cooking spray; let rise in a warm place until doubled, about 45 minutes. Beat egg and garlic salt; brush gently over dough. Sprinkle with onion and sesame seeds. Bake at 350° for 25-30 minutes or until golden brown. Remove from pan; cool on a wire rack. Split lengthwise.

Combine mayonnaise, mustard and horseradish; spread over cut sides of loaf. Layer with remaining filling ingredients. Cut into wedges. **Yield:** 12 servings.

Southwestern Bean Salad

(Pictured at right)

I've used this zippy salad many times and received compliments. When it comes to bean salad, most people think of the sweet, three-bean variety, so this change-of-pace recipe is a nice surprise.
—Lila Jean Allen, Portland, Oregon

  1 **can (16 ounces) kidney beans, rinsed and drained**
  1 **can (15 ounces) black beans, rinsed and drained**
  1 **can (15 ounces) garbanzo beans, rinsed and drained**
  2 **celery ribs, sliced**
  1 **medium red onion, diced**
  1 **medium tomato, diced**
  1 **cup frozen corn, thawed**
DRESSING:
 3/4 **cup thick and chunky salsa**
 1/4 **cup vegetable oil**
 1/4 **cup lime juice**
1-1/2 **teaspoons chili powder**
  1 **teaspoon salt**
 1/2 **teaspoon ground cumin**

In a bowl, combine beans, celery, onion, tomato and corn. In a small bowl, combine salsa, oil, lime juice, chili powder, salt and cumin; mix well. Pour dressing over the bean mixture and toss to coat. Cover salad and chill for at least 2 hours. **Yield:** 10 servings.

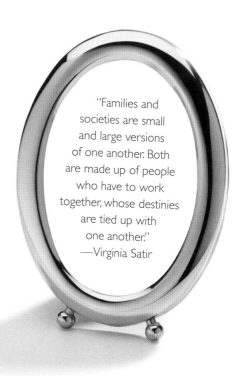

"Families and societies are small and large versions of one another. Both are made up of people who have to work together, whose destinies are tied up with one another."
—Virginia Satir

Sirloin Caesar Salad

(Pictured above)

A tangy sauce that combines bottled salad dressing, lemon juice and Dijon mustard flavors this filling main-dish salad. You save on cleanup time because both the steak and bread are cooked on the grill.
—Carol Sinclair, St. Elmo, Illinois

1 **boneless top sirloin steak (1 pound)**
1 **cup Caesar salad dressing**
1/4 **cup Dijon mustard**
1/4 **cup lemon juice**
6 **slices French bread (1 inch thick)**
12 **cups torn romaine**
1 **medium tomato, chopped**

Place steak in a large resealable plastic bag or shallow glass container. In a bowl, combine the salad dressing, mustard and lemon juice; set aside 3/4 cup. Pour remaining dressing mixture over the steak. Seal or cover and refrigerate for 1 hour, turning occasionally. Brush both sides of bread with 1/4 cup of the reserved dressing mixture. Grill bread, uncovered, over medium heat for 1-2 minutes on each side or until lightly toasted. Wrap in foil and set aside.

Drain steak, discarding marinade. Grill, covered, for 5-8 minutes on each side or until meat reaches desired doneness (for rare, a meat thermometer should read 140°; medium, 160°; well-done, 170°). Place romaine and tomato on a serving platter. Slice steak diagonally; arrange over salad. Serve with the bread and remaining dressing. **Yield:** 6 servings.

Soups, Salads & Sandwiches

Zucchini Soup

When there's an abundance of zucchini in our garden, I know it's time for this great-tasting soup.
—Mrs. R.C. Friend, Lynden, Washington

1 cup chopped onion
1 cup thinly sliced celery
1 garlic clove, minced
1/4 cup chopped green pepper
1 tablespoon vegetable oil
2 pounds zucchini, chopped
2 medium tomatoes, chopped
3 cups chicken broth
1/2 teaspoon dried basil
1/4 teaspoon dried thyme
1 cup half-and-half cream *or* milk

In a large saucepan, saute onion, celery, garlic and green pepper in oil until tender. Add zucchini, tomatoes, broth, basil and thyme; bring to a boil. Reduce heat; simmer, uncovered, for 20-30 minutes or until the vegetables are tender. Stir in cream; heat through. Serve hot or cold. **Yield:** 8 servings (2 quarts).

Slow-Cooked Chili

This hearty chili can cook up to 10 hours on low in the slow cooker. It's so good to come home to its wonderful aroma after a long day away.
—Sue Call, Beech Grove, Indiana

2 pounds ground beef
2 cans (16 ounces *each*) kidney beans, rinsed and drained
2 cans (14-1/2 ounces *each*) diced tomatoes, undrained
1 can (8 ounces) tomato sauce

2 medium onions, chopped
1 green pepper, chopped
2 garlic cloves, minced
2 tablespoons chili powder
2 teaspoons salt, optional
1 teaspoon pepper
Shredded cheddar cheese, optional

In a skillet, cook beef over medium heat until no longer pink; drain. Transfer to a slow cooker. Add the next nine ingredients. Cover and cook on low for 8-10 hours or on high for 4 hours. Garnish individual servings with cheese if desired. **Yield:** 10 servings.

Shrimp Salad Bagels

Dill adds fresh taste to this creamy spread. I usually prepare these hot open-faced sandwiches when I want a fast lunch. You can heat them in the microwave or pop them under the broiler if you'd like crispy bagels.
—Angie Hansen, Gildford, Montana

1 package (3 ounces) cream cheese, softened
3 tablespoons mayonnaise
1 tablespoon lemon juice
1/2 teaspoon dill weed
1 can (6 ounces) small shrimp, rinsed and drained
2 bagels, split and toasted
1/4 cup shredded Swiss cheese

In a bowl, combine cream cheese, mayonnaise, lemon juice and dill. Stir in the shrimp; spread over the bagels. Microwave, uncovered, on high for 1-1/2 to 2 minutes or broil 4 in. from the heat until hot and bubbly. Sprinkle with Swiss cheese. **Yield:** 4 servings.

SIZZLING RICE SOUP

(Pictured at right)

My family enjoys food with flair like this unique Oriental soup. Whenever I serve it, it's a hit.
—Mary Woodke, Gardiner, New York

- 1 **cup uncooked long grain rice**
- 8 **cups chicken broth**
- 2 **cups cubed cooked chicken**
- 2 **cups sliced fresh mushrooms**
- 1/4 **cup chopped green onions**
- 1 **can (8 ounces) bamboo shoots, drained**
- 1 **can (8 ounces) sliced water chestnuts, drained**
- 4 **chicken bouillon cubes**
- 1/2 **teaspoon garlic powder**
- 1 **package (10 ounces) frozen peas**
- 1/4 **cup vegetable oil**

Cook rice according to package directions. Spread on a greased 15-in. x 10-in. x 1-in. baking pan. Bake at 325° for 2 hours or until dried and browned, stirring occasionally; set aside.

In a large soup kettle or Dutch oven, combine the broth, chicken, mushrooms, onions, bamboo shoots, water chestnuts, bouillon and garlic powder. Cover and simmer for 1 hour. Add peas; cook for 15 minutes.

Just before serving, heat oil in a skillet. Fry rice in hot oil until it is slightly puffed. Ladle soup into serving bowls. Immediately spoon some hot rice into each bowl and it will sizzle. **Yield:** 10-12 servings (3 quarts).

Family-Tested Tip

Stretch your chili further for parties with a "Mexican pile-up." Stack ingredients in this order: crushed tortilla chips, rice, chili, beans, chopped lettuce, chopped tomatoes, sliced black olives, sliced jalapenos, shredded cheese, salsa and sour cream.
—Terri Gilmore, Roswell, New Mexico

ONION VINAIGRETTE SALAD

The recipe for this pretty dressing was given to me by my sister-in-law. We love the onion flavor.
—Harriet Stichter, Milford, Indiana

- 1 **cup sugar**
- 1 **cup vinegar**
- 1/2 **cup vegetable oil**
- 1/4 **cup chopped onion**
- 1-1/2 **teaspoons salt**
- 1/4 **teaspoon paprika**
- 1/4 **teaspoon ground mustard**
- **Dash pepper**
- **Torn salad greens**
- **Cherry tomatoes, sliced cucumber and grated carrots *or* vegetables of your choice**

In a jar with a tight-fitting lid, combine the first eight ingredients; shake well. In a salad bowl, combine greens and vegetables. Drizzle with dressing and toss to coat. Store any leftover dressing in the refrigerator. **Yield:** 2-1/2 cups dressing.

BEEF BARLEY SOUP

When making this versatile soup, I tend to clean out the refrigerator by adding leftovers. My family says they have to watch out for the kitchen sink!
—Sharon Kolenc, Jasper, Alberta

   2 **cups beef broth**
   8 **cups water**
   2 **cups chopped cooked roast beef**
 1/2 **cup chopped carrots**
   3 **celery ribs, chopped**
 1/2 **cup chopped onion**
   1 **can (14-1/2 ounces) diced tomatoes, undrained**
   1 **cup quick-cooking barley**
   1 **teaspoon dried oregano**
 1/2 **teaspoon pepper**
   1 **can (10-3/4 ounces) condensed tomato soup, undiluted**
 1/2 **cup frozen *or* canned peas**
 1/2 **cup frozen *or* canned cut green *or* wax beans**
Seasoned salt to taste

In a large kettle or Dutch oven, combine the first 10 ingredients; bring to a boil. Reduce heat; cover and simmer for 25 minutes, stirring occasionally. Add soup, peas and beans. Simmer, uncovered, for 10 minutes. Add seasoned salt. **Yield:** 12-14 servings (about 3-1/2 quarts).

SPICY SAUSAGE SANDWICHES

(Pictured at right)

These hearty sandwiches made with English muffins are packed with flavor and terrific for breakfast, lunch or a light supper. The pretty corn and pepper salsa is a garden-fresh topper for the sausage patties.
—Eileen Sullivan, Lady Lake, Florida

SALSA:
   2 **jalapeno peppers**
   1 **large fresh banana pepper**
 1/2 **cup diced sweet red pepper**
 1/2 **cup diced Vidalia *or* sweet onion**
 1/2 **cup fresh *or* frozen corn**
   1 **tablespoon chopped fresh cilantro**
SANDWICH:
   1 **pound bulk pork sausage**
   6 **English muffins, split and toasted**
   6 **slices Colby/Jack cheese**

Remove seeds and membranes from jalapeno and banana peppers if desired (for a less spicy salsa). Dice peppers and place in a bowl; add remaining salsa ingredients and mix well. Cover and refrigerate until ready to serve.

Form the sausage into six patties; cook in a skillet over medium heat until meat is no longer pink. Place each on an English muffin half; top with 1 tablespoon salsa and a slice of cheese. Cover with other muffin half. Serve remaining salsa on the side. **Yield:** 6 servings.

Editor's Note: When cutting or seeding hot peppers, use rubber or plastic gloves to protect your hands. Avoid touching your face.

TOASTED TURKEY SANDWICHES

(Pictured above)

With a special cranberry sauce, these sandwiches make a yummy supper. I often add a slice of cheddar cheese to the sandwiches for another flavor.
—*Patricia Kile, Greentown, Pennsylvania*

- 12 slices buttered French bread (1/2 inch thick)
- 6 thin slices cooked turkey
- 6 thin slices fully cooked ham
- 2 eggs, lightly beaten
- 1/2 cup milk
- 2 tablespoons butter
- 1/2 cup mayonnaise
- 1/3 cup whole-berry cranberry sauce

Make six sandwiches, dividing turkey and ham evenly between bread slices. In a shallow bowl, beat eggs and milk. Dip the sandwiches, turning to coat both sides.

In a large skillet over medium heat, melt butter. Brown sandwiches on both sides. Combine the mayonnaise and cranberry sauce; mix well. Serve with sandwiches. **Yield:** 6 servings.

BLACK BEAN SAUSAGE CHILI

I came up with this recipe when I wasn't sure what to do with a can of black beans. I threw a bunch of things together, and out came a new chili.
—*Nanci Keatley, Salem, Oregon*

- 1 pound bulk Italian sausage
- 3 garlic cloves, minced
- 1/2 cup chopped green pepper
- 1/2 cup chopped onion
- 1 can (15 ounces) black beans, rinsed and drained
- 1 can (14-1/2 ounces) diced tomatoes, undrained
- 1 can (11 ounces) whole kernel corn, drained
- 1 can (8 ounces) tomato sauce
- 1 can (6 ounces) tomato paste
- 1/2 cup water
- 1 tablespoon chili powder
- 1 teaspoon dried oregano
- 3/4 teaspoon salt
- 1/2 teaspoon dried basil
- 1/4 teaspoon pepper

Shredded cheddar cheese, optional

In a 3-qt. saucepan over medium heat, cook sausage and garlic. Add green pepper and onion. Cook and stir until meat is no longer pink and onion is tender; drain.

Add beans, tomatoes, corn, tomato sauce and paste, water, chili powder, oregano, salt, basil and pepper; bring to a boil. Reduce heat; cover and simmer for 30 minutes. Garnish with cheese if desired. **Yield:** 6 servings (1-3/4 quarts).

Family-Tested Tip

To keep bagged lettuce, carrots and cabbage crisp longer, add a few dry paper towels to the bag before putting it in the refrigerator. When the towels become wet, replace them with dry ones.
—*Alma Dalinsky, Lancaster, Pennsylvania*

SPECTACULAR OVERNIGHT SLAW

(Pictured below)

To create this crowd-pleasing coleslaw, I combined a number of different recipes and added some ideas of my own. As it chills overnight in the refrigerator, the flavor just keeps getting better. The slaw is a convenient option for busy-day events because you prepare the recipe ahead of time.
—Ruth Lovett, Bay City, Texas

1 medium head cabbage, shredded
1 medium red onion, thinly sliced
1/2 cup chopped green pepper
1/2 cup chopped sweet red pepper
1/2 cup sliced stuffed olives
1/2 cup white wine vinegar
1/2 cup vegetable oil
1/2 cup sugar
2 teaspoons Dijon mustard
1 teaspoon *each* salt, celery seed and mustard seed

In a 4-qt. bowl, combine the cabbage, onion, peppers and olives. In a saucepan, combine remaining ingredients; bring to a boil. Cook and stir for 1 minute. Pour over vegetables and stir gently. Cover and refrigerate overnight. Mix well before serving. **Yield:** 12-16 servings.

COMFORTING CHICKEN NOODLE SOUP

(Pictured above)

This rich, comforting soup is so simple to fix. I like to give a pot of it, along with the recipe, to new mothers so they don't have to worry about dinner.
—Joanna Sargent, Sandy, Utah

    2 quarts water
    8 chicken bouillon cubes
6-1/2 cups uncooked wide egg noodles
    2 cans (10-3/4 ounces *each*) condensed
       cream of chicken soup, undiluted
    3 cups cubed cooked chicken
    1 cup (8 ounces) sour cream
Minced fresh parsley

In a large saucepan, bring water and bouillon to a boil. Add noodles; cook, uncovered, until tender, about 10 minutes. Do not drain. Add soup and chicken; heat through.

Remove from heat; stir in the sour cream. Sprinkle with minced parsley. **Yield:** 10-12 servings (about 2-1/2 quarts).

ZESTY SLOPPY JOES

At big family gatherings, these sandwiches are a hit. A fantastic blend of seasonings in a hearty sandwich means no one can eat just one.
—Sandy Abrams, Greenville, New York

    4 pounds ground beef
    1 cup chopped onion
    1 cup finely chopped green pepper
    2 cans (10-3/4 ounces *each*) condensed
       tomato soup, undiluted
    1 can (15 ounces) thick and zesty tomato
       sauce
    1 can (8 ounces) tomato sauce
  3/4 cup packed brown sugar
  1/4 cup ketchup
    3 tablespoons Worcestershire sauce
    1 tablespoon prepared mustard
    1 tablespoon ground mustard
    1 teaspoon chili powder
    1 teaspoon garlic salt
   20 to 25 hamburger buns

In a large saucepan or Dutch oven, cook beef and onion over medium heat until meat is no longer pink. Add green pepper. Cook and stir for 5 minutes; drain. Add the next 10 ingredients; bring to a boil. Reduce heat; cover and simmer for 1 hour, stirring occasionally. Serve on buns. **Yield:** 20-25 servings.

"The presidency is temporary— but the family is permanent."
—Yvonne de Gaulle

LAYERED BASIL SALAD

(Pictured at right)

The basil in the dressing makes this salad stand out from the usual layered ones. The colorful ingredients look beautiful and taste wonderful together. It's especially impressive on a potluck buffet.
—Marcy Cella, L'Anse, Michigan

- 4 cups torn assorted salad greens
- 4 medium carrots, julienned
- 1-1/2 cups cooked macaroni shells
- 2 cups frozen peas, thawed
- 1 medium red onion, diced
- 3/4 pound fully cooked ham, cubed
- 1/3 cup shredded Swiss cheese
- 1/3 cup shredded cheddar cheese

DRESSING:
- 1 cup mayonnaise
- 1/2 cup sour cream
- 2 teaspoons Dijon mustard
- 1-1/2 teaspoons chopped fresh basil *or* 1/2 teaspoon dried basil
- 1/2 teaspoon salt
- 1/4 teaspoon pepper
- 2 hard-cooked eggs, cut into wedges, optional

In a 3-1/2-qt. glass bowl, layer the greens, carrots, macaroni, peas, onion, ham and cheeses. In a small bowl, combine the first six dressing ingredients; spread over the salad. Garnish with eggs if desired. Cover and chill for several hours. **Yield:** 12-14 servings.

ORANGE GELATIN SALAD

Our family loves to work together in the kitchen. With sweet mandarin orange segments, tangy pineapple and crunchy carrots, this pretty gelatin is one of our favorites to make—and eat!
—Joan Parker, Charlotte, North Carolina

- 1 package (3 ounces) orange gelatin
- 1 cup boiling water
- 1 can (8 ounces) crushed pineapple in juice
- 1 can (11 ounces) mandarin oranges, drained
- 1 cup grated carrots

In a bowl, dissolve gelatin in water. Drain pineapple, reserving juice; set the pineapple aside. Add enough water to the juice to make 1 cup; stir into gelatin. Chill until partially set. Fold in oranges, carrots and pineapple. Pour into a 5-cup serving bowl. Chill until firm. **Yield:** 4-6 servings.

Family-Tested Tips

Give sloppy joes a sweet-and-sour twist by adding a can of crushed pineapple, juice and all.
—Lana Cook, Bend, Oregon

To make flavored gelatin even more of a treat, substitute the same amount of ice cream for the cold water. Stir until the ice cream melts, then chill.
—Kim Friez, Mott, North Dakota

LAYERED ROAST BEEF SALAD

(Pictured at right)

I've prepared this fast-to-fix salad for my bridge club several times, and I always get requests for the recipe. If I don't have leftover roast beef on hand, I use sliced roast beef from the deli with equally tasty results.
—Susan Graham, Cherokee, Iowa

  8 **cups torn salad greens**
  1 **pound cooked roast beef, cut**
      into 3/4-inch strips
  1 **cup grated carrots**
1/2 **cup thinly sliced red onion**
  3 **hard-cooked eggs, sliced**
  1 **cup (8 ounces) sour cream *or* plain**
      yogurt
1/2 **cup mayonnaise**
  1 **tablespoon minced fresh parsley**
  1 **tablespoon minced fresh basil**

In a 3-qt. salad bowl, layer a third of the greens, beef, carrots, onion and eggs. Repeat layers twice. Combine remaining ingredients; spread over salad. Toss just before serving. **Yield:** 6-8 servings.

SUMMER SUB SANDWICH

(Pictured at right)

Being originally from the Northeast, we love submarine sandwiches. I created this hearty ham-and-cheese combination that's good either hot or cold.
—Jennifer Beck, Concord, Ohio

  1 **loaf (1 pound) unsliced French bread**
  1 **package (3 ounces) cream cheese,**
      softened
  8 **slices fully cooked ham**
  6 **slices provolone cheese**
  1 **jar (4 ounces) sliced mushrooms,**
      drained
1-1/2 **cups shredded lettuce**
  2 **medium tomatoes, thinly sliced**
  1 **small onion, thinly sliced**
  2 **banana peppers, thinly sliced**

Cut the loaf of bread in half horizontally. Spread bottom half with cream cheese; layer with ham, provolone and mushrooms. Replace top. Cut loaf in half; wrap in paper towels. Microwave on high for 45-60 seconds. Remove top; add lettuce, tomatoes, onion and peppers. Replace top. Cut into serving-size pieces. **Yield:** 4 servings.

    Editor's Note: When cutting or seeding hot peppers, use rubber or plastic gloves to protect your hands. Avoid touching your face.

BLT SOUP

(Pictured at right)

The BLT is a family favorite, so I came up with a soup that has all the fabulous flavor of the sandwich. But I gave it extra zip by adding picante sauce.
—Sharon Richardson, Dallas, Texas

  3 **tablespoons butter**
  2 **teaspoons vegetable oil**
  3 **cups cubed French bread**
  1 **pound sliced bacon, diced**
  2 **cups finely chopped celery**
  1 **medium onion, finely chopped**
  2 **tablespoons sugar**
  6 **tablespoons all-purpose flour**
  5 **cups chicken broth**
  1 **jar (16 ounces) picante sauce**
  1 **can (8 ounces) tomato sauce**
1/8 **teaspoon pepper**
  3 **cups shredded lettuce**

In a Dutch oven or large saucepan, heat butter and oil over medium heat. Add bread cubes; stir until crisp and golden brown. Remove and set aside. In same pan, cook bacon until crisp. Drain, reserving 1/4 cup drippings; set bacon aside.

    Saute celery and onion in drippings until tender. Add sugar; cook and stir for 1 minute. Stir in flour; cook and stir for 1 minute. Add broth, picante sauce, tomato sauce and pepper; bring to a boil. Boil and stir for 2 minutes. Just before serving, add lettuce and heat through. Garnish with the croutons and bacon. **Yield:** 8 servings (2 quarts).

SHREDDED PORK SANDWICHES

(Pictured at right)

With a zippy homemade sauce, these big sandwiches really stand out from the crowd. I received the recipe from my sister Linda, who's an excellent cook.
—Judi Jones, Wadsworth, Ohio

- 1 boneless pork shoulder roast (3 to 4 pounds)
- 1-1/4 cups ketchup
- 1/2 cup water
- 1/2 cup chopped celery
- 1/4 cup chopped onion
- 1/4 cup lemon juice
- 3 tablespoons vinegar
- 2 tablespoons Worcestershire sauce
- 2 tablespoons brown sugar
- 1-1/2 teaspoons ground mustard
- 1 teaspoon salt
- 1/2 teaspoon pepper
- 12 to 14 hamburger buns, split

Place roast in a Dutch oven or large kettle. In a bowl, combine the ketchup, water, celery, onion, lemon juice, vinegar, Worcestershire sauce, brown sugar, mustard, salt and pepper; pour over roast.

Cover and cook over medium-low heat for 4-6 hours or until meat is tender and pulls apart easily. Shred meat with two forks. Serve on buns. **Yield:** 12-14 servings.

GERMAN HOT NOODLE SALAD

Here's a tasty takeoff on German potato salad. This dish has all the tangy flavor of the traditional salad but uses egg noodles in place of potatoes. Everyone enjoys this simple variation.
—Gordon Kremer, Sacramento, California

- 2 cups wide egg noodles
- 3 bacon strips
- 1/4 cup chopped onion
- 1 tablespoon sugar
- 1 tablespoon all-purpose flour
- 1/4 teaspoon salt
- 1/8 teaspoon ground mustard
- 1/2 cup water
- 1/4 cup cider vinegar
- 1 cup sliced celery
- 2 tablespoons chopped fresh parsley

Cook noodles according to package directions. Meanwhile, in a skillet, cook the bacon until crisp. Crumble and set aside.

Reserve 1 tablespoon of drippings in the skillet; saute onion until tender. Stir in sugar, flour, salt and mustard; add water and vinegar. Cook and stir until thickened and bubbly, about 2-3 minutes.

Rinse and drain noodles; add to skillet. Stir in celery and parsley; heat through. Transfer to a serving bowl; sprinkle with bacon. **Yield:** 4 servings.

TURKEY FRUIT SALAD

(Pictured below)

This salad is a great way to use leftover turkey after Thanksgiving dinner or anytime. The citrus fruits make it refreshing, and the apples and toasted nuts give it a nice crunch. Just add a basket of breadsticks or rolls to round out your lunch or light supper.
—Mary Anne Mayberry, Fairmont, Minnesota

1/2 cup mayonnaise
2 tablespoons honey
1/8 teaspoon ground ginger
2 cups cubed cooked turkey
1 can (11 ounces) mandarin oranges, drained
1 cup chopped unpeeled apple
1 cup grape halves
1 can (8-1/4 ounces) pineapple chunks, drained
1/2 cup pecan halves, toasted

In a large bowl, combine mayonnaise, honey and ginger. Stir in turkey, oranges, apple, grapes and pineapple. Refrigerate for 1 hour. Sprinkle with pecans just before serving. **Yield:** 8 servings.

TOMATO DILL SOUP

Most often, I make this ahead of time and keep it in the fridge. The soup is particularly good alongside tuna or grilled cheese sandwiches. It has warm-you-up appeal served hot but is also delicious cold.
—Patty Kile, Greentown, Pennsylvania

1 medium onion, thinly sliced
1 garlic clove, minced
2 tablespoons vegetable oil
1 tablespoon butter
1/2 teaspoon salt
Pinch pepper
3 large tomatoes, sliced
1 can (6 ounces) tomato paste
1/4 cup all-purpose flour
2 cups water, *divided*
3/4 cup heavy whipping cream, whipped
1 to 2 tablespoons finely minced fresh dill *or* 1 to 2 teaspoons dill weed

In a large saucepan over low heat, cook onion and garlic in oil and butter until tender. Add salt, pepper and tomatoes; cook over medium-high heat for 3 minutes. Remove from the heat and stir in tomato paste.

In a small bowl, combine the flour and 1/2 cup of water; stir until smooth. Stir into saucepan. Gradually stir in the remaining water until smooth; bring to a boil over medium heat. Cook and stir for 2 minutes.

Place the mixture in a sieve over a bowl. With the back of a spoon, press the vegetables through the sieve to remove the seeds and skin; return puree to pan. Add cream and dill; cook over low heat just until heated through (do not boil). **Yield:** 4 servings (1 quart).

SAVORY CRESCENT BUNDLES

(Pictured below)

Each time I prepare this full-flavored recipe, I'm reminded fondly of my mother, who made it often for me and my seven brothers and sisters. It was her favorite—and now it's ours, too.
—Margaret Pache, Mesa, Arizona

1 package (3 ounces) cream cheese, softened
3 tablespoons butter, melted, *divided*
2 cups cooked cubed chicken *or* turkey
2 tablespoons milk
1 tablespoon chopped chives
1 tablespoon chopped pimientos
1/4 teaspoon salt
1/8 teaspoon pepper
1 tube (8 ounces) refrigerated crescent rolls
1/2 cup seasoned bread crumbs
Additional chives

In a mixing bowl, beat cream cheese and 2 tablespoons butter until smooth. Stir in chicken, milk, chives, pimientos, salt and pepper.

Separate crescent dough into four rectangles; firmly press the perforations to seal. Spoon 1/2 cup chicken mixture into the center of each rectangle. Bring four corners of the dough together and twist;

pinch the edges to seal.

Brush the tops of bundles with the remaining butter. Sprinkle with bread crumbs. Place on an ungreased baking sheet. Bake at 350° for 20-25 minutes or until golden brown. Tie a chive around each. **Yield:** 4 servings.

TACO PUFFS

I received this recipe years ago and still serve these hot and cheesy sandwiches regularly for dinner.
—Jan Schmid, Hibbing, Minnesota

1 pound ground beef
1/2 cup chopped onion
1 envelope taco seasoning
2 tubes (16.3 ounces *each*) large refrigerated flaky biscuits
8 ounces cheddar cheese, cut into 16 slices *or* 2 cups (8 ounces) shredded cheddar cheese

In a large skillet, cook beef and onion over medium heat until meat is no longer pink; drain. Add the taco seasoning and prepare according to package directions. Cool slightly.

Flatten half of the biscuits into 4-in. circles; place in greased 15-in. x 10-in. x 1-in. baking pans. Spoon 1/4 cup meat mixture onto each; top with two cheese slices or 1/4 cup shredded cheese. Flatten the remaining biscuits; place on top and pinch edges to seal tightly. Bake at 400° for 15 minutes or until golden brown. **Yield:** 8 servings.

MINESTRONE STEW

(Pictured above)

I add green chilies to this slow-cooked stew made from convenient pantry ingredients. You're sure to like the taste.
—Janie Hoskins, Red Bluff, California

1 pound ground beef
1 small onion, chopped
1 can (19 ounces) ready-to-serve minestrone soup
1 can (15 ounces) pinto beans, rinsed and drained
1 can (14-1/2 ounces) stewed tomatoes
1 can (11 ounces) whole kernel corn, drained
1 can (4 ounces) chopped green chilies

1 teaspoon salt
1/2 teaspoon garlic powder
1/2 teaspoon onion powder

In a skillet, cook beef and onion over medium heat until meat is no longer pink; drain. Transfer to a slow cooker. Add the remaining ingredients; mix well. Cover and cook on low for 4-6 hours or until heated through. **Yield:** 8 servings.

SPIRAL PASTA SALAD

(Pictured below)

I have two kids and am always on the go, so I appreciate recipes that I can prepare ahead of time. This super salad topped with a homemade dressing is easy to fix when I have a few spare moments. It's perfect for taking along on picnics or just about any outing.
—Darlene Kileel, Riverview, New Brunswick

    3 **cups cooked spiral pasta**
  1/2 **cup chopped green pepper**
  1/2 **cup sliced celery**
  1/2 **cup chopped tomato**
  1/2 **cup shredded carrot**
DRESSING:
  1/4 **cup vegetable oil**
  1/4 **cup cider vinegar**
  1/4 **cup chopped onion**
  2 **tablespoons ketchup**
  4 **teaspoons sugar**
  1/2 **teaspoon salt**
  1/4 **teaspoon ground mustard**
  1/4 **teaspoon paprika**
  1/4 **teaspoon garlic powder**
  1/4 **teaspoon dried oregano**

In a large bowl, combine pasta, green pepper, celery, tomato and carrot. In a jar with tight-fitting lid, combine dressing ingredients; shake well. Pour over salad and toss. Chill. **Yield:** 8 servings.

BAKED POTATO SALAD

I was tired of the ordinary potato salads served so often in summer, so I came up with this hearty flavorful variation. My family has enjoyed it now for several years, and I'm asked to make it whenever there's a get-together or cookout. I'm sure you'll like it as much as we do.
—Barbara O'Kane, Greenwood Lake, New York

4-1/2 **pounds potatoes, peeled and cut into 3/4-inch chunks**
  1/4 **cup olive oil**
  2 **envelopes Italian salad dressing mix**
  1 **medium green pepper, chopped**
  1 **medium sweet red pepper, chopped**
  1 **bunch green onions, chopped**
  2 **large tomatoes, chopped**
  4 **hard-cooked eggs, chopped**
  5 **bacon strips, cooked and crumbled**
1-1/2 **cups mayonnaise**
  1 **tablespoon vinegar**
  1 **tablespoon lemon juice**
  2 **teaspoons dried basil**
  1 **teaspoon salt**
  1/2 **teaspoon pepper**
  1/4 **teaspoon garlic powder**

In a large bowl, toss the potatoes with oil and dressing mixes. Place in two greased 13-in. x 9-in. x 2-in. baking pans. Bake, uncovered, at 400° for 45 minutes or until tender. Cool. Transfer to a large bowl; add peppers, onions, tomatoes, eggs and bacon. Toss gently.

Combine the remaining ingredients in a small bowl; mix well. Pour over the salad and stir gently. Cover and refrigerate for at least 1 hour. **Yield:** 16-20 servings.

PANFISH CHOWDER

(Pictured at right)

With my husband being an avid hunter and fisherman, I can never have enough new fish and wild game recipes. We especially enjoy this rich chowder with its chunks of fish, potatoes and bacon.
—Cyndi Fliss, Bevent, Wisconsin

    6 bacon strips, cut into 1-inch pieces
  2/3 cup chopped onion
  1/2 cup chopped celery
    3 medium potatoes, peeled and cubed
    2 cups water
  1/2 cup chopped carrots
    2 tablespoons minced fresh parsley
    1 tablespoon lemon juice
  1/2 teaspoon dill weed
  1/4 teaspoon garlic salt
  1/8 teaspoon pepper
    1 pound panfish fillets (perch, sunfish *or* crappie), cut into 1-inch chunks
    1 cup half-and-half cream

In a 3-qt. saucepan, cook the bacon until crisp. Remove bacon and set aside. Drain, reserving 2 tablespoons of drippings. Saute onion and celery in reserved drippings until tender.

Add the next eight ingredients. Simmer until vegetables are tender, about 30 minutes. Add fish and bacon; simmer for 5 minutes or just until fish flakes with a fork. Add cream and heat through. **Yield:** 4-6 servings.

"You don't choose your family.
They are God's gift to you,
as you are to them."
—Desmond Tutu

CRAN-RASPBERRY GELATIN

You'll love the sweet-tart flavor and beautiful ruby-red color of this chunky fruit salad. It's great served with a Thanksgiving turkey or with most any kind of meat.
—Kathy Jarvis, Bear Creek, Wisconsin

    1 package (3 ounces) raspberry gelatin
1-1/2 cups boiling water
    1 cup fresh *or* frozen cranberries
  1/2 cup raspberry jam *or* spreadable fruit
    1 can (8 ounces) crushed pineapple, undrained

In a bowl, dissolve gelatin in water. Place cranberries, jam and gelatin mixture in a blender or food processor; cover and process until the cranberries are coarsely chopped. Transfer to a bowl; stir in pineapple. Refrigerate until set. **Yield:** 8 servings.

SPINACH CHEESE SWIRLS

(Pictured above)

My family loves these super-easy sandwiches brimming with spinach and onion flavor. Using refrigerated pizza dough shaves minutes off prep time and creates a golden brown crust. The cheesy slices taste terrific warm or cold.
—Mary Nichols, Dover, New Hampshire

  1 package (10 ounces) frozen chopped spinach, thawed and drained
  2 cups (8 ounces) shredded mozzarella cheese
  1 cup finely chopped onion
  1 garlic clove, minced
  1 tube (10 ounces) refrigerated pizza crust

In a bowl, combine the first four ingredients and mix well. On a greased baking sheet, roll the pizza crust dough into a 14-in. x 10-in. rectangle; seal any holes.

Spoon filling over crust to within 1 in. of edge. Roll up, jelly-roll style, starting with a long side; seal the ends and place the seam side down. Bake at 400° for 25-27 minutes or until golden brown. Cut into slices. **Yield:** 4 servings.

TURKEY TORTILLA ROLL-UPS

To keep lunches new and exciting for my family, I like to make these roll-ups. They can be prepared ahead, so they're perfect for brown-bag lunches.
—Darlene Markel, Sublimity, Oregon

  3/4 cup sour cream
    6 flour tortillas (8 inches)
1-1/2 cups diced cooked turkey
    1 cup (4 ounces) finely shredded cheddar cheese
    1 cup shredded lettuce
  1/2 cup chopped ripe olives
  1/2 cup chunky salsa

Spread 2 tablespoons sour cream over each tortilla. Top with turkey, cheese, lettuce, olives and salsa. Roll up each tortilla tightly; wrap in plastic wrap. Refrigerate until serving. **Yield:** 6 servings.

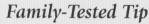

CHICKEN TORTILLA CHOWDER

(Pictured at right)

This recipe helps me have a hot meal on the table when my husband gets home. He's a real meat-and-potatoes man, but he loves this thick, creamy chowder with tortilla strips that puff up like homemade noodles.
—*Jennifer Gouge, Lubbock, Texas*

- 1 can (14-1/2 ounces) chicken broth
- 1 can (10-3/4 ounces) condensed cream of chicken soup, undiluted
- 1 can (10-3/4 ounces) condensed cream of potato soup, undiluted
- 1-1/2 cups milk
- 2 cups cubed cooked chicken
- 1 can (11 ounces) Mexicorn
- 1 jar (4-1/2 ounces) sliced mushrooms, drained
- 1 can (4 ounces) chopped green chilies
- 1/4 cup thinly sliced green onions
- 4 flour tortillas (6 to 7 inches), cut into 1/2-inch strips
- 1-1/2 cups (6 ounces) shredded cheddar cheese

In a Dutch oven or soup kettle, combine broth, soups and milk. Add the chicken, corn, mushrooms, chilies and onions; mix well. Bring to a boil. Add the tortilla strips.

Reduce heat; simmer, uncovered, for 8-10 minutes or until heated through. Add cheese; stir just until melted. Serve immediately. **Yield:** 8-10 servings (2-1/2 quarts).

CREAM OF CRAB SOUP

One of our Chesapeake Bay delicacies is the Maryland Blue Crab. It's abundant from May through October and used in a variety of dishes, like this rich soup.
—*Wanda Weller, Westminster, Maryland*

- 1/2 cup butter
- 1/2 cup all-purpose flour
- 1 to 2 tablespoons seafood seasoning
- 1 teaspoon salt
- 1/2 teaspoon curry powder
- 4 cups milk
- 1 pound cooked crabmeat *or* 3 cans (6 ounces *each*) crabmeat, drained
- 2 tablespoons minced fresh parsley

Additional milk and parsley, optional

Melt butter in a 3-qt. saucepan; stir in flour, seafood seasoning, salt and curry powder. Cook until thickened and bubbly. Gradually add milk; cook and stir until mixture is hot (do not boil).

Remove cartilage from crab if necessary. Add crab and parsley to soup; cook and stir just until crab is heated. If desired, thin soup with additional milk; garnish with parsley. **Yield:** 6-8 servings.

APPLE-HAM GRILLED CHEESE

(Pictured above)

After discovering this grilled cheese recipe years ago, I altered it to fit our tastes by adding chopped apples and walnuts. It only takes a few moments to mix in those two extra ingredients, and the results are well worth it. Our whole family loves these special sandwiches.
—Shirley Brazel, Rocklin, California

    1   cup chopped tart apples
    1/3 cup mayonnaise
    1/4 cup finely chopped walnuts
    8   slices process cheese (Velveeta)
    8   slices sourdough bread
    4   slices fully cooked ham
    1/4 cup butter, softened

Combine apples, mayonnaise and walnuts. Place a slice of cheese on four slices of bread. Layer each with 1/3 cup of the apple mixture, a slice of ham and another slice of cheese; cover with remaining bread. Butter the outsides of the sandwiches. Cook in a large skillet over medium heat on each side until bread is golden brown and cheese is melted. **Yield:** 4 servings.

"Love is the greatest gift that one generation can leave to another."
—Richard Garnett

ZESTY MACARONI SOUP

The recipe for this thick, zippy soup first caught my attention for two reasons—it calls for ingredients that are found in my pantry, and it can be prepared in a jiffy. A chili macaroni mix provides this dish with a little spice, but sometimes I jazz it up with green chilies.
—Joan Hallford, North Richland Hills, Texas

- 1 pound ground beef
- 1 medium onion, chopped
- 5 cups water
- 1 can (15 ounces) pinto beans, rinsed and drained
- 1 can (14-1/2 ounces) diced tomatoes, undrained
- 1 can (7 ounces) whole kernel corn, drained
- 1 can (4 ounces) chopped green chilies, optional
- 1/2 teaspoon ground mustard
- 1/2 teaspoon salt
- 1/8 teaspoon pepper
- 1 package (7-1/2 ounces) chili macaroni dinner mix

Salsa con queso dip

In a saucepan, cook beef and onion over medium heat until meat is no longer pink; drain. Stir in water, beans, tomatoes, corn and chilies if desired. Stir in mustard, salt, pepper and contents of macaroni sauce mix. Bring to a boil. Reduce heat; cover and simmer for 10 minutes.

Stir in contents of macaroni packet. Cover and simmer 10-14 minutes longer or until macaroni is tender, stirring once. Serve with salsa con queso dip. **Yield:** 8-10 servings (about 2-1/2 quarts).

Editor's Note: This recipe was tested with Hamburger Helper brand chili macaroni. Salsa con queso dip can be found in the international food section or snack aisle of most grocery stores.

SPINACH APPLE SALAD

(Pictured below and on the front cover)

Whenever Mom made this salad, it was the first thing on my plate. With spinach, apples, raisins and a light dressing, this beautiful harvest salad is a feast for the eyes as well as the palate.
—Darlis Wilfer, Phelps, Wisconsin

- 2 tablespoons cider vinegar
- 2 tablespoons vegetable oil
- 1/4 teaspoon salt
- 1/4 teaspoon sugar
- 1 cup diced unpeeled apple
- 1/4 cup chopped sweet onion
- 1/4 cup raisins
- 2 cups torn fresh spinach
- 2 cups torn romaine

In a small bowl, combine vinegar, oil, salt and sugar; mix well. Add apple, onion and raisins; toss lightly to coat. Cover and let stand for 10 minutes. Just before serving, combine spinach and romaine in a large salad bowl; add dressing and toss. **Yield:** 4-6 servings.

BAKED SOUTHWEST SANDWICHES

(Pictured below)

I like to make these special sandwiches for lunch with family and friends. The southwestern flavor created by a variety of toppings is out of this world. I'm often asked for a copy of the recipe.
—Holly Sorensen, Reedley, California

1 can (4-1/4 ounces) chopped ripe olives, drained
1/2 teaspoon chili powder
1/2 teaspoon ground cumin
1/4 teaspoon salt
1/2 cup mayonnaise
1/3 cup sour cream
1/3 cup chopped green onions
8 slices Italian bread
3/4 to 1 pound thinly sliced cooked turkey
2 medium tomatoes, thinly sliced
2 ripe avocados, sliced
3/4 cup shredded cheddar cheese
3/4 cup shredded Monterey Jack cheese

In a bowl, combine the olives, chili powder, cumin and salt; set aside 2 tablespoons. Add the mayonnaise, sour cream and onions to the remaining olive mixture.

Place bread on an ungreased baking sheet; spread 1 tablespoon of mayonnaise mixture on each slice. Top with turkey and tomatoes. Spread with another tablespoon of mayonnaise mixture; top with avocados and cheeses. Sprinkle with reserved olive mixture. Bake at 350° for 15 minutes or until heated through. **Yield:** 8 servings.

ALMOND CHICKEN SALAD

My mother used to prepare this salad for an evening meal during the hot summer months. It also serves well as a delicious but quick luncheon or potluck dish.
—Kathy Kittell, Lenexa, Kansas

4 cups cubed cooked chicken
1-1/2 cups halved green grapes
1 cup chopped celery
3/4 cup sliced green onions
3 hard-cooked eggs, chopped
1/2 cup mayonnaise
1/4 cup sour cream
1 tablespoon prepared mustard
1 teaspoon salt
1/2 teaspoon pepper
1/4 teaspoon onion powder
1/4 teaspoon celery salt
1/8 teaspoon ground mustard
1/8 teaspoon paprika
1/2 cup slivered almonds, toasted
1 kiwifruit, peeled and sliced, optional

In a large bowl, combine chicken, grapes, celery, onions and eggs. In another bowl, combine the next nine ingredients; stir until smooth. Pour over the chicken mixture and toss gently. Stir in almonds and serve immediately, or refrigerate and add the almonds just before serving. Garnish with kiwi if desired. **Yield:** 6-8 servings.

Best-Ever Potato Soup

(Pictured at right)

You'll be surprised at the taste of this rich, cheesy concoction—it's not a typical potato soup. I came up with the recipe after enjoying baked potato soup at one of our favorite restaurants. I added bacon, and we think that makes it even better.
—Coleen Morrissey, Sweet Valley, Pennsylvania

  6 bacon strips, diced
  3 cups cubed peeled potatoes
  1 can (14-1/2 ounces) chicken broth
  1 small carrot, grated
1/2 cup chopped onion
  1 tablespoon dried parsley flakes
1/2 teaspoon *each* celery seed, salt and pepper
  3 tablespoons all-purpose flour
  3 cups milk
  8 ounces process cheese (Velveeta), cubed
  2 green onions, thinly sliced, optional

In a large saucepan, cook bacon until crisp; drain. Add potatoes, broth, carrot, onion, parsley, celery seed, salt and pepper. Cover and simmer until potatoes are tender, about 15 minutes.

Combine flour and milk until smooth; add to soup. Bring to a boil; boil and stir for 2 minutes. Add cheese; stir until cheese is melted and the soup is heated through. Garnish with green onions if desired. **Yield:** 8 servings (2 quarts).

Zippy Radish Salad

I admit it—the first time I prepared this salad for my husband, he was skeptical! He loved it, though. Served with a rich entree or hot barbecue, it makes a light and refreshing side dish.
—Carol Stevens, Basye, Virginia

  2 cups thinly sliced radishes
1/2 cup cubed Swiss cheese
  2 green onions, thinly sliced
  1 garlic clove, minced
  1 tablespoon tarragon vinegar
1/2 teaspoon Dijon mustard
1/4 teaspoon salt
1/8 teaspoon pepper
  3 tablespoons olive oil
Leaf lettuce

In a bowl, combine radishes, cheese and onions. In a small bowl, combine garlic, vinegar, mustard, salt and pepper; whisk in oil until smooth. Pour over radish mixture; toss to coat. Chill for 2 hours. Serve on a bed of lettuce. **Yield:** 4 servings.

Chapter four

Look through any family collection of recipes,

and you'll likely find plenty of dishes featuring beef.

From classic grilled hamburgers and comforting

casseroles to old-fashioned meat loaves and Sunday

roasts, these menu mainstays will satisfy even

the heartiest appetites at the table.

Classic Swiss Steak
(Recipe on page 70)

♥ Beef & Ground Beef

STUFFED FLANK STEAK

(Pictured below)

This elegant slow-cooked meal is nice for family as well as for company. I like to make it on special occasions. The tasty tender steak cuts easily into appetizing spirals for serving, and extra stuffing cooks conveniently in a foil packet on top of the steak.
—Diane Hixon, Niceville, Florida

    1 package (8 ounces) crushed corn bread
         stuffing
    1 cup chopped onion
    1 cup chopped celery
  1/4 cup minced fresh parsley
  1/2 cup egg substitute
1-1/4 cups beef broth
  1/3 cup butter, melted
  1/2 teaspoon seasoned salt
  1/2 teaspoon pepper
1-1/2 pounds flank steak

In a large bowl, combine stuffing, onion, celery and parsley. In a small bowl, beat the egg substitute; stir in broth and butter. Pour over stuffing mixture. Sprinkle with seasoned salt and pepper; stir well.

Pound steak to 1/2-in. thickness. Spread 1-1/2 cups stuffing mixture over steak. Roll up, starting with a short side; tie with string. Place in a 5-qt. slow cooker. Remaining stuffing can be wrapped tightly in foil and placed over the rolled steak. Cover and cook on low for 6-8 hours or until a meat thermometer inserted in stuffing reads 165°. Remove string before slicing. **Yield:** 6 servings.

Editor's Note: No liquid is added to the slow cooker. The moisture comes from the meat.

CLASSIC SWISS STEAK

(Pictured on page 69)

When I prepare this dish for my husband and me, I always serve rolls or bread to dip in the sauce. We enjoy it to the last drop! For a large group, the recipe can be doubled and served as a casserole.
—Lorraine Dyda, Rancho Palos Verdes, California

    2 large carrots, sliced
    2 tablespoons vegetable oil, *divided*
    1 pound boneless round steak *or* sirloin
         steak
    1 can (14-1/2 ounces) diced tomatoes,
         undrained
    1 can (8 ounces) tomato sauce
    1 teaspoon sugar
  1/2 teaspoon dried oregano
  1/2 cup chopped onion
  1/2 cup chopped celery
    1 can (4 ounces) sliced mushrooms,
         drained
Hot cooked egg noodles

In a large skillet, saute carrots in 1 tablespoon oil until crisp-tender; remove and set aside. Cut meat into four pieces. Add meat and remaining oil to skillet; cook over medium-high heat until browned on both sides. Add tomatoes, tomato sauce, sugar and oregano; cover and simmer for 1 hour.

Add the onion, celery, mushrooms and carrots; cover and simmer for 45 minutes or until the meat and vegetables are tender. Thicken if desired. Serve over noodles. **Yield:** 4 servings.

to six 3/4-in.-thick patties (the mixture will be moist). In a bowl, combine the remaining cola and salad dressing; set aside.

Grill patties, uncovered, over medium-hot heat for 3 minutes on each side. Brush with cola mixture. Grill 8-10 minutes longer or until juices run clear, basting and turning occasionally. Serve on buns. **Yield:** 6 servings.

Editor's Note: Diet cola is not recommended for this recipe.

COLA BURGERS

(Pictured above)

The unusual combination of cola and French salad dressing added to the ground beef gives these hamburgers fabulous flavor. The mixture is also used as a basting sauce on the moist burgers, which are a family favorite.
—Melva Baumer, Millmont, Pennsylvania

  1 **egg**
1/2 **cup cola,** *divided*
1/2 **cup crushed saltines (about 15)**
  6 **tablespoons French salad dressing,** *divided*
  2 **tablespoons grated Parmesan cheese**
1/4 **teaspoon salt**
1-1/2 **pounds ground beef**
  6 **hamburger buns, split**

In a bowl, combine the egg, 1/4 cup cola, cracker crumbs, 2 tablespoons salad dressing, Parmesan cheese and salt. Add beef and mix well. Shape in-

PEPPERED BEEF TENDERLOIN

This tempting, well-seasoned tenderloin is perfect for folks who really savor a hearty beef dinner. It's important to let it rest for about 10 minutes before carving to allow the juices to work through the meat.
—Margaret Ninneman, La Crosse, Wisconsin

  1 **teaspoon dried oregano**
  1 **teaspoon paprika**
  1 **teaspoon dried thyme**
  1 **teaspoon salt**
1/2 **teaspoon garlic powder**
1/2 **teaspoon onion powder**
1/2 **teaspoon pepper**
1/2 **teaspoon white pepper**
1/8 **to 1/4 teaspoon cayenne pepper**
  1 **beef tenderloin (3 pounds)**

Combine seasonings and rub over entire tenderloin. Place on a rack in a roasting pan. Bake, uncovered, at 425° until meat is cooked as desired. Allow approximately 45-50 minutes for rare or until a meat thermometer reads 140°, 62-65 minutes for medium (160°) and 67-70 minutes for well-done (170°). Let stand 10 minutes before carving. **Yield:** 8-10 servings.

Editor's Note: After seasoning, the uncooked tenderloin may be wrapped tightly and refrigerated overnight for a more intense flavor.

CIDER BEEF STEW

(Pictured below)

When I was a new bride, this recipe was inside a serving dish I received as a gift. It's great on winter evenings paired with a loaf of fresh-from-the-oven bread.
—Carol Hendrickson, Laguna Beach, California

3 tablespoons all-purpose flour
1 teaspoon salt
1/2 teaspoon pepper
1 pound beef stew meat, cut into 1-inch pieces
2 tablespoons vegetable oil
1 cup apple cider
1/2 cup water
1 tablespoon vinegar
1/2 teaspoon dried thyme
2 large carrots, cut into 1-inch pieces
1 celery rib, cut into 1-inch pieces
1 large potato, peeled and cubed
1 medium onion, sliced

In a bowl or bag, combine flour, salt and pepper; add beef and toss to coat. In a saucepan, brown beef in oil. Add cider, water, vinegar and thyme; bring to a boil. Reduce heat; cover and simmer for 1 hour and 45 minutes or until meat is tender.

Add the carrots, celery, potato and onion; return to a boil. Reduce heat; cover and simmer for 45 minutes or until the vegetables are tender. **Yield:** 4 servings.

Beef & Ground Beef

Yankee Pot Roast

Rubbing garlic onto the roast before browning adds lots of flavor. With this recipe, the meat and vegetables turn out moist, tender and delicious.
—*Bill Schultz, Walden, New York*

     2 garlic cloves, minced
     1 beef chuck roast (3 to 3-1/2 pounds)
   1/4 cup all-purpose flour
   1/4 cup vegetable oil
     1 cup tomato juice
     4 medium carrots, sliced
     2 medium onions, chopped
     1 cup thinly sliced celery
     2 bay leaves
     1 teaspoon salt
   1/2 teaspoon dried thyme
   1/4 teaspoon pepper
     4 medium potatoes, peeled and quartered

Rub garlic onto roast, then coat with flour. In a large Dutch oven, brown roast in oil. Add the tomato juice, carrots, onions, celery, bay leaves, salt, thyme and pepper; bring to a boil. Reduce heat; cover and simmer for 3-1/2 hours, turning the meat occasionally.

Add potatoes; simmer for 30 minutes or until tender. Remove bay leaf. Remove roast and slice; serve with vegetables and gravy. **Yield:** 4-6 servings.

Bohemian Beef Dinner

One of my favorite things to do when I was growing up was to help my mother in the kitchen while she prepared traditional Czech dishes like this. It's a savory stick-to-your-ribs meal with beef and sauerkraut covered in a creamy sauce.
—*Carl Wanasek, Rogers, Arkansas*

   3/4 cup all-purpose flour
     1 teaspoon salt
   1/4 teaspoon pepper

     2 pounds beef stew meat, cut into 1-inch cubes
     2 tablespoons vegetable oil
     2 medium onions, chopped
     1 garlic clove, minced
     1 teaspoon dill weed
     1 teaspoon caraway seed
     1 teaspoon paprika
   1/2 cup water
     1 cup (8 ounces) sour cream
     1 can (27 ounces) sauerkraut
Additional paprika

In a bowl or plastic bag, combine flour, salt and pepper. Add beef; dredge or shake to coat. In a Dutch oven, brown the beef, half at a time, in oil; drain. Add onions, garlic, dill, caraway, paprika and water. Cover and simmer for 2 hours or until meat is tender, stirring occasionally.

Stir in sour cream; heat through but do not boil. Heat sauerkraut; drain and spoon onto a serving platter. Top with the beef mixture. Sprinkle with paprika. **Yield:** 6 servings.

"A family is a unit composed not only of children, but of men, women, an occasional animal and the common cold."
—Ogden Nash

paste, ketchup, garlic, brown sugar, onion, vinegar, mustard, salt and remaining water; mix well. Pour over ribs; bring to a boil. Reduce heat; cover and simmer for 1 hour or until meat is tender. Serve over noodles. **Yield:** 4-6 servings.

RED FLANNEL HASH

This is an old-fashioned meal that satisfies big appetites with its hearty mix of ingredients. It gets its name from the rosy color the dish picks up from the beets.
—Jesse and Anne Foust, Bluefield, West Virginia

- 3 tablespoons vegetable oil
- 1 can (15 ounces) sliced beets, drained and chopped
- 2 cups chopped cooked corned beef
- 2-1/2 cups diced cooked potatoes
- 1 medium onion, chopped
- 1/4 cup half-and-half cream
- 2 tablespoons butter, melted
- 2 teaspoons dried parsley flakes
- 1 teaspoon Worcestershire sauce
- 1/4 teaspoon salt
- 1/8 teaspoon pepper

Heat oil in a 12-in. skillet. Add all remaining ingredients. Cook and stir over low heat for 20 minutes or until lightly browned and heated through. **Yield:** 4 servings.

BARBECUED BEEF SHORT RIBS

(Pictured above)

For a real straight-from-the-chuckwagon beef meal, you can't rope a better main dish than this! It's the recipe I rely on when feeding a hungry group. The wonderfully tangy sauce is lip-smacking good.
—Mildred Sherrer, Bay City, Texas

- 3 to 4 pounds bone-in beef short ribs
- 1 tablespoon vegetable oil
- 2-1/2 cups water, *divided*
- 1 can (6 ounces) tomato paste
- 1 cup ketchup
- 1 garlic clove, minced
- 3/4 cup packed brown sugar
- 1/2 cup chopped onion
- 1/2 cup vinegar
- 2 tablespoons prepared mustard
- 1-1/2 teaspoons salt
- Hot cooked noodles

In a Dutch oven, brown ribs in oil. Add 2 cups water; bring to a boil. Reduce heat; cover and simmer for 1-1/2 hours. Drain. Combine the tomato

Family-Tested Tip

Give beef stew southwestern zest by adding canned green chilies, ground cumin and Mexican-style stewed tomatoes to the basic recipe. For extra flair, top each serving with some shredded cheddar cheese and a little sour cream.
—Anne Elmore-De Vinny, Orlando, Florida

BEEF 'N' BISCUIT BAKE

I think this quick-and-easy recipe is a great example of Midwest cuisine because it just tastes good!
—Erin Schneider, St. Peters, Missouri

1 pound ground beef
1 can (16 ounces) kidney beans, rinsed and drained
1 can (15-1/4 ounces) whole kernel corn, drained
1 can (10-3/4 ounces) condensed tomato soup, undiluted
1/4 cup milk
2 tablespoons minced onion
1/2 teaspoon chili powder
1/4 teaspoon salt
1 cup cubed process cheese (Velveeta)
1 tube (12 ounces) refrigerated biscuits
2 to 3 tablespoons butter, melted
1/3 cup yellow cornmeal

In a saucepan over medium heat, cook the beef until no longer pink; drain. Add the beans, corn, soup, milk, onion, chili powder and salt; bring to a boil. Remove from the heat; stir in cheese until melted. Spoon into a greased 2-1/2-qt. baking dish. Bake, uncovered, at 375° for 10 minutes.

Meanwhile, brush all sides of biscuits with butter; roll in cornmeal. Place on top of bubbling meat mixture. Return to the oven for 10-12 minutes or until biscuits are lightly browned and cooked through. **Yield:** 6-8 servings.

ZIPPY BEEF BAKE

(Pictured at right)

With its south-of-the-border flavor, this filling meal-in-one is a much-requested recipe in our home. In fact, we like it so much we have it about once a week!
—Gay Kelley, Tucson, Arizona

3/4 pound ground beef
1 tablespoon butter
2 medium zucchini, thinly sliced
1/4 pound fresh mushrooms, sliced
2 tablespoons sliced green onions
1-1/2 teaspoons chili powder
1 teaspoon salt
1/8 teaspoon garlic powder
1-1/2 cups cooked rice
1 can (4 ounces) chopped green chilies
1/2 cup sour cream
1 cup (4 ounces) shredded Monterey Jack cheese, *divided*

In a large skillet over medium heat, cook beef until no longer pink. Add butter, zucchini, mushrooms and onions; cook and stir until the vegetables are tender. Drain.

Stir in chili powder, salt and garlic powder. Add rice, chilies, sour cream and half of the cheese. Transfer to a greased 2-qt. baking dish; top with remaining cheese. Bake, uncovered, at 350° for 20 minutes or until cheese is melted. **Yield:** 4 servings.

TOMATO-FRENCH BREAD LASAGNA

(Pictured below)

For a big hearty meal, I make this as a side dish to go with veal cutlets or a roast. But you could also serve the beefy lasagna as a main dish. Just pair it with a tossed green salad and loaf of garlic bread.
—Patricia Collins, Imbler, Oregon

      1 pound ground beef
    1/3 cup chopped onion
    1/3 cup chopped celery
      2 garlic cloves, minced
     14 slices French bread (1/2 inch thick)
      4 large tomatoes, sliced 1/2 inch thick
      1 teaspoon dried basil
      1 teaspoon dried parsley flakes
      1 teaspoon dried oregano
      1 teaspoon dried rosemary, crushed
      1 teaspoon garlic powder
    3/4 teaspoon salt
    1/2 teaspoon pepper
      2 teaspoons olive oil, *divided*
      3 tablespoons butter
      3 tablespoons all-purpose flour
  1-1/2 cups milk
    1/3 cup grated Parmesan cheese
      2 cups (8 ounces) shredded mozzarella cheese

In a skillet, cook beef, onion, celery and garlic over medium heat until beef is no longer pink; drain and set aside. Toast bread; line bottom of an ungreased 13-in. x 9-in. x 2-in. baking dish with 10 slices. Top with half of the meat mixture and half of the tomatoes.

Combine seasonings; sprinkle half over tomatoes. Drizzle with 1 teaspoon oil. Crumble remaining bread over top. Repeat layers of meat, tomatoes, seasonings and oil.

In a saucepan over medium heat, melt the butter; stir in flour until smooth. Gradually stir in milk; bring to a boil. Cook and stir until thickened and bubbly, about 2 minutes. Remove from the heat; stir in Parmesan. Pour over casserole. Top with mozzarella. Bake, uncovered, at 350° for 40-45 minutes or until bubbly and cheese is golden brown. **Yield:** 8-10 servings.

BEEF 'N' RICE HOT DISH

Ground beef and rice star in this satisfying casserole. It's prepared on the stovetop…meaning dinner's ready in no time.
—Elma Katainen, Menahga, Minnesota

      1 pound ground beef
      1 medium onion, chopped
    1/2 cup chopped green pepper
    1/2 teaspoon salt
  Pinch pepper
  1-1/2 cups uncooked instant rice
      1 can (14-1/2 ounces) stewed tomatoes
      1 can (8 ounces) tomato sauce
  1-1/2 cups hot water
      1 teaspoon prepared mustard

In a skillet, cook beef over medium heat until no longer pink; drain. Add onion, green pepper, salt and pepper; cook and stir over medium heat until vegetables are tender. Add remaining ingredients; bring to a boil. Reduce heat; cover and simmer for 10 minutes. **Yield:** 4 servings.

COUNTRY-FRIED STEAKS

(Pictured above)

This down-home recipe calls for cube steak instead of round steak, so there's no need to pound the meat.
—Bonnie Malloy, Norwood, Pennsylvania

5 tablespoons all-purpose flour, *divided*
1/4 cup cornmeal
1/2 teaspoon salt
1/4 teaspoon pepper
4 beef cube steaks (about 1 pound)
1 egg white
1 teaspoon water
2 tablespoons vegetable oil, *divided*
GRAVY:
1 tablespoon butter
2 tablespoons all-purpose flour
1-1/2 cups milk
1 teaspoon beef bouillon granules
1/2 teaspoon dried marjoram
1/4 teaspoon dried thyme
1/8 teaspoon pepper

Combine 3 tablespoons flour, cornmeal, salt and pepper; set aside. Coat steaks with remaining flour. Beat egg white and water; dip steaks, then dredge in cornmeal mixture.

In a skillet over medium-high heat, cook two steaks in 1 tablespoon oil for 5-7 minutes on each side or until crisp, lightly browned and cooked as desired. Remove steaks and keep warm. Repeat with the remaining oil and steaks.

Meanwhile, for gravy, melt butter in a saucepan; stir in flour until well blended. Gradually add milk; bring to a boil over medium heat. Boil for 2 minutes, stirring constantly; reduce heat to medium-low. Add bouillon, marjoram, thyme and pepper; simmer, uncovered, for 4-5 minutes, stirring occasionally. Serve over steaks. **Yield:** 4 servings.

Family-Tested Tip

Have extra liquid at the bottom of the salsa jar? Save the liquid and add it to ground beef to give hamburgers, meat loaves or casseroles extra zip.
—Wendy Nowakowski, Rama, Saskatchewan

In a Dutch oven, brown beef in oil. Add the beef broth, onions, garlic and seasonings. Cover and simmer for 2-1/2 hours or until beef is tender; reduce heat.

Combine water and flour until smooth; gradually stir into the beef mixture. Cook and stir for 2 minutes. Add sour cream and heat through (do not boil). Serve over rice with sauerkraut on the side. **Yield:** 6-8 servings.

BAVARIAN BEEF DINNER

(Pictured above)

I've had this recipe for quite a number of years. I won second place with it in a cooking contest that was sponsored by our local newspaper.
—Dot Christiansen, Bettendorf, Iowa

    2 pounds boneless chuck roast, cut
       into 1-inch cubes
    2 tablespoons vegetable oil
1-1/2 cups beef broth
    2 medium onions, sliced
    1 garlic clove, minced
    1 teaspoon *each* dill seed, caraway seed,
       paprika and salt
  1/4 teaspoon pepper
  1/4 cup cold water
    3 tablespoons all-purpose flour
    1 cup (8 ounces) sour cream
Hot cooked rice
    1 can (14 ounces) sauerkraut, warmed

SUPREME ROAST BEEF

This fix-and-forget roast is one of our family's favorite Sunday meals. With just five ingredients, it's simple to prepare and leaves plenty of leftovers that we can enjoy later in the week.
—Jackie Holland, Gillette, Wyoming

    1 large onion, sliced into rings
    2 tablespoons Worcestershire sauce
    4 to 5 teaspoons coarsely ground pepper
    1 boneless rump roast (4 to 5 pounds)
    6 to 8 bay leaves

Place onion in a greased shallow roasting pan. Rub Worcestershire sauce and pepper over the roast. Place over the onion; top with bay leaves. Cover and bake at 325° for 1-3/4 to 2-1/4 hours or until meat reaches desired doneness.

Discard bay leaves. Let stand for 10-15 minutes before carving. Thicken pan juices if desired. **Yield:** 8 servings.

CHILI NACHO SUPPER

(Pictured at right)

This creamy, chili-like dish can be served over corn chips and eaten with a fork...or kept warm in a slow cooker and served as a hearty dip at parties.
—Laurie Withers, Wildomar, California

2-1/2 pounds ground beef
 3 cans (15 ounces *each*) tomato sauce
 2 cans (16 ounces *each*) pinto beans, rinsed and drained
 1 can (10 ounces) diced tomatoes and green chilies, undrained
 2 envelopes chili mix
 2 pounds process cheese (Velveeta), cubed
 1 cup heavy whipping cream
 2 packages (16 ounces *each*) corn chips
Sour cream

In a Dutch oven, cook the beef until no longer pink; drain. Add tomato sauce, beans, tomatoes and chili mix; heat through. Add cheese and cream; cook until the cheese is melted. Serve over chips. Top with sour cream. **Yield:** 14-16 servings.

BEST MEAT LOAF

My husband loves meat loaf. Everyone who's tried this one agrees that it lives up to its name.
—Dorothy Pritchett, Wills Point, Texas

 1/3 cup chopped onion
 1/3 cup chopped sweet red pepper
 1/3 cup chopped green pepper
 3 tablespoons minced fresh parsley
 3 garlic cloves, minced
1-1/4 teaspoons chili powder
1-1/4 teaspoons dried sage
1-1/4 teaspoons salt
 1 teaspoon pepper
 2 pounds ground beef
 3/4 cup milk
 2 eggs, beaten
 1/4 cup Worcestershire sauce

 2/3 cup dry bread crumbs
 4 bacon strips
SAUCE:
 1/4 cup chopped canned tomatoes
 1/4 cup ketchup
 2 tablespoons brown sugar
 1 teaspoon salt
 1 teaspoon ground mustard
 1/2 teaspoon pepper

In a large bowl, combine the first nine ingredients. Crumble beef over mixture; mix well. Combine the milk, eggs and Worcestershire sauce; mix into the beef mixture. Add crumbs.

Grease a large sheet of foil. Place bacon on foil. Mold meat mixture into a loaf and place over bacon. Seal foil tightly around loaf. Refrigerate for 2 hours or overnight.

Place wrapped loaf on a baking sheet. Bake at 350° for 1 hour. Open foil; drain juices. Combine sauce ingredients and spoon over loaf. Bake, uncovered, 30 minutes longer or until no pink remains and a meat thermometer reads 160°. **Yield:** 8 servings.

FOUR-CHEESE LASAGNA

(Pictured at right)

This tempting cheese-packed lasagna can be prepared ahead of time and baked later.
—Janet Myers, Napanee, Ontario

1 pound ground beef
1 medium onion, chopped
2 garlic cloves, minced
1 can (28 ounces) diced tomatoes, undrained
1 can (8 ounces) sliced mushrooms, drained
1 can (6 ounces) tomato paste
1 teaspoon salt
1 teaspoon dried oregano
1 teaspoon dried basil
1/2 teaspoon pepper
1/2 teaspoon fennel seed
1 carton (16 ounces) cottage cheese
2/3 cup grated Parmesan cheese
1/4 cup shredded mild cheddar cheese
1-1/2 cups (6 ounces) shredded mozzarella cheese, *divided*
2 eggs
1 pound lasagna noodles, cooked and drained

In a skillet, cook beef, onion and garlic over medium heat until meat is no longer pink and onion is tender; drain. In a blender, process the tomatoes until smooth. Stir into beef mixture along with mushrooms, tomato paste and seasonings; simmer 15 minutes.

In a bowl, combine cottage cheese, Parmesan, cheddar, 1/2 cup mozzarella and eggs. Spread 2 cups meat sauce in bottom of an ungreased 13-in. x 9-in. x 2-in. baking dish. Arrange half the noodles over sauce. Spread cheese mixture over noodles. Top with remaining noodles and sauce.

Cover and bake at 350° for 45 minutes. Uncover; sprinkle with remaining mozzarella. Return to the oven for 15 minutes or until cheese is melted. **Yield:** 12 servings.

"What can you do to promote world peace? Go home and love your family."
—Mother Teresa

HEARTY HAMBURGER SUPPER

My husband and I are retired and enjoy home cooking. This hearty stovetop meal proves that it doesn't have to be time-consuming.
—Georgene Remm, Wausa, Nebraska

3/4 **pound ground beef**
  1 **small onion, chopped**
  4 **cups diced cabbage**
1/4 **cup all-purpose flour**
1-1/2 **teaspoons salt**
1/4 **teaspoon paprika**
  2 **cups milk**
Hot mashed potatoes
Additional paprika, optional

In a large saucepan, cook the beef and onion over medium heat until the meat is no longer pink and onion is tender; drain. Add cabbage; cook and stir for 2 minutes. Sprinkle with flour, salt and paprika; mix well.

Gradually add milk. Bring to a boil; boil and stir for 2 minutes. Reduce heat; cover and simmer for 10-12 minutes or until the cabbage is tender. Serve over potatoes. Sprinkle with paprika if desired. **Yield:** 4 servings.

COLORFUL STUFFED PEPPERS

(Pictured at right)

You're sure to enjoy this tasty twist on traditional stuffed peppers. Crisp-tender pepper cups hold a colorful filling that gets south-of-the-border flavor from salsa and cumin.
—Angie Dierikx, State Center, Iowa

  1 **pound ground beef**
  2 **cups salsa**
  1 **cup frozen corn**
1/4 **cup water**
3/4 **teaspoon ground cumin**
3/4 **teaspoon dried oregano**
  1 **teaspoon salt**
1/2 **teaspoon pepper**
1/2 **cup uncooked instant rice**

  1 **cup (4 ounces) shredded cheddar cheese,** *divided*
  4 **medium green peppers, halved lengthwise**
Sliced canned jalapeno peppers, optional

Crumble beef into a 2-qt. microwave-safe dish. Cover and microwave on high for 2 minutes; stir. Cook on high 1-2 minutes longer or until the meat is no longer pink; drain.

Stir in salsa, corn, water, cumin, oregano, salt and pepper. Cover and microwave on high for 3 minutes or until mixture bubbles around the edges. Stir in rice and 1/2 cup cheese. Cover and let stand for 5 minutes; stir.

Spoon 1/2 cupful into each pepper half. Place on a 12-in. round microwave-safe plate. Cover loosely and cook on high for 8-10 minutes or until peppers are tender, rotating a half turn once. Cover and let stand for 4 minutes. Sprinkle with remaining cheese; top with jalapenos if desired. **Yield:** 4 servings.

Editor's Note: This recipe was tested in an 850-watt microwave.

Potato-Topped Chili Loaf

(Pictured at right)

Here's a meat loaf that constitutes a complete meal, even for the biggest appetites. No one leaves the table hungry when I serve this tasty combination of beef, potatoes, corn and beans.
—Glenn Schildknecht, Savannah, Missouri

3/4 cup diced onion
1/3 cup saltine crumbs
  1 egg
  3 tablespoons milk
  1 tablespoon chili powder
1/2 teaspoon salt
1-1/2 pounds ground beef
TOPPING:
  3 cups hot mashed potatoes (with milk and butter)
  1 can (11 ounces) Mexicorn, drained
  1 can (15-1/2 ounces) kidney beans, rinsed and drained
1/4 cup thinly sliced green onions
  1 cup (4 ounces) shredded cheddar *or* taco cheese, *divided*

Combine the first six ingredients; crumble beef over mixture and mix well. Press into an ungreased 9-in. square baking pan. Bake at 375° for 25 minutes or until no longer pink; drain.

Combine the potatoes, corn, beans, onions and 1/2 cup of cheese; spread over meat loaf. Sprinkle with the remaining cheese. Bake 15 minutes longer or until the potato layer is lightly browned and heated through. **Yield:** 6 servings.

Family-Tested Tip

To easily cut flank steak into thin, uniform pieces for use in stir-fries, fajitas or other dishes, do the cutting while the steak is partially frozen.
—Elizabeth Wood, Veazie, Maine

Mexican Chip Casserole

This satisfying casserole relies on convenient packaged ingredients to create an entree with savory Southwestern flair. There's nothing tricky about the preparation, and I have time to set the table while it's in the oven.
—Doris Heath, Franklin, North Carolina

  1 pound ground beef
  1 medium onion, chopped
  1 garlic clove, minced
  1 can (10-3/4 ounces) condensed cream of mushroom soup, undiluted
  1 can (11 ounces) Mexicorn
  1 can (4 ounces) chopped green chilies
  1 package (10-1/2 ounces) corn chips
  1 can (10 ounces) enchilada sauce
  1 to 2 cups (4 to 8 ounces) shredded Colby-Monterey Jack cheese

In a skillet, cook beef, onion and garlic over medium heat until meat is no longer pink and onion is tender; drain. Add soup, corn and chilies; mix well. In an ungreased shallow 3-qt. baking dish, layer meat mixture, chips and sauce; top with cheese. Bake, uncovered, at 350° for 8-10 minutes or until heated through. **Yield:** 6 servings.

TRADITIONAL BOILED DINNER

When St. Patrick's Day rolls around each year, my family and I look forward to having a traditional hearty meal of corned beef and cabbage.
—Joy Strasser, Mukwonago, Wisconsin

1 corned beef brisket with spice packet (3 pounds)
1 teaspoon whole black peppercorns
2 bay leaves
2 medium potatoes, peeled and quartered
3 medium carrots, quartered
1 medium onion, cut into 6 wedges
1 small head green cabbage, cut into 6 wedges
Prepared horseradish *or* mustard, optional

Place the brisket and contents of spice packet in a large kettle or Dutch oven. Add the peppercorns, bay leaves and enough water to cover; bring to a boil. Reduce heat; cover and simmer for 2 hours or until meat is almost tender.

Add the potatoes, carrots and onion; bring to a boil. Reduce heat; cover and simmer for 10 minutes. Add cabbage; cover and simmer for 15-20 minutes or until tender. Discard the bay leaves and peppercorns. Thinly slice the meat; serve with the vegetables and horseradish or mustard if desired. **Yield:** 6 servings.

SCOTT'S BEEF BRISKET

(Pictured at right)

My brother and I made special grills to cook and smoke 20 briskets at a time for parties. I created this recipe to achieve a similar fork-tender, sweet and spicy brisket using the oven.
—Scott Post, Clayton, North Carolina

1/2 teaspoon *each* ground allspice, chili powder, garlic powder, onion powder, paprika, seasoned salt and sugar
1/4 teaspoon pepper
1 fresh beef brisket (3 to 4 pounds)
1/2 cup cola
1/3 cup Worcestershire sauce
1/2 cup cider vinegar
1/2 cup butter, melted
1/3 cup soy sauce
3/4 cup barbecue sauce
Additional barbecue sauce, optional

Combine the dry seasonings; cover and set aside. Place brisket in a shallow dish or large heavy-duty resealable plastic bag. Combine the cola and Worcestershire sauce; pour over meat. Cover or seal and refrigerate overnight.

Drain meat; discard marinade. Rub seasoning mix over brisket; place in a large shallow roasting pan. Combine vinegar, butter and soy sauce; pour over meat. Cover and bake at 325° for 2 hours, basting occasionally.

Drain drippings. Pour barbecue sauce over meat. Cover and bake for 1 hour or until the meat is tender. Remove meat from pan; let stand 15 minutes before slicing. Serve with additional barbecue sauce if desired. **Yield:** 6-8 servings.

Editor's Note: This is a fresh brisket, not corned beef.

DEEP-DISH PIZZA

(Pictured at right)

My family quickly devours this crusty pan pizza that has delicious toppings. With plenty of ground beef, it also satisfies everyone's appetite. Use a combination of green, red and yellow peppers for added color.
—Patricia Howson, Carstairs, Alberta

  1 package (1/4 ounce) active dry yeast
  1 cup warm water (110° to 115°)
  1 teaspoon sugar
  1 teaspoon salt
  2 tablespoons vegetable oil
2-1/2 cups all-purpose flour
  1 pound ground beef, cooked and drained
  1 can (10-3/4 ounces) condensed tomato soup, undiluted
  1 teaspoon *each* dried basil, oregano and thyme
  1 teaspoon dried rosemary, crushed
1/4 teaspoon garlic powder
  1 small green pepper, julienned
  1 can (8 ounces) mushroom stems and pieces, drained
  1 cup (4 ounces) shredded mozzarella cheese

In a bowl, dissolve yeast in water. Stir in sugar, salt, oil and flour. Beat vigorously 20 strokes. Cover and let rest for 20 minutes.

On a floured surface, roll into a 13-in. x 9-in. rectangle. Transfer to a greased 13-in. x 9-in. x 2-in. baking pan. Sprinkle with beef.

Combine soup and seasonings; spoon over beef. Top with green pepper, mushrooms and cheese. Bake at 425° for 20-25 minutes or until crust and cheese are lightly browned. **Yield:** 8 servings.

SHEPHERD'S PIE

(Pictured at right)

Instead of using a pastry crust, this recipe creates a savory crust with mashed potatoes. The bacon flavor in the filling is fabulous! Just add a tossed salad or green vegetable and dessert, and you'll have a complete meal that's sure to please your family.
—Chris Eschweiler, Dallas, Texas

  1 pound ground beef
  3 bacon strips, diced
  1 small onion, chopped
  2 garlic cloves, minced
1/4 teaspoon dried oregano
1/2 cup tomato sauce
  1 can (2-1/4 ounces) chopped ripe olives, drained
5-1/2 cups hot mashed potatoes (prepared without milk and butter)
  2 eggs, beaten
  2 tablespoons butter, softened
  1 tablespoon minced fresh cilantro
1/4 teaspoon salt
Additional butter, melted

In a skillet, cook beef over medium heat until no longer pink; drain and set aside. In the same skillet, cook bacon, onion, garlic and oregano until bacon is crisp. Stir in tomato sauce, olives and beef. Simmer for 10 minutes.

Meanwhile, combine the mashed potatoes, eggs, butter, cilantro and salt; mix well. Spread half of the potato mixture onto the bottom and up the sides of a greased 9-in. pie plate. Top with the beef mixture and remaining potato mixture. Bake at 375° for 20 minutes.

Brush the pie with the melted butter. Bake 10 minutes longer or until top is golden brown. **Yield:** 6-8 servings.

BEEF BURRITOS

(Pictured at right)

Living in Arizona, we enjoy all sorts of foods with Southwestern flair, such as these beef-stuffed tortillas. The recipe is easy to make and easy to serve. Folks can assemble their own burritos with their choice of garnishes.
—Amy Martin, Waddell, Arizona

2 **chuck pot roasts (2-1/2 to 3 pounds** *each***)**
2 **tablespoons vegetable oil**
1 **cup water**
1 **large onion, chopped**
4 **garlic cloves, minced**
2 **teaspoons dried oregano**
2 **teaspoons salt**
1 **teaspoon pepper**
1 **can (28 ounces) diced tomatoes, undrained**
2 **cans (4 ounces** *each***) chopped green chilies**
2 **tablespoons all-purpose flour**
1/4 **cup cold water**
4 **to 6 drops hot pepper sauce**
18 **flour tortillas (8 inches), warmed**
Shredded cheddar cheese, sour cream and salsa

In a Dutch oven over medium heat, brown roasts in oil; drain. Add water, onion, garlic, oregano, salt and pepper; bring to a boil. Reduce heat; cover and simmer for 2 to 2-1/2 hours or until meat is tender. Remove roasts; cool.

Remove the meat from the bone and cut into bite-size pieces. Skim the fat from the pan juices. Add tomatoes and chilies; mix well. Add meat; bring to a boil. Reduce heat; simmer, uncovered, for 30 minutes.

Combine flour and cold water; mix well. Stir into beef mixture. Cook over medium heat, stirring constantly, until thickened and bubbly. Add hot pepper sauce. Spoon down the center of tortillas; fold top and bottom of tortilla over filling and roll up. Serve with cheese, sour cream and salsa.
Yield: 18 servings.

TERIYAKI KABOBS

It takes just seconds to stir up this delicious marinade, which flavors the beef and vegetables wonderfully. Marinate the meat a few hours or overnight— whatever suits your schedule.
—Candy VanderWaal, Elkhart Lake, Wisconsin

1/3 **cup soy sauce**
2 **tablespoons vegetable oil**
1 **tablespoon brown sugar**
1 **garlic clove, minced**
1 **teaspoon ground ginger**

1 teaspoon seasoned salt
1-1/2 pounds boneless sirloin steak, cut into 1-1/4-inch cubes
12 whole fresh mushrooms
1 large green pepper, cut into 1-1/2-inch pieces
1 large onion, cut into wedges
12 cherry tomatoes
Hot cooked rice, optional

In a bowl, combine soy sauce, oil, brown sugar, garlic, ginger and salt; mix well. Pour half of the marinade into a large resealable plastic bag or shallow glass container; add beef and turn to coat. Seal or cover; refrigerate for 4-8 hours, turning occasionally. Cover and refrigerate the remaining marinade.

Drain the meat, discarding the marinade. On metal or soaked bamboo skewers, alternate meat, mushrooms, green pepper, onion and tomatoes. Grill, uncovered, over medium heat for 3 minutes on each side.

Baste with reserved marinade. Continue turning and basting for 8-10 minutes or until meat reaches desired doneness (for rare, a meat thermometer should read 140°; medium, 160°; well-done, 170°). Serve meat and vegetables over rice if desired. **Yield:** 6 servings.

CHILIES RELLENOS CASSEROLE

I love to cook with green chilies and often use recipes featuring them when I entertain. This beefy main dish has a big pepper taste in every bite. Time and again, the casserole has proven to be a winner.
—Nadine Estes, Alto, New Mexico

1 can (7 ounces) whole green chilies
1-1/2 cups (6 ounces) shredded Colby-Monterey Jack cheese
3/4 pound ground beef
1/4 cup chopped onion
1 cup milk
4 eggs
1/4 cup all-purpose flour
1/4 teaspoon salt
1/8 teaspoon pepper

Split chilies and remove seeds; dry on paper towels. Arrange chilies on the bottom of a greased 2-qt. baking dish. Top with cheese. In a skillet, cook beef and onion over medium heat until meat is no longer pink; drain. Spoon over the cheese.

In a mixing bowl, beat the milk, eggs, flour, salt and pepper until smooth; pour over the beef mixture. Bake, uncovered, at 350° for 45-50 minutes or until a knife inserted near the center comes out clean. Let stand 5 minutes before serving. **Yield:** 6 servings.

Editor's Note: When cutting or seeding hot peppers, use rubber or plastic gloves to protect your hands. Avoid touching your face.

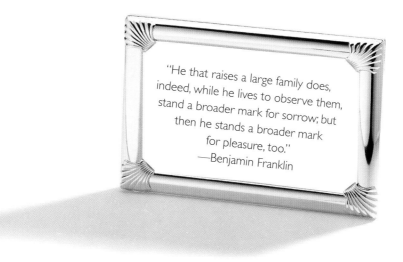

"He that raises a large family does, indeed, while he lives to observe them, stand a broader mark for sorrow; but then he stands a broader mark for pleasure, too."
—Benjamin Franklin

MEATY MAC 'N' CHEESE

(Pictured below)

I don't have a lot of time to spend in the kitchen, so I came up with this tasty way to beef up macaroni and cheese. Corn, olives and salsa provide extra flavor.
—Charlotte Kremer, Pahrump, Nevada

- 1 package (7-1/4 ounces) macaroni and cheese
- 1 pound ground beef
- 1/4 cup chopped onion
- 1-1/2 cups salsa
- 1/2 cup fresh *or* frozen corn
- 1 can (2-1/4 ounces) sliced ripe olives, drained
- 3 tablespoons diced pimientos

Shredded cheddar cheese
Chopped tomato

Set aside cheese sauce mix from macaroni and cheese; cook macaroni according to package directions. Meanwhile, in a large saucepan, cook beef and onion until meat is no longer pink; drain. Add the salsa, corn, olives and pimientos; heat through. Drain macaroni; add to beef mixture with contents of cheese sauce mix. Mix well; heat through. Garnish with cheese and tomato. **Yield:** 4-6 servings.

Editor's Note: The milk and butter listed on the macaroni and cheese package are not used in this recipe.

CUBE STEAK PARMIGIANA

I received this recipe when I was newly married, and it became an instant favorite. Now my family of six loves these saucy, cheese-topped steaks so much that I have to double the recipe! I like to serve them with pasta.
—Kathryn Bray, Westfield, Indiana

- 3 tablespoons all-purpose flour
- 1/2 teaspoon salt
- 1/4 teaspoon pepper
- 1 egg
- 1 tablespoon water
- 1/3 cup grated Parmesan cheese
- 1/3 cup finely crushed saltines (about 10)
- 1/2 teaspoon dried basil
- 6 cube steaks (about 4 ounces *each*)
- 2 tablespoons vegetable oil

SAUCE:
- 1 can (15 ounces) tomato sauce
- 1 tablespoon sugar
- 1 garlic clove, minced
- 1/2 teaspoon dried oregano, *divided*
- 3 slices mozzarella cheese, halved
- 1/3 cup grated Parmesan cheese

In three shallow bowls, combine flour, salt and pepper; beat egg and water; and combine Parmesan cheese, saltines and basil. Dip steaks in the flour mixture and egg mixture, then roll in the cheese mixture.

In a large skillet, heat 1 tablespoon of oil over medium-high heat. Brown three steaks on both sides. Remove to a greased 13-in. x 9-in. x 2-in. baking pan. Repeat with the remaining steaks, adding additional oil as needed. Bake, uncovered, at 375° for 25 minutes. Drain any pan juices.

Combine the tomato sauce, sugar, garlic and 1/4

teaspoon of oregano; pour over steaks. Bake 20 minutes longer. Place mozzarella cheese on steaks. Sprinkle with Parmesan and remaining oregano. Return to the oven for 5 minutes or until cheese is melted. **Yield:** 6 servings.

MEXICAN BEEF BURGERS

(Pictured above)

One night for dinner, half of the family said they wanted hamburgers and the other half requested tacos. So my daughter-in-law and I came up with a compromise to satisfy everyone. These flavor-packed burgers are wrapped in tortillas and have tasty toppings.
—Stanny Barta, Pisek, North Dakota

2 eggs, beaten
2 cans (4 ounces *each*) chopped green chilies
1/4 cup finely minced onion
1/3 cup salsa
1 teaspoon salt
1/2 teaspoon pepper
1 garlic clove, minced

3/4 cup finely crushed corn chips
2 pounds ground beef
8 flour tortillas (10 inches), warmed
TOPPINGS:
Chopped tomatoes
Chopped ripe olives
Shredded cheddar cheese
Shredded lettuce
Salsa
Sour cream

In a bowl, combine the first seven ingredients. Add chips and beef; mix well. Shape into eight patties. Pan-fry, grill or broil until no longer pink. Wrap burgers and desired toppings in tortillas. **Yield:** 8 servings.

SLOPPY JOE UNDER A BUN

I usually keep a can of sloppy joe sauce in the pantry because our family loves sloppy joes. But sometimes I don't have buns on hand. With this fun casserole, we can still enjoy the flavor that we love in a flash. The bun-like top crust is made with biscuit mix, sprinkled with sesame seeds and baked until golden.
—Trish Bloom, Romeo, Michigan

1-1/2 pounds ground beef
1 can (15-1/2 ounces) sloppy joe sauce
2 cups (8 ounces) shredded cheddar cheese
2 cups biscuit/baking mix
2 eggs, beaten
1 cup milk
1 tablespoon sesame seeds

In a skillet, cook beef over medium heat until no longer pink; drain. Stir in sloppy joe sauce; mix well. Transfer to a lightly greased 13-in. x 9-in. x 2-in. baking dish; sprinkle with cheese.

In a bowl, combine biscuit mix, eggs and milk just until blended. Pour over cheese; sprinkle with sesame seeds. Bake, uncovered, at 400° for 25 minutes or until golden brown. **Yield:** 8 servings.

meat. Press the remaining bread crumbs onto butter mixture.

Place meat on a rack in a shallow roasting pan. Bake, uncovered, at 350° for 15 minutes. Cover and bake for 1 hour or until meat reaches desired doneness (for rare, a meat thermometer should read 140°; medium, 160°; well-done, 170°). Let stand for 10 minutes and remove toothpicks before slicing. **Yield:** 6-8 servings.

MUSHROOM-STUFFED TENDERLOIN

(Pictured above)

These tender beef slices are filled with a tasty mixture of mushrooms, bacon and bread crumbs.
—Marie Steeber, Mishicot, Wisconsin

    3 bacon strips
    1 cup chopped fresh mushrooms
    2 tablespoons chopped onion
    1 garlic clove, minced
  3/4 cup dry bread crumbs, *divided*
    2 tablespoons minced fresh parsley
    1 beef tenderloin (about 2 pounds), trimmed
    1 tablespoon butter, melted
    1 tablespoon grated Parmesan cheese

In a skillet, cook bacon until crisp. Remove bacon; crumble and set aside. Drain, reserving 1 tablespoon drippings. In the drippings, saute the mushrooms, onion and garlic until tender. Remove from the heat; stir in 1/2 cup of bread crumbs, parsley and bacon.

Cut a slit lengthwise three-quarters of the way through the tenderloin. Lightly place stuffing in the pocket; close with toothpicks. Combine butter and Parmesan cheese; spread over top and sides of

GRILLED STEAK PINWHEELS

I've been serving this recipe to family and friends for 20 years, and very seldom do I have leftovers. We try to keep the house cool, so we grill out often. I get most of the herbs for this recipe from my son's garden.
—Mary Hills, Scottsdale, Arizona

    2 flank steaks (1 pound *each*), trimmed
  1/2 pound sliced bacon, cooked and crumbled
    1 cup finely chopped fresh mushrooms
    1 cup finely chopped green onions
  1/4 cup finely chopped fresh basil
       or 4 teaspoons dried basil
    2 tablespoons minced fresh chives

Pound flank steaks on each side. Combine bacon, mushrooms, onions, basil and chives; spread evenly over steaks. Roll the meat up and secure with skewers or toothpicks. Cut each roll into 1/2- to 3/4-in. slices and secure with a toothpick or skewer. Grill over medium-hot heat for 4-6 minutes on each side or until meat reaches desired doneness. Remove picks before serving. **Yield:** 6-8 servings.

Family-Tested Tip

Making shepherd's pie? Instead of preparing mashed potatoes, combine a can of cream of celery soup with milk and frozen hash browns, then layer that mixture on top of the meat and vegetables.
—*Tanya Sheets, Stoney Creek, Ontario*

STEAK STIR-FRY

(Pictured below)

No one would guess this elegant entree is a snap to prepare at the last minute. To save even more prep time, use frozen mixed veggies instead of fresh. Sometimes I substitute chicken, chicken bouillon and curry for the beef, beef bouillon and ginger.
—Janis Plourde, Smooth Rock Falls, Ontario

1 teaspoon beef bouillon granules
1 cup boiling water
2 tablespoons cornstarch
1/3 cup soy sauce
1 pound boneless sirloin steak, cut into thin strips
1 garlic clove, minced
1 teaspoon ground ginger
1/4 teaspoon pepper
2 tablespoons vegetable oil, *divided*
1 large green pepper, julienned
1 cup sliced carrots *or* celery
5 green onions, cut into 1-inch pieces
Hot cooked rice

Dissolve bouillon in water. Combine the cornstarch and soy sauce until smooth; add to bouillon. Set aside. Toss beef with garlic, ginger and pepper. In a large skillet or wok over medium-high heat, stir-fry beef in 1 tablespoon oil until cooked as desired; remove and keep warm.

Heat remaining oil; stir-fry vegetables until crisp-tender. Stir soy sauce mixture and add to the skillet; bring to a boil. Cook and stir for 2 minutes. Return meat to pan and heat through. Serve over rice. **Yield:** 4 servings.

SWEDISH MEATBALLS

(Pictured below)

I can still remember how happy it made my mom to cook something special for a family gathering. My parents were ranchers all their lives, so almost every main dish featured beef. This is Mom's recipe for tender Swedish meatballs with a thick, savory gravy.
—Donna Hanson, Lusk, Wyoming

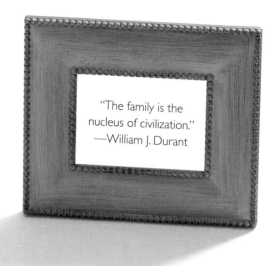

"The family is the nucleus of civilization."
—William J. Durant

    4 eggs
    1 cup milk
    8 slices white bread, torn
    2 pounds ground beef
  1/4 cup finely chopped onion
    4 teaspoons baking powder
    1 to 2 teaspoons salt
    1 teaspoon pepper
    2 tablespoons shortening
    2 cans (10-3/4 ounces *each*) condensed
       cream of chicken soup, undiluted
    2 cans (10-3/4 ounces *each*) condensed
       cream of mushroom soup, undiluted
    1 can (12 ounces) evaporated milk
Minced fresh parsley

In a large bowl, beat eggs and milk. Add bread; mix gently and let stand for 5 minutes. Add beef, onion, baking powder, salt and pepper; mix well (mixture will be soft). Shape into 1-in. balls. In a large skillet, brown meatballs, a few at a time, in shortening. Place in an ungreased 3-qt. baking dish. In a bowl, stir soups and milk until smooth; pour over meatballs. Bake, uncovered, at 350° for 1 hour. Sprinkle with parsley. **Yield:** 8-10 servings.

ONE-SKILLET SPAGHETTI

I call this medley my "homemade hamburger helper." Everything—including the spaghetti—cooks right in the same skillet. I serve this meal often to my family. It's so convenient, and they all really love it.
—Joanne Shew Chuk, St. Benedict, Saskatchewan

    1 pound ground beef
    2 medium onions, chopped
    1 package (7 ounces) ready-cut spaghetti
    1 can (28 ounces) diced tomatoes,
       undrained
  3/4 cup chopped green pepper
  1/2 cup water
    1 can (8 ounces) sliced mushrooms,
       drained
    1 teaspoon chili powder
    1 teaspoon dried oregano
    1 teaspoon sugar
    1 teaspoon salt
    1 cup (4 ounces) shredded cheddar cheese

In a large skillet, cook beef and onions over medium heat until meat is no longer pink; drain. Stir in uncooked spaghetti and the next eight ingredients; bring to a boil. Reduce heat; cover and simmer for 30 minutes or until the spaghetti is tender. Sprinkle with cheese; cover and heat until melted. **Yield:** 4-6 servings.

BARBECUED CHUCK ROAST

Whether I serve this roast for church dinners, company or family, it is always a hit. If there's ever any left over, it makes good sandwiches, too.
—Ardis Gautier, Lamont, Oklahoma

1/3 cup cider vinegar
1/4 cup ketchup
  2 tablespoons vegetable oil
  2 tablespoons soy sauce
  1 tablespoon Worcestershire sauce
  1 teaspoon garlic powder
  1 teaspoon prepared mustard
  1 teaspoon salt
1/4 teaspoon pepper
  1 boneless chuck roast (2-1/2 to 3 pounds)
1/2 cup applesauce

In a large resealable plastic bag or shallow glass container, combine the first nine ingredients; mix well. Add roast and turn to coat. Seal bag or cover container; refrigerate for at least 3 hours, turning occasionally.

  Remove roast. Pour marinade into a small saucepan; bring to a boil. Reduce heat; simmer for 15 minutes. Meanwhile, grill roast, covered, over indirect heat for 20 minutes, turning occasionally.

  Add applesauce to marinade; brush over roast. Continue basting and turning the roast several times for 1 to 1-1/2 hours or until meat reaches desired doneness (for rare, a meat thermometer should read 140°; medium, 160°; well-done, 170°). **Yield:** 6-8 servings.

SWEET-AND-SOUR POT ROAST

(Pictured above)

I was so pleased to receive this recipe since it gives pot roast a new mouth-watering flavor.
—Erica Warkentin, Dundas, Ontario

12 small white potatoes, peeled
  1 boneless beef chuck roast
    (about 3 pounds)
  1 tablespoon vegetable oil
  1 cup chopped onion
  1 can (15 ounces) tomato sauce
1/4 cup packed brown sugar
  2 to 3 tablespoons Worcestershire sauce
  2 tablespoons cider vinegar
  1 teaspoon salt

Place the potatoes in a slow cooker. Trim fat from roast; brown in oil on all sides in a skillet. Place meat in the slow cooker. Discard all but 1 tablespoon drippings from skillet; saute onion until tender. Stir in tomato sauce, brown sugar, Worcestershire sauce, vinegar and salt. Pour over the meat and potatoes.

  Cover and cook on high for 4-5 hours or until meat is tender. Before serving, pour sauce into a skillet. Cook and stir over medium-high heat until thickened; serve with potatoes and meat. **Yield:** 6-8 servings.

Chapter five

Time and again, family cooks who want a sure

winner rely on popular poultry. Try finger-lickin'

fried chicken, delicious skillets, traditional stuffed

turkeys, taste-tempting bakes or any of the other

unbeatable entrees in this chapter. Whichever you

fix, rest assured it's a tried-and-true hit.

Stuffed Chicken Breasts
(Recipe on page 96)

♥Chicken & Turkey

TARRAGON CHICKEN CASSEROLE

(Pictured above)

For a quick, satisfying main dish that's ideal when the weather's warm, try this casserole. With cooked chicken, it bakes in just half an hour. People love the tasty sauce and cheese on top.
—Bob Breno, Strongsville, Ohio

 2 cans (10-3/4 ounces *each*) condensed cream of chicken soup, undiluted
 2 cups half-and-half cream
 4 teaspoons dried tarragon
 1/2 teaspoon pepper
 1 package (16 ounces) linguine *or* spaghetti, cooked and drained
 6 cups cubed cooked chicken
 1/2 cup grated Parmesan cheese
Paprika, optional

In a large bowl, combine soup, cream, tarragon and pepper. Stir in the linguine and chicken. Transfer to an ungreased 4-qt. baking dish. Sprinkle with the Parmesan cheese and paprika if desired. Bake, uncovered, at 350° for 30 minutes or until heated through. **Yield:** 12 servings.

STUFFED CHICKEN BREASTS

(Pictured on page 95)

Mushroom-and-rice stuffing turns plain chicken breasts into a terrific main dish that your family will remember.
—Pat Neu, Gainesville, Texas

 1-1/2 cups sliced fresh mushrooms
 1-1/3 cups uncooked instant rice
 1/4 cup chopped onion
 1/4 cup chopped celery leaves
 1/4 cup butter
 1-1/2 cups water
 1-1/2 teaspoons salt
 1/2 teaspoon dried oregano
 1/2 teaspoon rubbed sage
 1/2 teaspoon dried thyme
 1/4 teaspoon pepper
 1/3 cup chopped pecans, toasted
 6 bone-in chicken breast halves

In a saucepan, saute mushrooms, rice, onion and celery leaves in butter until onion is tender. Add water and seasonings; bring to a boil. Reduce heat; cover and simmer for 5-7 minutes or until rice is tender and liquid is absorbed. Stir in pecans.

Stuff 1/2 cup of the rice mixture under the skin of each chicken breast half. Place in a greased 13-in. x 9-in. x 2-in. baking dish. Bake, uncovered, at 350° for 1-1/2 hours or until juices run clear. **Yield:** 6 servings.

"Put together all the existing families, and you have society."
—Virginia Satir

CHICKEN AND BARLEY BOILED DINNER

(Pictured below)

I began putting this meal-in-one on my menu because it's nutritious and adequately feeds the big appetites in my family. For a hearty home-style dinner, it's surprisingly easy to prepare. That's especially nice when I don't have a lot of time to spend in the kitchen.
—Susan Greeley, Morrill, Maine

2 broiler-fryer chickens (about 3 pounds *each*), cut up and skinned
3 tablespoons vegetable oil
2 quarts chicken broth
1 cup uncooked brown rice
1/2 cup medium pearl barley
1 medium onion, chopped
2 bay leaves
1/2 teaspoon dried basil
2 teaspoons salt
1/4 teaspoon pepper
8 carrots, cut into 1-inch pieces
2-1/2 cups frozen cut green beans
2 celery ribs, cut into 1-inch pieces

In an 8-qt. kettle or Dutch oven, brown chicken in oil. Remove chicken and set aside. Drain. In the same kettle, combine the broth, rice, barley, onion, bay leaves, basil, salt and pepper; bring to a boil. Reduce heat. Return chicken to pan; cover and simmer for 45 minutes.

Stir in the carrots, beans and celery. Cook over medium heat for 30 minutes or until the chicken and grains are tender. Remove bay leaves before serving. **Yield:** 6-8 servings.

cup mozzarella cheese, basil and remaining salt. Top with chicken. Cover and bake at 400° for 25 minutes or until chicken juices run clear. Uncover; sprinkle with remaining cheese. Bake 10 minutes longer or until cheese is melted. **Yield:** 4 servings.

BAKED CHICKEN AND ZUCCHINI

I like zucchini, and this colorful dish is one of my favorites. I make it often in summer. It's especially good with tomatoes fresh from the garden.
—*Sheryl Goodnough, Eliot, Maine*

1 egg
1 tablespoon water
3/4 teaspoon salt, *divided*
1/8 teaspoon pepper
1 cup dry bread crumbs
4 boneless skinless chicken breast halves
4 tablespoons olive oil, *divided*
5 medium zucchini, sliced
4 medium tomatoes, sliced
1 cup (4 ounces) shredded mozzarella cheese, *divided*
2 teaspoons minced fresh basil

In a shallow bowl, beat egg, water, 1/2 teaspoon salt and pepper. Set aside 2 tablespoons bread crumbs. Place the remaining crumbs in a large re-sealable plastic bag. Dip chicken in egg mixture, then place in bag and shake to coat.

In a skillet, cook the chicken in 2 tablespoons oil for 2-3 minutes on each side or until golden brown; remove and set aside. In the same skillet, saute the zucchini in remaining oil until crisp-tender; drain. Transfer to a greased 13-in. x 9-in. x 2-in. baking dish.

Sprinkle the reserved bread crumbs over the zuc-chini. Top with the tomato slices; sprinkle with 2/3

CHICKEN AVOCADO MELT

(Pictured below)

Avocados are used in many Southwestern recipes, so I feel this represents my region well. It's very easy to prepare and has great flavor. Everyone loves it.
—*Pat Cade, Canyon Lake, Texas*

4 boneless skinless chicken breast halves
1/3 cup cornstarch
1 teaspoon ground cumin
1 teaspoon garlic powder
1 teaspoon salt
1/8 teaspoon cayenne pepper
1 egg
2 tablespoons water
1/2 cup cornmeal

1/4 cup vegetable oil
1 medium avocado, thinly sliced
2 cups (8 ounces) shredded Monterey Jack cheese
Sour cream, salsa and sliced green onions, optional

Pound chicken to 1/4-in. thickness; set aside. In a shallow bowl, combine cornstarch, cumin, garlic powder, salt and cayenne. In another bowl, beat egg and water. Dip chicken into egg, then into the cornstarch mixture; coat with cornmeal.

In a large skillet, brown chicken in oil until golden brown on both sides. Place in a greased 13-in. x 9-in. x 2-in. baking dish; arrange avocado evenly on top. Bake, uncovered, at 350° for 10-15 minutes or until juices run clear. Sprinkle with cheese. Serve with sour cream, salsa and green onions if desired. **Yield:** 4 servings.

TURKEY POTPIE

(Pictured at right)

Family and guests rave about this hearty potpie and its light flaky crust. The "secret" crust ingredients are Parmesan cheese and instant mashed potato flakes. On busy days, I prepare this entree in the morning and just bake it in the evening.
—Cheryl Arnold, Lake Zurich, Illinois

1 can (10-3/4 ounces) condensed cream of mushroom soup, undiluted
1 can (5 ounces) evaporated milk
1/4 cup minced fresh parsley *or* 1 tablespoon dried parsley flakes
1/2 teaspoon dried thyme
3 cups cubed cooked turkey
1 package (10 ounces) frozen mixed vegetables, thawed
1/4 teaspoon salt
1/4 teaspoon pepper
CRUST:
3/4 cup instant mashed potato flakes
3/4 cup all-purpose flour
1/4 cup grated Parmesan cheese
1/3 cup butter
1/4 cup ice water
Half-and-half cream

In a bowl, combine the first four ingredients. Stir in turkey, vegetables, salt and pepper. Spoon into a greased 11-in. x 7-in. x 2-in. baking dish.

For the crust, combine the potato flakes, flour and Parmesan in a bowl; cut in the butter until crumbly. Add water, 1 tablespoon at a time, tossing lightly with a fork until the dough forms a ball. On a lightly floured surface, roll the dough to fit the baking dish. Cut vents in the crust, using a small tree or star cutter if desired. Place over the filling; flute the edges.

Brush pastry with cream. Bake at 400° for 25-30 minutes or until golden brown. If necessary, cover edges of crust with foil to prevent overbrowning. **Yield:** 6 servings.

CHICKEN WITH POTATO STUFFING

(Pictured above)

*This is a great Sunday meal or "company dish"—as long as you're prepared with second helpings!
The aroma of this chicken roasting makes folks ask, "When will dinner be ready?"*
—Carla Kreider, Quarryville, Pennsylvania

6 **medium red potatoes, cut into 1-inch cubes**
1 **pound Italian sausage**
1 **cup finely chopped onion**
1 **tablespoon butter**
4 **teaspoons dried parsley flakes,** *divided*
1 **teaspoon salt**
3/4 **teaspoon dried rosemary, crushed**
2-3/4 **teaspoons dried thyme,** *divided*
1/2 **teaspoon pepper**
1 **roasting chicken (7 to 7-1/2 pounds)**
1 **tablespoon vegetable oil**
1 **cup water**

Cook the potatoes in boiling salted water until almost tender; drain and set aside. Cook the sausage in boiling water for 10 minutes; drain. Halve each sausage lengthwise, then cut into 1/2-in. pieces.

In a large skillet over medium heat, cook potatoes, sausage and onion in butter until sausage is browned and onion is tender. Add 2 teaspoons parsley, salt, rosemary, 3/4 teaspoon thyme and pepper. Stuff the chicken. Place the remaining stuffing in a greased 1-1/2-qt. baking dish; cover and refrigerate.

Place chicken in a roasting pan; brush with oil and sprinkle with remaining parsley and thyme. Add water to pan. Bake, uncovered, at 350° for 1-1/2 hours. Place baking dish of stuffing in oven. Bake chicken and stuffing for 45 minutes or until a meat thermometer reads 180°. Thicken pan drippings for gravy if desired. **Yield:** 8 servings.

CHICKEN BROCCOLI CASSEROLE

Broccoli is a popular vegetable in our home. This is one dish that always gets rave reviews. Serve it for dinner or even brunch.
—Colleen Lewis, Cottonwood, Arizona

  3 cups broccoli florets
  2 cups cubed cooked chicken *or* turkey
  1 can (10-3/4 ounces) condensed cream of chicken soup, undiluted
1/2 cup mayonnaise
1/2 cup grated Parmesan cheese
1/2 teaspoon curry powder
  1 cup cubed fresh bread
  2 tablespoons butter, melted

In a covered saucepan, cook broccoli in water until crisp-tender; drain. Place in a greased 11-in. x 7-in. x 2-in. baking dish; set aside.

Combine chicken, soup, mayonnaise, Parmesan cheese and curry powder; spoon over broccoli. Top with bread cubes and butter. Bake, uncovered, at 350° for 25-30 minutes or until heated through. **Yield:** 6 servings.

POPOVER WITH HOT TURKEY SALAD

(Pictured at right)

Whether I present this hot turkey dish to my family or to dinner guests, there are never any leftovers. The popover "bowl" that holds the salad is a unique way of serving it and always draws compliments.
—Mary Anne Mayberry, Fairmont, Minnesota

  2 eggs, room temperature
  1 cup milk, room temperature
  1 cup all-purpose flour
1/2 teaspoon salt

  4 cups diced cooked turkey
  2 cups diced celery
  2 cups (8 ounces) shredded cheddar cheese
  1 can (2-1/4 ounces) sliced ripe olives, drained
  1 cup mayonnaise
1/4 cup milk
1/8 teaspoon pepper
Pinch onion powder
1-1/2 cups crushed potato chips
Tomato wedges, optional

In a mixing bowl, beat eggs until lemon-colored and foamy. Add milk, flour and salt; beat just until smooth (do not overbeat). Pour into a greased 10-in. glass pie plate. Bake at 400° for 35-40 minutes or until deep golden brown. Immediately prick with a fork in the center to allow steam to escape.

Combine the next eight ingredients in a saucepan; cook and stir over low until heated through. Stir in potato chips. Spoon into popover. Garnish with tomato wedges if desired. Serve immediately. **Yield:** 10-12 servings.

Chicken 'N' Dumplings With Sour Cream Gravy

(Pictured at right)

This wonderful home-style recipe has been in my family for years. I remember my mother, who is of Czech descent, preparing this saucy chicken dinner when I was a child. Now my daughters like to make it for their own families.
—Doris Butler, Burbank, Illinois

1 cup all-purpose flour
3 teaspoons paprika, *divided*
2 teaspoons salt
5 pounds broiler-fryer chicken pieces
1/4 cup butter
1/2 cup *each* chopped celery, onion and green pepper
2-1/2 cups chicken broth
DUMPLINGS:
1-1/4 cups all-purpose flour
1-1/2 teaspoons baking powder
1/2 teaspoon salt
1 egg
1/2 cup milk
GRAVY:
2 tablespoons cornstarch
2 tablespoons water
1 cup (8 ounces) sour cream
2 tablespoons minced fresh parsley

Combine flour, 2 teaspoons of paprika and salt; dredge chicken. Brown in a Dutch oven in butter, a few pieces at a time. Remove and set aside.

In the same pan, saute celery, onion and green pepper until tender. Add broth, chicken and remaining paprika. Cover and simmer for 45 minutes or until chicken juices run clear. Remove chicken to a serving platter and keep warm.

For dumplings, combine flour, baking powder and salt. Beat egg and milk; stir into flour mixture and mix well. Drop dough, 2 tablespoonfuls at a time, into simmering broth. Cover and simmer for 10 minutes. Remove dumplings to platter and keep warm.

For gravy, combine cornstarch and water; stir into broth. Bring to a boil; cook for 2 minutes. Reduce heat; add sour cream and parsley. Serve with chicken and dumplings. **Yield:** 6 servings.

Chicken Sausage Saute

(Pictured at right)

I received this meaty recipe many years ago. Since then, I've served it for meals ranging from weeknight suppers to potlucks. It's a one-dish dinner that disappears quickly and never disappoints.
—Susan Lynn Hauser, Etters, Pennsylvania

4 medium potatoes (about 1-1/2 pounds), peeled and cut into 1-inch pieces
1 pound Italian sausage, cut into 1-inch pieces
Vegetable oil, optional
3 boneless skinless chicken breast halves, cut into 1-inch pieces
1 *each* large green pepper, sweet red pepper and onion, cut into 1-inch pieces
1 package (10 ounces) frozen green beans, thawed
1/2 cup water
1 teaspoon dried oregano
3/4 teaspoon salt
1/4 teaspoon pepper

In a large skillet over medium heat, brown potatoes and sausage in oil if desired for 15-20 minutes. Add chicken, peppers and onion; saute for 15 minutes or until chicken is browned. Add beans, water, oregano, salt and pepper. Reduce heat; cover and simmer for 15 minutes or until vegetables are tender and meat juices run clear. **Yield:** 6 servings.

CHICKEN RICE BURRITOS

(Pictured below)

*For a nice alternative to beef and bean burritos,
I use this recipe. If I fix the chicken mixture the
night before, the next day's dinner is a snap.*
—Suzanne Adams, Laguna Niguel, California

1/3 cup sliced green onions
  1 garlic clove, minced
  2 tablespoons butter
  7 cups shredded cooked chicken
  1 tablespoon chili powder
2-1/2 cups chicken broth, *divided*
  1 jar (16 ounces) picante sauce, *divided*
  1 cup uncooked long grain rice
1/2 cup sliced ripe olives
  3 cups (12 ounces) shredded cheddar
     cheese, *divided*
 12 flour tortillas (10 inches), warmed
Additional picante sauce and cheddar cheese

In a skillet, saute onions and garlic in butter until
tender. Stir in the chicken, chili powder, 1/4 cup
of broth and 3/4 cup of picante sauce. Heat
through; set aside.

In a medium saucepan, bring rice and remaining broth to a boil. Reduce heat; cover and simmer for 20 minutes. Stir in remaining picante sauce; cover and simmer 5-10 minutes or until rice is tender. Stir into chicken mixture. Add olives and 2 cups cheese.

Spoon 1 cup filling, off center, on each tortilla. Fold sides and ends over filling, then roll up. Arrange burritos in two ungreased 13-in. x 9-in. x 2-in. baking dishes. Sprinkle with the remaining cheese. Cover and bake at 375° for 10-15 minutes or until heated through. Garnish with picante sauce and cheese. **Yield:** 6 servings.

CHICKEN IN PLUM SAUCE

*The secret is in the sauce in this delicious main dish.
Honey, plums and garlic combine to make a sauce
that adds mouth-watering flavor to tender, juicy chicken.*
—Patricia Collins, Imbler, Oregon

  1 broiler/fryer chicken (3-1/2 to 4
     pounds), cut up
3/4 cup all-purpose flour
  3 tablespoons vegetable oil
  2 cans (16-1/2 ounces *each*) whole plums,
     pitted
1/2 cup honey
  1 tablespoon vinegar
  1 to 2 garlic cloves, minced

Coat chicken pieces with flour; brown in oil in a large skillet over medium heat. Transfer to a greased 13-in. x 9-in. x 2-in. baking pan. Drain plums, reserving syrup; remove pits and coarsely chop plums in a food processor. Pour into a measuring cup; add enough syrup to equal 2 cups. Place in a saucepan. Add honey, vinegar and garlic; bring to a boil. Cook and stir for 2 minutes. Pour over chicken. Bake, uncovered, at 350° for 45 minutes or until chicken juices run clear. **Yield:** 4-6 servings.

CHICKEN HOT DISH

When my brother and his wife came over to visit after our third child was born, they brought this comforting, creamy dish for supper. It's become a favorite since then.
—Amber Dudley, New Prague, Minnesota

- 1 package (26 ounces) frozen shredded hash brown potatoes, thawed
- 1 package (24 ounces) frozen California-blend vegetables
- 3 cups cubed cooked chicken
- 1 can (10-3/4 ounces) condensed cream of chicken soup, undiluted
- 1 can (10-3/4 ounces) condensed cream of mushroom soup, undiluted
- 1 cup chicken broth
- 3/4 cup french-fried onions

In a greased 13-in. x 9-in. x 2-in. baking dish, layer the potatoes, vegetables and chicken. In a bowl, combine soups and broth; pour over the chicken (dish will be full).

Cover and bake at 375° for 1 hour. Uncover; sprinkle with french-fried onions. Bake 10 minutes longer or until heated through. **Yield:** 6 servings.

TURKEY DRUMSTICK DINNER

(Pictured above right)

I love this recipe because it uses economical turkey drumsticks to make a savory meat-and-potatoes meal everyone loves. The flavorful sauce and plentiful vegetables turn plain turkey into a feast.
—Alice Balliet, Kane, Pennsylvania

- 4 uncooked turkey drumsticks (about 3 pounds)
- 2 tablespoons vegetable oil
- 1 tablespoon butter
- 1 medium onion, sliced
- 1 can (14-1/2 ounces) stewed tomatoes
- 3 chicken bouillon cubes
- 1 teaspoon garlic salt
- 1/2 teaspoon dried oregano
- 1/2 teaspoon dried basil
- 4 large potatoes, peeled, cooked and quartered
- 2 medium zucchini, cut into 3/4-inch slices
- 2 tablespoons cornstarch
- 2 tablespoons water

Snipped fresh parsley

In a large skillet, brown drumsticks in oil and butter. Place in a 3-qt. Dutch oven. Top with onion slices. In the same skillet, heat tomatoes, bouillon and seasonings until bouillon is dissolved. Pour over the drumsticks.

Cover and bake at 325° for 2 hours, basting once or twice. Add potatoes and zucchini. Cover and bake for 20 minutes. Remove drumsticks and vegetables to a serving dish and keep warm.

Combine the cornstarch and water until smooth; stir into tomato mixture. Return to the oven, uncovered, for 10-15 minutes or until slightly thickened. Pour over drumsticks and vegetables. Sprinkle with parsley. **Yield:** 4 servings.

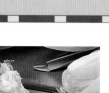

chicken. Cover and bake at 350° for 45 minutes. Drain, reserving 1/2 cup sauce.

Stir sour cream into sauce; pour over the chicken. Combine bread crumbs with the remaining butter; sprinkle over chicken. Bake, uncovered, 15 minutes more or until meat juices run clear. **Yield:** 4 servings.

CHICKEN BREAST CACCIATORE

I make this moist chicken often in summer when we want something quick and yummy. With its golden coating, this entree is special enough for company.
—Roni Goodell, Spanish Fork, Utah

1 can (8 ounces) tomato sauce
1 teaspoon Italian seasoning
1/4 teaspoon garlic powder
1/2 cup cornflake crumbs
1/4 cup grated Parmesan cheese
1 teaspoon dried parsley flakes
6 boneless skinless chicken breast halves
1 egg, beaten
2/3 cup shredded mozzarella cheese

In a microwave-safe bowl, combine tomato sauce, Italian seasoning and garlic powder. Cover and microwave on high for 2 minutes; stir. Cook at 50% power for 3-5 minutes or until mixture simmers, stirring once; set aside.

In a bowl, combine the crumbs, Parmesan and parsley. Dip the chicken into egg, then roll in the crumb mixture. Place in a lightly greased shallow 3-qt. microwave-safe dish. Cover and microwave on high for 10-12 minutes, rotating a half turn after 5 minutes.

Pour tomato mixture over chicken; sprinkle with mozzarella. Cook, uncovered, at 50% power for 3-5 minutes or until meat juices run clear. **Yield:** 6 servings.

Editor's Note: This recipe was tested in an 850-watt microwave.

BAKED ALMOND CHICKEN

(Pictured above)

This is a tasty dish that my family just loves. The almonds give the chicken a wonderful flavor.
—Diana Frankford, Sarasota, Florida

1 broiler-fryer chicken (3 to 3-1/2 pounds), cut up
3/4 cup all-purpose flour
8 tablespoons butter, melted, *divided*
1 teaspoon *each* salt, paprika and celery salt
3/4 cup sliced almonds
1-1/2 cups half-and-half cream
1 cup (8 ounces) sour cream
3 tablespoons dry bread crumbs

Place the chicken and flour in a large resealable plastic bag. Seal bag; turn to coat chicken. In a shallow dish, combine 7 tablespoons butter with salt, paprika and celery salt. Add chicken pieces and turn to coat.

Transfer to a greased 13-in. x 9-in. x 2-in. baking dish. Sprinkle with almonds. Pour cream around

JUICY ROAST TURKEY

(Pictured below)

I can't wait to serve this juicy turkey at Thanksgiving—so I make it several times a year. The aroma that wafts through the house during baking is almost as mouth-watering as the turkey dinner itself.
—Terrie Herman, N. Myrtle Beach, South Carolina

1/4 cup ground mustard
  2 tablespoons Worcestershire sauce
  2 tablespoons olive oil
1/2 teaspoon white vinegar
  1 teaspoon salt
1/8 teaspoon pepper
  1 turkey (10 to 12 pounds)
  1 medium onion, quartered
  2 celery ribs, quartered lengthwise
Fresh parsley sprigs
  2 bacon strips

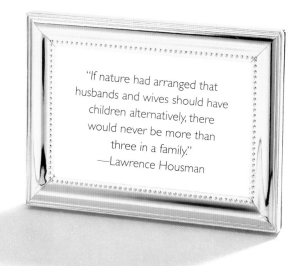

"If nature had arranged that husbands and wives should have children alternatively, there would never be more than three in a family."
—Lawrence Housman

1/4 cup butter, softened
Additional olive oil
Cheesecloth, optional
  2 cups chicken broth
  1 cup water

Combine the first six ingredients in a small bowl; stir to form a smooth paste. Brush over inside and outside of turkey. Cover or place in a 2-gal. resealable plastic bag; refrigerate for 1-24 hours.

Place the turkey on a rack in a large roasting pan. Place the onion, celery and parsley inside turkey cavity. Lay the bacon across breast. Spread butter between legs and body. Tie drumsticks together. Brush the turkey with oil, or take a piece of cheesecloth large enough to cover the turkey and soak it in oil; place over the turkey. Pour broth and water into pan.

Bake, uncovered, at 325° for 3-1/2 to 4 hours or until a meat thermometer reads 185°, basting frequently. Remove from oven; discard cheesecloth and bacon. Let stand 20 minutes before carving. Thicken pan juices for gravy if desired. **Yield:** 10-12 servings.

Editor's Note: Cheesecloth is available in the housewares section of your grocery store. This recipe can be prepared without the cheesecloth.

TURKEY BOW TIE SKILLET

(Pictured above)

*I came up with this satisfying stovetop dish after modifying a different recipe. I knew this was a hit
when our grandchildren tried it and asked for seconds.*
—Ruth Peterson, Jenison, Michigan

1/2	pound ground turkey breast
1-1/2	teaspoons vegetable oil
3/4	cup chopped celery
1/2	cup chopped onion
1/2	cup chopped green pepper
1	garlic clove, minced
1	can (14-1/2 ounces) chicken broth
2	cups uncooked bow tie pasta
1	can (14-1/2 ounces) stewed tomatoes
1	tablespoon white vinegar
3/4	teaspoon sugar
1/2	teaspoon chili powder
1/2	teaspoon garlic salt
2	tablespoons grated Parmesan cheese
1	tablespoon minced fresh parsley

In a large skillet or Dutch oven, cook turkey in oil over medium heat until no longer pink. Add the celery, onion, green pepper and garlic; cook until vegetables are tender. Remove the turkey and vegetables with a slotted spoon and keep warm.

Add chicken broth to the pan; bring to a boil. Add bow tie pasta; cook for 10 minutes or until tender. Reduce heat; stir in the stewed tomatoes, vinegar, sugar, chili powder, garlic salt and turkey mixture. Simmer for 10 minutes or until heated through. Sprinkle with Parmesan cheese and fresh parsley. **Yield:** 6 servings.

PASTA WITH CHICKEN AND SQUASH

This is a special dish that we enjoy often. A bed of noodles is covered with a creamy cheese sauce, tender squash and strips of chicken that've been stir-fried with flavorful herbs. It's delicious and pretty, too!
—Pam Hall, Elizabeth City, North Carolina

  1 package (16 ounces) spiral pasta
  2 cups heavy whipping cream
  1 tablespoon butter
  2 cups (8 ounces) shredded Mexican cheese blend
  1 small onion, chopped
  1 garlic clove, minced
  5 tablespoons olive oil, *divided*
  2 medium zucchini, julienned
  2 medium yellow summer squash, julienned
1-1/4 teaspoons salt, *divided*
  1/8 teaspoon pepper
  1 pound boneless skinless chicken breasts, julienned
  1/4 teaspoon *each* dried basil, marjoram and savory
  1/4 teaspoon dried rosemary, crushed
  1/8 teaspoon rubbed sage

Cook pasta according to package directions. Meanwhile, heat cream and butter in a large saucepan until butter melts. Add cheese; cook and stir until melted. Rinse and drain pasta; add to cheese mixture. Cover and keep warm.

In a skillet over medium heat, saute the onion and garlic in 3 tablespoons of oil until onion is tender. Add the squash; cook until tender. Add 1 teaspoon of salt and pepper; remove from the heat and keep warm.

Add remaining oil to skillet; stir-fry chicken with herbs and remaining salt until juices run clear. Place pasta on a serving platter; top with chicken and squash. **Yield:** 8 servings.

TURKEY POTATO PANCAKES

(Pictured below)

My husband and our four children like pancakes, and I appreciate quick suppers...so this recipe is one that I turn to often. Adding turkey to golden potato pancakes creates a simple main dish we all savor.
—Kathi Duerr, Fulda, Minnesota

  3 eggs
  3 cups shredded peeled potatoes
1-1/2 cups finely chopped cooked turkey
  1/4 cup sliced green onions with tops
  2 tablespoons all-purpose flour
1-1/2 teaspoons salt
Vegetable oil
Cranberry sauce, optional

In a bowl, beat the eggs. Add potatoes, turkey, onions, flour and salt; mix well. Heat about 1/4 in. of oil in a large skillet. Pour batter by 1/3 cupfuls into hot oil. Fry 5-6 minutes on each side or until potatoes are tender and pancakes are golden brown. Serve with cranberry sauce if desired. **Yield:** 12 pancakes.

LATTICE-TOP CHICKEN STEW

(Pictured above)

Convenient crescent roll dough turns into the pretty topping on this creamy casserole filled with chicken and vegetables. While it's baking, I prepare a simple salad and dessert. It's a nice meal for company, too.
—Janet Aselage, Sidney, Ohio

 1 **package (16 ounces) frozen
    California-blend vegetables, thawed
    and drained**
 2 **cups cubed cooked chicken**
 1 **cup milk**
 1 **can (10-3/4 ounces) condensed cream of
    potato soup, undiluted**
 1/2 **cup shredded cheddar cheese**
 1/2 **cup french-fried onions**
 1/2 **teaspoon seasoned salt**
 1 **tube (8 ounces) refrigerated crescent
    rolls**

In a bowl, combine the vegetables, chicken, milk, soup, cheese, onions and seasoned salt. Transfer to a greased 13-in. x 9-in. x 2-in. baking dish. Bake, uncovered, at 350° for 20 minutes. Meanwhile, separate crescent dough into two rectangles. Seal

perforations; cut each rectangle lengthwise into four strips. Working quickly, weave strips over warm filling, forming a lattice crust. Bake 15 minutes longer or until crust is golden brown. **Yield:** 6-8 servings.

GRILLED TURKEY BREAST

After marinating overnight, this turkey is grilled, then dressed up with a fast fruity sauce.
—Ravonda Mormann, Raleigh, North Carolina

 2 **boneless skinless turkey breast halves
    (about 2-1/2 pounds *each*)**
 1 **cup cranberry juice**
 1/4 **cup orange juice**
 1/4 **cup olive oil**
 1 **teaspoon salt**
 1 **teaspoon pepper**
SAUCE:
 1 **can (16 ounces) jellied cranberry sauce**
 1/4 **cup lemon juice**
 3 **tablespoons brown sugar**
 1 **teaspoon cornstarch**

Place the turkey in a large resealable plastic bag. Combine the next five ingredients; pour over the turkey. Seal and refrigerate for 8 hours or overnight, turning occasionally.

Drain and discard marinade. Grill turkey, cov-

Family-Tested Tips

To avoid dirtying additional dishes when reheating Thanksgiving leftovers, bundle the turkey and each side dish separately in aluminum foil and set them on a baking sheet. After baking, discard the foil.
—Louise Priest, El Cajon, California

Do you find it difficult to remove the skin from chicken? Try gripping the skin with a paper towel.
—Edna Ivey, Graham, North Carolina

ered, over indirect heat for 1-1/4 to 1-1/2 hours or until juices run clear and a meat thermometer reads 170°. Meanwhile, combine the sauce ingredients in a saucepan; cook and stir over medium heat until thickened, about 5 minutes. Serve with the turkey. **Yield:** 10 servings.

CHICKEN FAJITAS

(Pictured at right)

I was born and raised on a farm in Iowa but have been a California resident for many years. Southwestern recipes like these tasty chicken fajitas soon became family favorites. I like to serve them with salsa and guacamole.
—Betty Foss, San Marcos, California

3/4 cup lime juice
1/2 cup olive oil
  3 garlic cloves, minced
  2 teaspoons dried oregano
  1 teaspoon ground cumin
1/2 teaspoon pepper
1-1/2 pounds boneless skinless chicken breasts, cut into thin strips
  3 small zucchini, julienned
  2 small yellow summer squash, julienned
  2 medium green peppers, julienned
  2 medium sweet red peppers, julienned
 12 flour tortillas (10 inches), warmed

Combine the first six ingredients; divide the mixture between two large resealable plastic bags. Add chicken to one and vegetables to the other; seal bags and turn to coat. Refrigerate for 2-4 hours, turning bags occasionally.

Drain the chicken and vegetables, discarding the marinade. In a large skillet over medium heat, saute chicken for 6-7 minutes or until juices run clear. Remove chicken and keep warm. Drain skillet. Saute vegetables for 3-4 minutes or until crisp-tender; drain. Spoon chicken and vegetables onto tortillas; fold in sides. Serve immediately. **Yield:** 12 servings.

CHICKEN WITH CRANBERRIES

When cranberries are in season, I like to stock the freezer so I can make this dish year-round. The sauce's tangy flavor complements the chicken very well.
—Pauline Olsson, Edina, Minnesota

3/4 cup all-purpose flour
1/2 teaspoon salt
1/4 teaspoon pepper
  6 boneless skinless chicken breast halves
1/4 cup butter
  1 cup fresh *or* frozen cranberries
  1 cup water
1/2 cup packed brown sugar
  1 tablespoon red wine vinegar
Dash ground nutmeg

In a shallow bowl, combine flour, salt and pepper; dredge the chicken. In a large skillet, cook chicken in butter until browned on both sides. Remove chicken and set aside.

In the same skillet, combine the cranberries, water, brown sugar, vinegar and nutmeg; cover and simmer for 5 minutes. Place chicken on top; cover and simmer for 30 minutes. To serve, spoon cranberry mixture over chicken. **Yield:** 6 servings.

BAYOU CHICKEN PASTA

(Pictured at right)

This is a tasty main dish served in the bayou country of South Louisiana. Salsa and hot pepper sauce give this chicken its tempting zip. Add a tossed salad and French bread, and you have a hearty meal.
—Myrtle Anderson, Plaquemine, Louisiana

- 1 cup chopped onion
- 1 cup chopped celery
- 1/2 cup *each* chopped green and yellow pepper
- 3 tablespoons olive oil
- 1 pound boneless skinless chicken breasts, cubed
- 2 teaspoons garlic powder
- 1 jar (16 ounces) salsa
- 1 tablespoon cornstarch
- 1 tablespoon water
- 1 tablespoon dried parsley flakes
- 1/2 teaspoon salt
- 1/4 teaspoon hot pepper sauce
- Hot cooked pasta

In a large saucepan over medium-high heat, saute onion, celery and pepper in oil for 3-4 minutes or until crisp-tender. Add chicken and garlic powder; cook for 4-5 minutes or until chicken juices run clear. Stir in salsa.

Combine cornstarch and water; stir into the chicken mixture. Bring to a boil; cook and stir for 2 minutes or until mixture is thickened and bubbly. Add the parsley, salt and hot pepper sauce; mix well. Serve over pasta. **Yield:** 4 servings.

POTLUCK CHICKEN CASSEROLE

As the name suggests, this flavorful bake is perfect for potlucks...but I've found it goes over well anytime. Its homey taste, rich sauce and golden topping have a way of drawing people back for second helpings.
—Ruth Andrewson, Leavenworth, Washington

- 1/2 cup chopped fresh mushrooms
- 3 tablespoons finely chopped onion
- 2 garlic cloves, minced
- 4 tablespoons butter, *divided*
- 3 tablespoons all-purpose flour
- 1-1/4 cups milk
- 3/4 cup mayonnaise
- 4 cups cubed cooked chicken
- 3 cups cooked long grain rice
- 1 cup chopped celery
- 1 cup frozen peas, thawed
- 1 jar (2 ounces) diced pimientos, drained
- 2 teaspoons lemon juice
- 1 teaspoon salt
- 1/2 teaspoon pepper
- 3/4 cup coarsely crushed cornflakes

In a saucepan over medium heat, saute the mushrooms, onion and garlic in 3 tablespoons butter until tender. Stir in the flour until thoroughly combined. Gradually add the milk; bring to a boil. Cook and stir for 2 minutes or until thickened and bubbly.

Remove from the heat; stir in mayonnaise until smooth. Add chicken, rice, celery, peas, pimientos, lemon juice, salt and pepper; mix well. Spoon into an ungreased 13-in. x 9-in. x 2-in. baking dish. Melt remaining butter; toss with cornflakes. Sprinkle over casserole. Bake, uncovered, at 350° for 30-35 minutes or until bubbly. **Yield:** 8-10 servings.

BARBECUED CHICKEN

(Pictured below)

If you're like me, you can never have enough delicious ways to grill chicken. The savory sauce in this recipe gives chicken a wonderful herb flavor. It's easy to put together a great meal when you start with these golden pieces.
—Joanne Shew Chuk, St. Benedict, Saskatchewan

1 broiler-fryer chicken (3-1/2 to 4 pounds), quartered
1/4 cup white vinegar
1/4 cup butter
1/4 cup water
1/4 teaspoon *each* dried thyme, oregano, rosemary and garlic powder
1/8 teaspoon salt
1/8 teaspoon pepper

Place chicken in a shallow glass dish. In a small saucepan, combine all remaining ingredients; bring to a gentle boil. Remove from the heat. Pour over chicken. Cover and refrigerate for 4 hours, turning once. Drain and discard marinade. Grill chicken, covered, over medium heat for 30-40 minutes or until juices run clear. **Yield:** 4 servings.

Family-Tested Tip

When you have leftover canned pineapple juice, use it to make an easy marinade for chicken breasts. Just add a little vegetable oil, soy sauce and garlic, then let the chicken marinate overnight. Bake it in the marinade the next day for a terrific dinner.
—Lenora Cuccia, Tallahassee, Florida

APPLE-ALMOND STUFFED TURKEY

(Pictured at right)

I tried this terrific recipe for a dinner party a few years back. Everyone enjoyed the combination of flavors and unique ingredients. The currants and chopped apples give the stuffing a nice sweet flavor, and the toasted almonds provide a pleasing crunch.
—Laurel McLennan, Medicine Hat, Alberta

    1 loaf (1 pound) sliced bread
    3 medium onions, chopped
    3 medium tart apples, chopped
1-1/2 cups diced fully cooked ham
    1 cup sliced celery
    1 tablespoon dried savory
    2 teaspoons grated lemon peel
1-1/2 teaspoons grated orange peel
    1 teaspoon salt
  1/2 teaspoon pepper
  1/2 teaspoon fennel seed, crushed
  1/2 cup butter
1-1/2 cups slivered almonds, toasted
  1/2 cup dried currants
    1 cup turkey *or* chicken broth
  1/2 cup apple juice
    1 turkey (14 to 16 pounds)

Cut bread into 1/2-in. cubes and place in a single layer on ungreased baking sheets. Bake at 225° for 30-40 minutes, tossing occasionally until partially dried.

Meanwhile, in a skillet, saute the next 10 ingredients in butter until onions and apple are tender, about 15 minutes. Transfer to a large bowl. Add the bread cubes, almonds, currants, broth and juice; toss well. Just before baking, stuff the turkey. Skewer openings; tie drumsticks together. Place on a rack in a roasting pan.

Bake, uncovered, at 325° for 4-1/2 to 5 hours or until thermometer reads 185°. When turkey begins to brown, cover lightly with foil and baste if needed. **Yield:** 12 servings (12 cups stuffing).

Editor's Note: Stuffing may be baked separately in a greased 3-qt. baking dish. Cover and bake at 325° for 1 hour; uncover and bake 10 minutes more.

TURKEY TENDERLOIN SUPREME

We're a busy hockey and figure skating family, so we're always on the go. Served over rice, this skillet supper makes a good home-cooked meal when I don't have a lot of time to spend in the kitchen.
—Nancy Levin, Chesterfield, Missouri

    6 turkey breast tenderloin slices (3/4 inch thick and 4 ounces *each*)
    1 tablespoon butter
    3 green onions, thinly sliced
    1 can (10-3/4 ounces) condensed cream of chicken soup, undiluted
  1/4 cup water

In a large skillet, brown turkey in butter. Add onions; cook for 1-2 minutes. Combine soup and water; pour over turkey. Bring to a boil. Reduce heat; cover and simmer for 8-10 minutes or until meat juices run clear. **Yield:** 6 servings.

Chicken 'n' Biscuits

(Pictured below)

This cheesy chicken casserole gets its vibrant color from frozen vegetables and its unique flavor from crumbled bacon. The biscuit-topped dish has become a regular at our dinner table since my sister-in-law shared it with us after the birth of our son.
—Debbie Vannette, Zeeland, Michigan

1 package (16 ounces) frozen mixed vegetables
2-1/2 cups cubed cooked chicken
1 can (10-3/4 ounces) condensed cream of chicken soup, undiluted
3/4 cup milk
1-1/2 cups (6 ounces) shredded cheddar cheese, *divided*
8 bacon strips, cooked and crumbled, optional

BISCUITS:
1-1/2 cups biscuit/baking mix
2/3 cup milk
1 can (2.8 ounces) french-fried onions

In a large bowl, combine the vegetables, chicken, soup, milk, 1 cup cheese and bacon if desired. Pour into an ungreased 13-in. x 9-in. x 2-in. baking dish. Cover and bake at 400° for 15 minutes.

Meanwhile, in another bowl, combine biscuit mix and milk. Drop the batter by tablespoonfuls onto the chicken mixture. Bake, uncovered, for 20-22 minutes or until biscuits are golden brown. Top with the onions and remaining cheese. Bake 3-4 minutes longer or until the cheese is melted. **Yield:** 6 servings.

Orange Onion Chicken

Everyone who tries this change-of-pace chicken likes it. Flavored with orange juice and orange sections, it's a refreshing dinner that appeals to all palates.
—Alcy Thorne, Los Molinos, California

4 boneless skinless chicken breast halves (1-1/4 pounds)
2 tablespoons vegetable oil
1-1/4 cups water, *divided*
1/2 cup orange juice
1/4 cup chopped onion
1/4 cup chicken broth
1/4 to 1/2 teaspoon ground ginger
2 tablespoons cornstarch
2 oranges, peeled and sectioned

In a skillet, brown the chicken in oil; drain. Add 1 cup water, orange juice, onion, broth and ginger. Cover and simmer until chicken juices run clear, 20-25 minutes. Remove chicken; keep warm.

Mix cornstarch with remaining water; stir into skillet. Cook and stir until thickened and bubbly; cook and stir for 2 minutes more. Add the orange sections and heat through. Serve over the chicken. **Yield:** 4 servings.

FIESTA FRY PAN DINNER

(Pictured below)

Taco seasoning mix adds fast flavor to this speedy skillet dish. It's so easy to make that I fix it frequently. All I need is salad and dessert, and the meal is ready.
—Leota Shaffer, Sterling, Virginia

  1 **pound ground turkey *or* beef**
1/2 **cup chopped onion**
  1 **envelope taco seasoning**
1-1/2 **cups water**
1-1/2 **cups sliced zucchini**
  1 **can (14-1/2 ounces) stewed tomatoes, undrained**
  1 **cup frozen corn**
1-1/2 **cups uncooked instant rice**
  1 **cup (4 ounces) shredded cheddar cheese**

In a skillet, cook turkey and onion until meat is no longer pink; drain if necessary. Stir in taco seasoning, water, zucchini, tomatoes and corn; bring to a boil. Add rice. Reduce heat; cover and simmer for 5 minutes or until rice is tender and liquid is absorbed. Sprinkle with cheese; cover and let stand until the cheese is melted. **Yield:** 8-10 servings.

SPICY GRILLED CHICKEN

Very near the top of the list of foods I prepare for company is this chicken. But it's also a recipe I often turn to for a simple, fail-proof family dinner. The marinating starts the day before, and all that's left to do the next day is the grilling.
—Edith Maki, Hancock, Michigan

3/4 **cup finely chopped onion**
1/2 **cup grapefruit juice**
  2 **tablespoons olive oil**
  2 **tablespoons soy sauce**
  1 **tablespoon honey**
  1 **garlic clove, minced**
1-1/2 **teaspoons salt**
1-1/2 **teaspoons rubbed sage**
1-1/2 **teaspoons dried thyme**
  1 **teaspoon ground allspice**
  1 **teaspoon garlic powder**
1/2 **teaspoon ground cinnamon**
1/2 **teaspoon ground nutmeg**
1/4 **teaspoon cayenne pepper**
1/4 **teaspoon pepper**
  6 **boneless skinless chicken breast halves**

In a large resealable plastic bag or shallow glass container, combine the first 15 ingredients; mix well. Reserve 1/3 cup for basting and refrigerate. Add the chicken to the remaining marinade and turn to coat. Seal the bag or cover the container; refrigerate overnight.

    Drain and discard marinade. Grill chicken, uncovered, over medium heat for 3 minutes on each side. Baste with reserved marinade. Continue grilling for 6-8 minutes or until juices run clear, basting and turning several times. **Yield:** 6 servings.

Cashew Chicken Stir-Fry

(Pictured at right)

The hardest part of making this dish is keeping the cashews in the cupboard! My family loves them.
—Vicki Hirschfeld, Hartland, Wisconsin

 2 cups chicken broth, *divided*
1/4 cup cornstarch
 3 tablespoons soy sauce
1/2 teaspoon ground ginger
 1 pound boneless skinless chicken breasts, cut into 1/2-inch strips
 2 garlic cloves, minced
1/2 cup thinly sliced carrots
1/2 cup sliced celery (1/2-inch pieces)
 3 cups broccoli florets
 1 cup fresh *or* frozen snow peas
1-1/2 cups cashews
Hot cooked rice

In a skillet, heat 3 tablespoons of broth. Meanwhile, combine the cornstarch, soy sauce, ginger and remaining broth until smooth; set aside. Add chicken to the skillet; stir-fry over medium heat until no longer pink, about 3-5 minutes. Remove with a slotted spoon and keep warm.

Add garlic, carrots and celery to skillet; stir-fry for 3 minutes. Add broccoli and peas; stir-fry for 4-5 minutes or until crisp-tender. Stir broth mixture; add to the skillet with the chicken. Cook and stir for 2 minutes. Stir in cashews. Serve over rice. **Yield:** 4 servings.

Chicken with Cucumbers

Although most often eaten raw, cucumbers taste great cooked in this creamy chicken dinner.
—Angela Avedon, Moorseville, North Carolina

 1 broiler/fryer chicken (3-1/2 to 4 pounds), cut up
 2 tablespoons vegetable oil
1/4 pound fresh mushrooms, sliced
 1 garlic clove, minced
 3 tablespoons all-purpose flour
1-3/4 cups water
 1 tablespoon chicken bouillon granules
 2 large cucumbers
 1 cup (8 ounces) sour cream

In a large skillet over medium heat, brown chicken in oil. Remove chicken and set aside. To drippings, add mushrooms and garlic; saute 2 minutes. Stir in flour until mushrooms are coated. Gradually add water and bouillon; cook and stir over medium heat until bubbly.

Return the chicken to the skillet; bring to a boil. Reduce heat; cover and simmer for 30 minutes, stirring occasionally. Meanwhile, slice one cucumber into thin slices; set aside. Peel the remaining cucumber; slice in half lengthwise and remove the seeds. Cut into 1-in. chunks. Add to skillet and simmer for 20 minutes or until chicken juices run clear.

Stir sour cream into sauce; heat through but do not boil. Garnish with reserved cucumber slices. **Yield:** 4-6 servings.

HERBED CHICKEN AND VEGGIES

(Pictured below)

*This subtly seasoned chicken and vegetable combination is a snap to prepare on a hectic working day.
A dessert is all that's needed to complete this satisfying supper.*
—Dorothy Pritchett, Wills Point, Texas

1 broiler-fryer chicken (3 to 4 pounds), cut up and skin removed
2 medium tomatoes, chopped
1 medium onion, chopped
2 garlic cloves, minced
1/2 cup chicken broth
2 tablespoons white wine *or* additional chicken broth
1 bay leaf
1-1/2 teaspoons salt
1 teaspoon dried thyme
1/4 teaspoon pepper
2 cups broccoli florets
Hot cooked rice

Place the chicken in a slow cooker. Top with the tomatoes, onion and garlic. Combine broth, wine or additional broth, bay leaf, salt, thyme and pepper; pour over the chicken. Cover and cook on low for 7-8 hours.

Add broccoli; cook 45-60 minutes longer or until the chicken juices run clear and the broccoli is tender. Discard bay leaf. Thicken pan juices if desired. Serve over rice. **Yield:** 4-6 servings.

SOUTHERN FRIED CHICKEN

(Pictured at right)

Here's a traditional main course that our region of the country is well known for. My husband operates a ham radio, and we've shared this lip-smacking chicken recipe with folks from all over the world.
—*Jo Ruh, Covington, Kentucky*

  2 **eggs**
  2 **tablespoons milk**
1-1/4 **cups all-purpose flour**
1-1/2 **teaspoons salt**
 1/2 **teaspoon pepper**
 1/4 **teaspoon ground cumin**
 1/4 **teaspoon dried oregano**
 1/4 **teaspoon paprika**
  2 **broiler-fryer chickens (3 to 3-1/2 pounds *each*), cut up**
  1 **cup shortening**
MILK GRAVY:
 1/4 **cup all-purpose flour**
 1/2 **teaspoon salt**
 1/8 **teaspoon pepper**
  1 **cup milk**
  1 **cup water**
 1/8 **teaspoon browning sauce, optional**
Fresh oregano, optional

In a medium bowl, beat eggs and milk. In another bowl, combine flour and seasonings. Dip chicken pieces in egg mixture, then in flour mixture.

Heat shortening in a large skillet; brown the chicken on both sides. Cover and cook the chicken over low heat for 45 minutes or until juices run clear. Remove chicken from the skillet; keep warm.

Reserve 1/4 cup drippings in skillet.

For gravy, stir in flour, salt and pepper. Cook and stir over medium heat for 5 minutes or until browned. Combine milk and water; add to skillet. Bring to a boil; boil and stir for 2 minutes. Add browning sauce if desired. Serve with chicken. Garnish with oregano if desired. **Yield:** 8 servings.

SEASONED TURKEY BURGERS

This fun mixture of turkey and dressing tastes almost like Thanksgiving dinner on a bun.
—*Vicki Engelhardt, Grand Rapids, Michigan*

 1/2 **cup herb-seasoned stuffing croutons**
  1 **pound ground turkey breast**
  1 **small onion, finely chopped**
  5 **hamburger buns, split**
Lettuce leaves, onion, tomato slices and fat-free mayonnaise, optional

Crush or process stuffing croutons into fine crumbs. In a bowl, combine crumbs, turkey and onion. Shape into five patties. Broil or grill over medium-hot heat for 8-10 minutes, turning once. Serve on buns with lettuce, onion, tomato and mayonnaise if desired. **Yield:** 5 servings.

TURKEY IN MUSHROOM SAUCE

(Pictured below)

If you like a traditional turkey dinner for Thanksgiving but don't like all the fuss, here's a recipe that fills the bill. It's easy to make and tastes very good.
—Rose Maldet, Johnstown, Pennsylvania

- 3/4 cup all-purpose flour
- 2 teaspoons salt
- 1/4 teaspoon pepper
- 6 turkey thighs (4 to 5 pounds)
- 3 tablespoons vegetable oil
- 2 cups chopped fresh mushrooms
- 3 green onions, sliced
- 1-1/2 teaspoons dried thyme
- 2 cups turkey *or* chicken broth
- 1/3 cup tomato paste
- 1 cup (8 ounces) sour cream
- Hot cooked noodles

In a bowl or resealable plastic bag, combine flour, salt and pepper. Add turkey, one piece at a time; dredge or shake to coat. In a skillet, brown turkey in oil. Add mushrooms, onions and thyme. Combine the broth and tomato paste until smooth; pour over turkey. Cover and simmer for 1-1/2 hours or until the turkey juices run clear; skim fat. Stir in sour cream; heat through (do not boil). Serve over noodles. **Yield:** 6 servings.

HARVEST STUFFED CHICKEN

This roasted chicken is simple enough to prepare every day, yet special enough for company. The corn bread and savory enhance the flavor of the homemade stuffing.
—Jodi Cigel, Stevens Point, Wisconsin

- 1 box (7-1/2 ounces) corn bread/muffin mix, prepared as directed and crumbled *or* 3 cups corn bread crumbs
- 3 cups unseasoned stuffing croutons
- 1/2 cup *each* chopped celery, fresh mushrooms and fully cooked ham
- 1/4 cup chopped sweet red pepper
- 1/4 cup chopped green onions
- 4 teaspoons chopped fresh savory *or* 1 teaspoon dried savory
- 3/4 teaspoon salt
- 1/2 teaspoon pepper
- 3 tablespoons vegetable oil
- 1 to 1-1/2 cups chicken broth
- 1 roasting chicken (6 to 7 pounds)

In a large bowl, combine corn bread crumbs and croutons. In a large skillet, saute the celery, mushrooms, ham, red pepper, onions, savory, salt and pepper in oil until vegetables are tender. Add to the crumb mixture. Stir in enough broth to moisten. Stuff the chicken. Place on a rack in a large roasting pan.

Bake, uncovered, at 325° for 2-1/2 to 3 hours or until juices run clear. Or bake stuffing separately in a greased 2-qt. covered casserole at 350° for 45 minutes. **Yield:** 6 servings.

CHICKEN NOODLE STIR-FRY

(Pictured above)

Rely on Ramen noodles to stretch this appealing stir-fry. You can use whatever vegetables you happen to have on hand. This dish is different every time I make it.
—Darlene Markel, Sublimity, Oregon

1   package (3 ounces) chicken-flavored
    Ramen noodles
1   pound boneless skinless chicken breasts,
    cut into strips
1   tablespoon vegetable oil
1   cup broccoli florets
1   cup cauliflowerets
1   cup sliced celery
1   cup coarsely chopped cabbage
2   medium carrots, thinly sliced
1   medium onion, thinly sliced
1/2 cup fresh *or* canned bean sprouts
1/2 cup teriyaki *or* soy sauce

Set aside seasoning packet from noodles. Cook noodles according to package directions. Meanwhile, in a large skillet or wok, stir-fry chicken in oil for 5-6 minutes or until no longer pink. Add the vegetables; stir-fry for 3-4 minutes or until crisp-tender.

Drain noodles; add to the pan with contents of seasoning packet and the teriyaki sauce. Stir well. Serve immediately. **Yield:** 4 servings.

Chapter six

Whether for holiday feasts or everyday fare,

succulent pork and lamb have long guaranteed

family menu success. Your loved ones will ask

for seconds when they sample hearty helpings

of the recipes here, such as home-style ham,

luscious lamb chops and savory sausages.

Roast Pork with Apple Topping
(Recipe on page 124)

♥ Pork & Lamb

ROAST PORK WITH APPLE TOPPING

(Pictured on page 123)

I enjoy cooking and am constantly on the lookout for new recipes to try. I feel very fortunate when I find a dish like this that becomes a family favorite.
—Virginia Barrett, Rochester, New York

  2 tablespoons all-purpose flour
1-3/4 teaspoons salt, *divided*
  1 teaspoon ground mustard
  1 teaspoon caraway seed
  1/2 teaspoon sugar
  1/4 teaspoon pepper
  1/4 teaspoon rubbed sage
  1 pork loin roast (4 to 5 pounds)
1-1/2 cups applesauce
  1/2 cup packed brown sugar
  1/4 teaspoon ground mace

In a small bowl, combine flour, 1-1/2 teaspoons salt, ground mustard, caraway seed, sugar, pepper and sage; rub over the roast. Cover and let stand for 30 minutes.

Place on a greased baking rack, fat side up, in a roasting pan. Bake, uncovered, at 325° for 1 hour.

"The family is the school of duties—founded on love."
—Felix Adler

Combine applesauce, brown sugar, mace and remaining salt; mix well. Spread over roast. Roast 1 hour longer or until the internal temperature reaches 160°-170°. Let stand 15 minutes before slicing. **Yield:** 8-10 servings.

ORANGE BLOSSOM LAMB

(Pictured at left)

After a long workday, I like to make supper simple. This is a special main dish that's easy, too.
—Felicia Johnson, Oak Ridge, Louisiana

  8 rib lamb chops (1 inch thick)
  2 tablespoons butter
  1 can (6 ounces) orange juice concentrate, thawed
  1 medium onion, sliced
  1 to 2 teaspoons soy sauce
  1 teaspoon salt
Dash pepper

In a large skillet, brown lamb chops in butter. Add remaining ingredients; mix well. Reduce heat; cover and simmer for 20-25 minutes or until the meat is tender, turning once. To serve, spoon sauce over the lamb. **Yield:** 4 servings.

onion and carrot; mix well. Dissolve the bouillon in water; pour over vegetables. Cover and cook over medium-high heat until the vegetables are tender, about 10-15 minutes. Reduce heat; stir in sour cream, salt and pepper. Heat through. Transfer to a serving bowl; add hot noodles and toss. Garnish with parsley if desired. **Yield:** 4-6 servings.

ITALIAN POTATO CASSEROLE

After one taste, you'll see why this delicious dish won grand prize in a local newspaper cooking contest. It's a great variation on traditional shepherd's pie.
—Jackie Jacoby, Gettysburg, Pennsylvania

  1 **pound bulk Italian sausage**
  3 **cups mashed potatoes**
  1 **cup chopped onion**
3/4 **cup chopped green pepper**
  2 **garlic cloves, minced**
  1 **tablespoon vegetable oil**
  2 **cups sliced fresh mushrooms**
  2 **cups chopped fresh tomatoes**
  1 **can (2-1/4 ounces) sliced ripe olives, drained**
  1 **teaspoon dried basil**
1/4 **teaspoon salt**
1/8 **teaspoon pepper**
1/4 **cup grated Parmesan cheese**
  1 **tablespoon chopped fresh parsley *or* 2 teaspoons dried parsley flakes**

In a skillet, cook sausage until no longer pink; drain. Place in a greased 9-in. square baking dish. Top with potatoes. In the same skillet, saute onion, green pepper and garlic in oil for 5 minutes or until vegetables are crisp-tender.

Stir in the mushrooms, tomatoes, olives, basil, salt and pepper. Spoon over the potatoes to within 1 in. of edge of dish. Sprinkle the Parmesan cheese and parsley on top. Bake, uncovered, at 350° for 30-35 minutes or until the top is lightly browned. **Yield:** 4-6 servings.

SAUSAGE 'N' NOODLE DINNER

(Pictured above)

I adapted this dish from a recipe my German grandmother gave me. It reminds me of my heritage whenever I make it.
—Phyllis Dennewitz, Frankfort, Ohio

  1 **pound bulk pork sausage**
  1 **medium head cabbage (about 1-1/2 pounds), thinly sliced**
  1 **large onion, thinly sliced**
  1 **large carrot, shredded**
  2 **teaspoons chicken bouillon granules**
1/4 **cup boiling water**
  2 **cups (16 ounces) sour cream**
3/4 **teaspoon salt**
1/2 **teaspoon pepper**
  8 **ounces noodles, cooked and drained**
Fresh parsley, optional

In a large skillet, cook the sausage over medium heat until no longer pink; drain. Add cabbage,

Sweet-and-Sour Ribs

(Pictured at right)

I like making this for family dinners and potlucks at work. It's a nice change from everyday fare.
—Kate Raleigh, Salt Lake City, Utah

      4 pounds pork spareribs
1-1/2 teaspoons salt, *divided*
  1/2 teaspoon pepper
  1/3 cup chopped celery
  1/3 cup chopped green pepper
      2 tablespoons butter
      1 can (20 ounces) pineapple tidbits
      2 tablespoons cornstarch
  1/3 cup vinegar
      2 tablespoons soy sauce
      1 tablespoon sugar
      1 garlic clove, minced
  1/2 teaspoon ground ginger

Cut ribs into serving-size pieces; place with bone side down on a rack in a greased shallow roasting pan. Sprinkle with 1 teaspoon salt and pepper. Cover and bake at 400° for 30 minutes; drain. Reduce heat to 350°; cover and bake 1 hour longer.

In a saucepan, saute celery and green pepper in butter until tender. Drain pineapple, reserving juice. Set pineapple aside. Combine juice and cornstarch; add to saucepan and bring to a boil. Cook and stir until thickened, about 2 minutes.

Add the pineapple, vinegar, soy sauce, sugar, minced garlic, ginger and remaining salt to the saucepan; mix well. Spoon over the ribs. Bake, uncovered, 25-30 minutes longer or until the meat is tender. **Yield:** 4 servings.

Family-Tested Tip

To create a quick marinade for pork chops, combine 1/2 cup *each* of soy sauce, water and honey. Pour the mixture over four chops, marinate in the refrigerator overnight and grill the next day.
—*Rhea Lease, Colman, South Dakota*

Greek Burgers

I tried these lamb patties at a barbecue party. After tasting them, I wouldn't leave without the recipe! The rosemary, garlic and mustard give these one-of-a-kind burgers fantastic flavor.
—Michelle Curtis, Baker City, Oregon

      1 pound ground lamb
      1 tablespoon Dijon mustard
      1 tablespoon lemon juice
      1 tablespoon minced onion
      1 garlic clove, minced
  1/2 teaspoon dried rosemary, crushed
  1/2 teaspoon salt
  1/4 teaspoon pepper
      4 hamburger buns *or* hard rolls, split
Sliced cucumbers and tomatoes, optional
Ranch salad dressing, optional

In a medium bowl, combine the first eight ingredients; mix well. Shape into four patties. Pan-fry, grill or broil until no longer pink. Serve on buns with cucumbers, tomatoes and ranch dressing if desired. **Yield:** 4 servings.

PORK POTPIE

(Pictured below)

The first time I put this tasty potpie on the table, my family said the recipe was a hands-down keeper.
—Linda Flor, Marmarth, North Dakota

CRUST:
    3 cups all-purpose flour
  1/2 teaspoon salt
    1 cup shortening
    5 to 6 tablespoons cold water
    1 egg
    1 tablespoon vinegar
FILLING:
1-1/2 cups cubed peeled potatoes
  1/2 cup thinly sliced carrots
  1/4 cup thinly sliced celery
  1/4 cup chopped onion
    1 cup water
    2 cups diced cooked pork
  3/4 cup pork gravy
  1/2 teaspoon dried rosemary, crushed, optional
  1/4 teaspoon salt
  1/8 teaspoon pepper
Half-and-half cream, optional

In a bowl, combine flour and salt; cut in shortening until the mixture resembles coarse crumbs.

Combine 5 tablespoons water, egg and vinegar; sprinkle over dry ingredients, 1 tablespoon at a time. Toss lightly with a fork until dough forms a ball; add additional water if necessary. Divide into two balls; chill while preparing filling.

In a saucepan, cook potatoes, carrots, celery and onion in water for 10 minutes or until crisp-tender; drain well. Add pork, gravy, rosemary if desired, salt and pepper; set aside.

On a floured surface, roll one ball of dough to fit a 9-in. pie plate. Fill with the meat mixture. Roll the remaining pastry to fit the top of pie. Cut slits in the top crust and place over the filling; seal and flute the edges. Brush pastry with cream if desired. Bake at 375° for 50-55 minutes or until golden brown. **Yield:** 6 servings.

BACON AND PEPPER PASTA

This snappy combination of bacon and linguine works as either a main dish or a side dish. It gets its fresh flavor and pretty color from onions, tomatoes and three kinds of peppers.
—Teri Rasey-Bolf, Cadillac, Michigan

  1/2 pound sliced bacon, diced
    2 medium onions, halved and sliced
    2 garlic cloves, minced
    1 medium green pepper, julienned
    1 medium sweet red pepper, julienned
    1 small jalapeno pepper, seeded and minced
    1 can (14-1/2 ounces) stewed tomatoes
    1 pound linguine *or* pasta of your choice, cooked and drained

In a large skillet, cook bacon until crisp. Remove with a slotted spoon and set aside; reserve drippings. Saute onions and garlic in drippings for 3 minutes. Add peppers; cook and stir for 3 minutes. Stir in tomatoes; heat through. Add bacon and mix well. Serve over pasta. **Yield:** 4 servings.

Editor's Note: When cutting and seeding hot peppers, use rubber or plastic gloves to protect your hands. Avoid touching your face.

HAM 'N' NOODLE HOT DISH

(Pictured above)

Frozen green peas add lovely color to this comforting meal-in-one. The easy, cheesy dish is a terrific way to use up extra baked ham from a holiday feast or dinner party. No one feels like they're eating leftovers when I serve this tasty bake.
—Renee Schwebach, Dumont, Minnesota

3 tablespoons butter, *divided*
2 tablespoons all-purpose flour
1 cup milk
1 cup (4 ounces) shredded process cheese (Velveeta)
1/2 teaspoon salt
2 cups diced fully cooked ham
1-1/2 cups medium noodles, cooked and drained
1 cup frozen peas, thawed
1/4 cup dry bread crumbs
1/2 teaspoon dried parsley flakes

In a saucepan, melt 2 tablespoons butter; stir in flour until smooth. Gradually add milk. Bring to a boil over medium heat; cook and stir for 2 minutes. Remove from the heat; stir in cheese and salt until cheese is melted.

Add the ham, noodles and peas. Pour into a greased 1-qt. baking dish. Melt remaining butter; add bread crumbs and parsley. Sprinkle over casserole. Bake, uncovered, at 350° for 30 minutes or until heated through. **Yield:** 4 servings.

HEARTY HAM LOAVES

This simple-to-prepare recipe yields two ham loaves—one you can enjoy right away and one to freeze for a later meal. They're so nicely flavored with a variety of seasonings that everyone raves about them.
—Audrey Thibodeau, Mesa, Arizona

1 cup crushed butter-flavored crackers (about 25 crackers)
2/3 cup finely chopped onion
1/2 cup finely chopped green pepper
2 eggs, beaten
2 tablespoons lemon juice
1 teaspoon ground mustard
1 teaspoon ground ginger
1 teaspoon Worcestershire sauce
1/4 teaspoon pepper
Dash ground nutmeg
Dash paprika
1-1/3 pounds finely ground fully cooked ham
1 pound bulk pork sausage
GLAZE:
1/2 cup packed brown sugar
1/4 cup cider vinegar
1/4 cup water
1 teaspoon ground mustard

In a large bowl, combine the first 11 ingredients. Add ham and sausage; mix well. Shape into two loaves. Place in ungreased 9-in. x 5-in. x 3-in. loaf pans. Bake one loaf at 350° for 1 hour.

Meanwhile, combine glaze ingredients in a small saucepan. Bring to a boil; boil for 2 minutes. Remove loaf from the oven; drain. Baste with half of the glaze. Bake 30-40 minutes longer or until a meat thermometer reads 160°-170°, basting occasionally.

Cover and freeze the remaining loaf and glaze for up to 2 months. To prepare, thaw in the refrigerator overnight and bake as directed. **Yield:** 2 loaves (6-8 servings each).

GREAT PORK CHOP BAKE

(Pictured below)

I first tried this hearty meat-and-potatoes dish when I returned home from the hospital with our youngest child. Since then, we've enjoyed it many times. It's a great meal to have on the table after a busy day.
—Rosie Glenn, Los Alamos, New Mexico

6 bone-in pork chops (3/4 inch thick)
1 tablespoon vegetable oil
1 can (10-3/4 ounces) condensed cream of chicken soup, undiluted
3 tablespoons ketchup
2 tablespoons Worcestershire sauce
1/2 teaspoon salt
1/4 teaspoon pepper
4 medium potatoes, cut into 1/2-inch wedges
1 medium onion, sliced into rings

In a skillet, brown pork chops in oil. Transfer to a greased 13-in. x 9-in. x 2-in. baking dish. In a bowl, combine the soup, ketchup, Worcestershire sauce, salt and pepper. Add potatoes and onion; toss to coat. Pour over the chops. Cover and bake at 350° for 55-60 minutes or until meat juices run clear and potatoes are tender. **Yield:** 6 servings.

1/2 hours, stirring occasionally.

Meanwhile, brown the sausage and garlic in a large skillet; drain. Cool slightly. Cut sausage into 1-in. pieces; return to the skillet. Add parsley, tomatoes and tomato paste; bring to a boil. Remove from the heat.

Spread half of the cornmeal mixture in a serving dish; top with half of the sausage mixture. Repeat layers. Sprinkle with Parmesan cheese. Serve immediately. **Yield:** 6-8 servings.

MEATY CORN-BREAD SQUARES

Working full time outside of the home doesn't allow me to cook as often as I'd like. So when I get a spare moment, I enjoy experimenting in the kitchen. These tasty squares are an all-time favorite.
—Rebecca Meyerkorth, Wamego, Kansas

- 1 can (10 ounces) diced tomatoes with green chilies, undrained
- 1 tablespoon cornstarch
- 1 pound diced fully cooked ham
- 1/4 cup chopped onion
- 2 teaspoons chili powder
- 1 garlic clove, minced
- 1 cup all-purpose flour
- 1/2 cup cornmeal
- 2 teaspoons baking powder
- 2 eggs
- 1 can (16 ounces) whole kernel corn, drained
- 3/4 cup milk
- 3 tablespoons vegetable oil
- 1-1/2 cups (6 ounces) shredded Monterey Jack cheese
- Salsa, optional

Drain tomatoes, reserving juice in a skillet; set tomatoes aside. Add cornstarch to juice; mix well. Add ham, onion, chili powder, garlic and tomatoes. Bring to a boil over medium heat; boil and stir for 2 minutes. Set aside.

In a bowl, combine flour, cornmeal and baking

POLENTA WITH ITALIAN SAUSAGE

(Pictured above)

This recipe came from my mom, who brought it over from Europe. When I first made it, everyone wanted to know where I got the recipe. I've copied it numerous times for friends.
—Peggy Ratliff, North Tazewell, Virginia

- 4 cups water
- 1 cup cornmeal
- 1 teaspoon salt
- 1 pound Italian sausage
- 2 garlic cloves, minced
- 2 tablespoons minced fresh parsley
- 1 can (14-1/2 ounces) Italian stewed tomatoes
- 1 can (6 ounces) tomato paste
- 1/4 cup shredded Parmesan cheese

Combine water, cornmeal and salt in a double boiler or heavy saucepan; bring to a boil, stirring constantly. Reduce heat; cover and simmer for 1-

powder. In another bowl, combine eggs, corn, milk and oil; stir into dry ingredients just until moistened. Spread half the batter into a greased 9-in. square baking dish. Spoon meat mixture over batter. Sprinkle with cheese. Spoon remaining batter on top.

Bake, uncovered, at 350° for 35-40 minutes or until golden brown. Let stand for 5 minutes before cutting. Serve with salsa if desired. **Yield:** 6 servings.

FARMHOUSE PORK AND APPLE PIE

(Pictured at right)

I've always loved pork and apples together, and this recipe combines them nicely to create a comforting main dish. It calls for a bit of preparation, but my family and I agree that its wonderful flavor makes it well worth the extra effort.
—Suzanne Strocsher, Bothell, Washington

     1 pound sliced bacon, cut into 2-inch pieces
     3 medium onions, chopped
     3 pounds boneless pork, cubed
   3/4 cup all-purpose flour
Vegetable oil, optional
     3 medium tart apples, peeled and chopped
     1 teaspoon rubbed sage
   1/2 teaspoon ground nutmeg
     1 teaspoon salt
   1/4 teaspoon pepper
     1 cup apple cider
   1/2 cup water
     4 medium potatoes, peeled and cubed
   1/2 cup milk
     5 tablespoons butter, *divided*
Additional salt and pepper
Snipped fresh parsley, optional

Cook bacon in an ovenproof 12-in. skillet until crisp. Remove with a slotted spoon to paper towels to drain. In drippings, saute onions until tender; remove with a slotted spoon and set aside. Dust pork lightly with flour. Brown a third at a time in drippings, adding oil if needed. Remove from the heat and drain.

To the pork, add the bacon, onions, apples, sage, nutmeg, salt and pepper. Stir in the cider and water. Cover and bake at 325° for 2 hours or until pork is tender.

In a saucepan, cook potatoes in boiling water until tender. Drain and mash with milk and 3 tablespoons butter. Add salt and pepper to taste. Remove skillet from the oven and spread potatoes over pork mixture.

Melt remaining butter; brush over potatoes. Broil 6 in. from the heat for 5 minutes or until topping is browned. Sprinkle with parsley if desired. **Yield:** 10 servings.

Family-Tested Tip

Need an easy holiday ham glaze? Combine 1 cup of whole-berry cranberry sauce, 3 tablespoons of brown sugar and 1-1/2 teaspoons of prepared mustard. Use it to baste the ham during baking.
—*Sandra Larrick, Hanover, Pennsylvania*

BRAISED LAMB SHANKS

(Pictured at left)

These lamb shanks become so tender and savory after simmering with the vegetables and herbs.
—Billie Moss, El Sobrante, California

  2 lamb shanks (about 2 pounds)
  2 tablespoons vegetable oil
  1 medium onion, diced
  2 garlic cloves, minced
  1 tablespoon all-purpose flour
  2 beef bouillon cubes
1/4 cup boiling water
  1 can (14-1/2 ounces) diced tomatoes, undrained
1/2 cup chopped celery
1/2 cup chopped carrot
1/2 teaspoon dried marjoram
1/4 teaspoon salt

In a large skillet, brown lamb in oil; remove and set aside. Add the onion and garlic; saute until tender. Stir in flour; cook and stir for 1 minute. Add bouillon and water; stir to dissolve. Return lamb to pan. Add remaining ingredients; bring to a boil. Reduce heat; cover and simmer for 1-1/2 hours or until meat is tender. **Yield:** 2 servings.

OLD-FASHIONED LAMB STEW

(Pictured at left)

This hearty stew is chock-full of tender lamb chunks and vegetables. Sometimes I prepare it in my slow cooker.
—Michelle Wise, Spring Mills, Pennsylvania

1/4 cup all-purpose flour
  1 teaspoon salt
1/2 teaspoon pepper
  3 pounds boneless lamb, cut into 3-inch pieces
  2 tablespoons vegetable oil
  1 can (28 ounces) diced tomatoes, undrained
  1 medium onion, cut into eighths
  1 tablespoon dried parsley flakes
  2 teaspoons dried rosemary, crushed
1/4 teaspoon garlic powder
  4 large carrots, cut into 1/2-inch pieces
  4 medium potatoes, peeled and cut into 1-inch pieces
  1 package (10 ounces) frozen peas
  1 can (4 ounces) mushroom stems and pieces, drained

In a large resealable plastic bag, combine flour, salt and pepper; add lamb and toss to coat. In a Dutch oven, brown the lamb in oil; drain. Add tomatoes, onion, parsley, rosemary and garlic powder. Cover and simmer for 2 hours. Add carrots and potatoes; cover and cook 1 hour longer or until meat is tender. Add peas and mushrooms; heat through. Thicken if desired. **Yield:** 10-12 servings.

MUSHROOM LAMB CHOPS

(Pictured at left)

Fresh lamb chops are a real treat for us, and this is how I always fix them.
—Ruth Andrewson, Leavenworth, Washington

  6 blade lamb chops (about 3 pounds)
  1 tablespoon olive oil
1/2 teaspoon dried thyme
1/2 teaspoon salt
1/4 teaspoon pepper
1/2 cup chopped celery
1/2 cup chopped green onions
  1 can (10-1/2 ounces) beef consomme, undiluted
  3 tablespoons all-purpose flour
1/4 cup water
  1 can (4 ounces) button mushrooms, drained
  1 tablespoon minced fresh parsley
Hot cooked noodles

In a large skillet, brown the chops in oil; drain. Sprinkle with thyme, salt and pepper. Add celery, onions and consomme; cover and simmer for 40-45 minutes or until meat is tender.

Remove chops and keep warm. Combine flour and water until smooth; gradually stir into skillet and bring to a boil. Cook and stir for 2 minutes. Add mushrooms and parsley; heat through. Serve over chops and noodles. **Yield:** 6 servings.

SAUSAGE-STUFFED LOAF

(Pictured below)

This bread is filled with cheese, spinach and sausage, making it a real crowd-pleaser. Tasty slices are terrific as a snack, a side dish with bowls of soup or an appetizer at your next pizza party.
—Suzanne Hansen, Arlington Heights, Illinois

  2 **loaves (1 pound *each*) frozen bread dough**
  1 **pound bulk Italian sausage**
  1 **package (10 ounces) frozen chopped spinach, thawed and squeezed dry**
  4 **cups (1 pound) shredded mozzarella cheese**
1/4 **cup grated Parmesan cheese**
  1 **teaspoon dried oregano**
1/2 **teaspoon garlic powder**
  2 **tablespoons butter, cubed**
  1 **egg, lightly beaten**

Thaw bread dough on a greased baking sheet according to package directions; let rise until doubled. Meanwhile, in a skillet over medium heat, cook the sausage until no longer pink. Drain and place in a bowl. Add spinach, cheeses, oregano and garlic powder; set aside.

Roll each loaf of bread into a 14-in. x 12-in.

rectangle. Spread the sausage mixture lengthwise down the center of each rectangle. Gently press the filling down; dot with butter. Bring edges of the dough to the center over filling; pinch to seal. Return to the baking sheet, placing the seam side down; tuck the ends under and form into a crescent shape. Brush with egg.

Bake at 350° for 20-25 minutes or until golden brown. Let stand for 5-10 minutes before cutting. If desired, cool one loaf on a wire rack; wrap in foil and freeze for up to 3 months.

To use frozen loaf: Thaw at room temperature for 2 hours. Unwrap and place on a greased baking sheet. Bake at 350° for 15-20 minutes or until heated through. **Yield:** 2 loaves.

POTATO-CRUST PIZZA

We grow potatoes and found this recipe is a great way to use up leftover mashed potatoes. It's also a favorite among our family and friends.
—Carol Gorentz, Park Rapids, Minnesota

    3 **cups mashed potatoes (prepared with milk)**
    1 **egg, beaten**
  1/2 **cup grated Parmesan cheese**
    2 **tablespoons butter, melted**
1-1/2 **teaspoons salt**
    1 **can (8 ounces) pizza sauce**
    3 **ounces sliced pepperoni**
    4 **fresh mushrooms, sliced**
    1 **cup (4 ounces) shredded mozzarella cheese**

In a mixing bowl, combine potatoes, egg, Parmesan cheese, butter and salt. Press onto the bottom and up the sides of a greased 10-in. pie plate. Spread pizza sauce over potato mixture to within 1/2 in. of edges. Top with pepperoni and mushrooms. Sprinkle with mozzarella cheese. Bake at 400° for 25-30 minutes or until heated through and cheese is melted. **Yield:** 4-6 servings.

Editor's Note: An 11-in. x 7-in. x 2-in. baking dish can be used instead of the pie plate.

cheese is melted, stirring occasionally. Add the macaroni; cook 5-10 minutes longer or until heated through. **Yield:** 6-8 servings.

HAM WITH CHERRY SAUCE

This tangy fruit sauce with almonds is so wonderful over baked ham…and the ruby-red color is gorgeous, too! I usually round out this dinner with sweet potatoes, coleslaw or applesauce and rolls.
—Joan Laurenzo, Johnstown, Ohio

1/2   fully cooked bone-in ham
      (6 to 7 pounds)
1   jar (12 ounces) cherry preserves
1/4   cup red wine vinegar
2   tablespoons light corn syrup
1/4   teaspoon *each* ground cloves, cinnamon
      and nutmeg
3   tablespoons slivered almonds

Place ham on a rack in a shallow roasting pan. If desired, remove skin from ham and score the surface with shallow diagonal cuts, making diamond shapes. Bake, uncovered, at 325° for 1-1/2 to 2 hours or until a meat thermometer reads 140°.

In a saucepan, combine the preserves, vinegar, corn syrup, cloves, cinnamon and nutmeg. Bring to a boil, stirring often. Reduce heat; simmer, uncovered, for 2 minutes. Remove from the heat; stir in almonds. Serve with the ham. **Yield:** 10-12 servings (1-1/2 cups sauce).

SMOKY MACARONI

(Pictured above)

Our two grandsons are big fans of macaroni and cheese. When they're hungry, I can have this tasty variation with little smoked sausages and peas finished and on the table in about 20 minutes.
—Perlene Hoekema, Lynden, Washington

1/4   cup chopped sweet red pepper
2   tablespoons chopped onion
1   can (10-3/4 ounces) condensed cheddar
      cheese soup, undiluted
1   cup milk
1   package (16 ounces) miniature smoked
      sausage links
8   ounces process cheese (Velveeta), cut
      into 1/2-inch cubes
1   cup frozen peas
4   cups cooked elbow macaroni

In a nonstick skillet, saute red pepper and onion until tender. Combine soup and milk; stir into skillet. Add sausage, cheese and peas. Reduce heat; simmer, uncovered, for 5-10 minutes or until the

---

Family-Tested Tip

To deliciously flavor a plain pork roast for dinner, insert slivers of garlic into small slits cut into the top of the roast. During the last 15 minutes of baking, brush the meat with a mixture of 3 tablespoons of lemon juice and 1/2 cup of maple syrup.
—Beverly Borges, Rockland, Massachusetts

Place ribs, meaty side up, on a rack in a greased 13-in. x 9-in. x 2-in. baking pan. Cover pan tightly with foil. Bake at 350° for 1-1/4 hours. Meanwhile, combine the next nine ingredients in a saucepan. Bring to a boil over medium heat. Reduce heat; simmer for 15 minutes, stirring occasionally.

Drain ribs; remove rack and return ribs to pan. Cover with sauce. Bake, uncovered, for 35 minutes, basting occasionally. Sprinkle with sesame seeds just before serving. **Yield:** 6 servings.

Marinated Pork Kabobs

This recipe was originally for lamb, but I changed it to pork and adjusted the spices. After tasting these flavorful kabobs, my husband couldn't stop raving about them. They're one of his first requests when the grill comes out for the season.
—Bobbie Jo Devany, Fernly, Nevada

- 2 cups plain yogurt
- 2 tablespoons lemon juice
- 4 garlic cloves, minced
- 1/2 teaspoon ground cumin
- 1/4 teaspoon ground coriander
- 2 pounds pork tenderloin, cut into 1-1/2-inch cubes
- 8 small white onions, halved
- 8 cherry tomatoes
- 1 medium sweet red pepper, cut into 1-1/2-inch pieces
- 1 medium green pepper, cut into 1-1/2-inch pieces

In a medium glass bowl, combine yogurt, lemon juice, garlic, cumin and coriander; mix well. Add pork; cover and refrigerate for 6 hours or overnight. Alternate pork, onions, tomatoes and peppers on eight skewers. Grill over medium heat for 30-35 minutes or until meat reaches desired doneness. **Yield:** 8 servings.

Maple-Glazed Ribs

(Pictured above)

My family and I love maple syrup…no matter if it's for breakfast, lunch or dinner! That ingredient really comes through in these lip-smacking spareribs. I make them often and never have any leftovers.
—Linda Kobeluck, Ardrossan, Alberta

- 3 pounds pork spareribs, cut into serving-size pieces
- 1 cup maple syrup
- 3 tablespoons orange juice concentrate
- 3 tablespoons ketchup
- 2 tablespoons soy sauce
- 1 tablespoon Dijon mustard
- 1 tablespoon Worcestershire sauce
- 1 teaspoon curry powder
- 1 garlic clove, minced
- 2 green onions, minced
- 1 tablespoon sesame seeds, toasted

Cauliflower and Ham Casserole

My mother made this recipe often while I was growing up. I remember leaning on the table to watch her.
—Rosemary Flexman, Waukesha, Wisconsin

- 1 tablespoon chopped onion
- 3 tablespoons butter, *divided*
- 2 tablespoons all-purpose flour
- 1/2 teaspoon salt

Pepper to taste

- 1 cup milk
- 1/2 cup shredded cheddar cheese
- 1 medium head cauliflower, cut into florets, cooked and drained
- 2 cups cubed fully cooked ham
- 1 jar (4-1/2 ounces) sliced mushrooms, drained
- 1 jar (2 ounces) diced pimientos, drained
- 6 saltines, crumbled

In a saucepan over medium heat, saute chopped onion in 2 tablespoons of butter until tender. Stir in flour, salt and pepper until smooth. Gradually add milk; cook and stir for 2 minutes or until thick and bubbly.

Remove from the heat; stir in cheese until melted. Fold in cauliflower, ham, mushrooms and pimientos. Pour into a greased 2-qt. casserole.

In a small saucepan, brown cracker crumbs in remaining butter; sprinkle over casserole. Cover and bake at 350° for 20 minutes. Uncover and bake 5-10 minutes longer or until heated through. **Yield:** 6 servings.

Farm-Style Sausage Bake

(Pictured at right)

This dish is a hearty meal all by itself. My family thinks it's fantastic. I hope yours does, too.
—Catherine O'Hara, Bridgeton, New Jersey

- 6 medium potatoes (about 2 pounds), peeled and cubed
- 3 to 4 green onions, sliced
- 2 garlic cloves, minced
- 2 tablespoons butter
- 3/4 cup milk
- 2 egg yolks

Dash *each* pepper and ground nutmeg

- 2 tablespoons dried parsley flakes
- 1 pound smoked sausage, sliced
- 1/2 cup diced mozzarella cheese
- 2 tablespoons grated Parmesan cheese
- 1 teaspoon dried thyme *or* sage

Cook the potatoes in boiling salted water until tender. Drain and transfer to a mixing bowl; mash the potatoes. Add green onions, garlic, butter, milk, egg yolks, pepper and nutmeg; beat until light and fluffy.

Stir in parsley, sausage and cheeses. Spoon into a greased 2-qt. baking dish. Sprinkle with thyme. Bake, uncovered, at 400° for 30 minutes or until lightly browned and heated through. **Yield:** 6 servings.

the fat side almost to the bone. Spoon about 1/4 cup stuffing into each pocket. Combine the remaining salt and pepper; rub over chops.

In a skillet, brown the chops in oil; transfer to a slow cooker. Pour wine or broth over the chops. Cover and cook on low for 8-9 hours or until meat juices run clear. **Yield:** 6 servings.

HERB-STUFFED CHOPS

(Pictured above)

Guests will think you stayed home all day when you serve these tender stuffed chops. I often share this recipe with new brides because I know it will become one of their favorites. It's so convenient, too—I can put the chops in my slow cooker in the morning, then let them cook until dinner.
—Diane Seeger, New Springfield, Ohio

3/4 cup chopped onion
1/4 cup chopped celery
  2 tablespoons butter
  2 cups day-old bread cubes
1/2 cup minced fresh parsley
1/3 cup evaporated milk
  1 teaspoon fennel seed, crushed
1-1/2 teaspoons salt, *divided*
1/2 teaspoon pepper, *divided*
  6 rib *or* loin pork chops (1 inch thick)
  1 tablespoon vegetable oil
3/4 cup white wine *or* chicken broth

In a skillet, saute onion and celery in butter until tender. Add bread cubes, parsley, milk, fennel, 1/4 teaspoon salt and 1/8 teaspoon pepper; toss to coat. Cut a pocket in each chop by slicing from

SAUSAGE SAUERKRAUT SUPPER

With big, tender chunks of sausage, potatoes and carrots, this meal-in-one has old-world flavor that will satisfy even the heartiest of appetites. It always disappears in a hurry, whether served at a family gathering or at an office potluck.
—Joalyce Graham, St. Petersburg, Florida

  4 cups carrot chunks (2-inch pieces)
  4 cups red potato chunks
  2 cans (14 ounces *each*) sauerkraut, rinsed and drained
2-1/2 pounds fresh Polish sausage, cut into 3-inch pieces
  1 medium onion, thinly sliced
  3 garlic cloves, minced
1-1/2 cups dry white wine *or* chicken broth
  1 teaspoon pepper
1/2 teaspoon caraway seed

In a 5-qt. slow cooker, layer carrots, potatoes and sauerkraut. In a skillet, brown the sausage; transfer to the slow cooker (slow cooker will be full). Reserve 1 tablespoon drippings in skillet; saute onion and garlic until tender.

Gradually add wine or broth to skillet. Bring to a boil; stir to loosen browned bits. Stir in pepper and caraway. Pour over sausage. Cover and cook on low for 8-9 hours or until vegetables are tender and sausage is no longer pink. **Yield:** 10-12 servings.

PORK TENDERLOIN DIANE

(Pictured below)

We have pork at least once a week, and this is one dish we especially enjoy. The moist, tender pork "medallions" are served up in a savory sauce for a combination that's irresistible. This recipe is also nice for busy days because it's quick and easy to prepare.
—Janie Thorpe, Tullahoma, Tennessee

1 **pork tenderloin (about 1 pound)**
1 **tablespoon lemon-pepper seasoning**
2 **tablespoons butter**
2 **tablespoons lemon juice**
1 **tablespoon Worcestershire sauce**
1 **teaspoon Dijon mustard**
1 **tablespoon minced fresh parsley**

Cut tenderloin into eight pieces; place each piece between two pieces of plastic wrap or waxed paper and flatten to 1/2-in. thickness. Sprinkle with lemon-pepper.

Melt butter in a large skillet over medium heat; cook pork for 3-4 minutes on each side or until no longer pink and juices run clear. Remove to a serving platter and keep warm.

To the pan juices, add lemon juice, Worcestershire sauce and mustard; heat through, stirring occasionally. Pour over the pork and sprinkle with parsley. **Yield:** 4 servings.

POTLUCK SPARERIBS

*These ribs are guaranteed pleasers at potlucks.
I always bring home an empty dish.*
—Sheri Kirkman, Lancaster, New York

6 pounds pork spareribs
1-1/2 cups ketchup
3/4 cup packed brown sugar
1/2 cup vinegar
1/2 cup honey
1/3 cup soy sauce
1-1/2 teaspoons ground ginger
1 teaspoon salt
3/4 teaspoon ground mustard
1/2 teaspoon garlic powder
1/4 teaspoon pepper

Cut ribs into serving-size pieces; place with the meaty side up on racks in two greased 13-in. x 9-in. x 2-in. baking pans. Cover tightly with foil. Bake at 350° for 1-1/4 hours or until meat is tender.

Drain; remove racks and return ribs to pans. Combine remaining ingredients; pour over ribs. Return to oven, uncovered, for 35 minutes or until sauce coats ribs, basting occasionally. Ribs can also be grilled over medium-hot heat for the last 35 minutes instead of baking. **Yield:** 12 servings.

MANDARIN PORK MEDALLIONS

(Pictured at right)

*My daughter demonstrated this recipe at the state
fair and received lots of compliments.*
—Dawn Doyle, Easton, Minnesota

1 pork tenderloin (about 1 pound)
1 tablespoon vegetable oil
3/4 cup orange juice
1 tablespoon cornstarch
1/4 cup orange marmalade
2 tablespoons lemon juice
1 teaspoon prepared horseradish
1/4 to 1/2 teaspoon salt

Hot cooked noodles
1 can (11 ounces) mandarin oranges, drained

Cut tenderloin into four pieces; pound until 1/3 in. thick. Brown in a large skillet in oil for 3 minutes on each side; remove and set aside.

Combine orange juice and cornstarch; add to the skillet along with marmalade, lemon juice, horseradish and salt. Bring to a boil. Reduce heat; cook and stir until sauce thickens, about 2 minutes.

Return the pork to the skillet; cover and cook for 8-10 minutes or until pork is no longer pink. Serve over noodles; garnish with mandarin oranges. **Yield:** 4 servings.

Family-Tested Tip

Leftover barbecued pork chops make wonderful sandwiches the next day. Just remove the meat from the bones and chop it in your food processor. Reheat the meat and serve it on buns.
—Deborah Imiolo-Schriver, Amherst, New York

Au Gratin Sausage Skillet

(Pictured at right)

Using frozen vegetables and a package of au gratin potatoes, I can get this satisfying stovetop supper on the table in no time. Even picky eaters will ask for second helpings when I dish out this cheesy sausage skillet…and I rarely have leftovers.
—Penny Greene, Lancaster, Ohio

> 1 **pound fully cooked kielbasa *or* Polish sausage, halved and sliced 1/2 inch thick**
> 2 **tablespoons vegetable oil**
> 1 **package (5-1/4 ounces) au gratin potatoes**
> 2-1/2 **cups water**
> 1 **package (8 ounces) frozen California-blend vegetables**
> 1 **to 2 cups (4 to 8 ounces) shredded cheddar cheese**

In a skillet, cook sausage in oil until lightly browned; drain. Add potatoes with contents of sauce mix and water. Cover and cook over medium heat for 18-20 minutes or until the potatoes are almost tender, stirring occasionally.

Add vegetables; cover and cook for 8-10 minutes or until potatoes and vegetables are tender. Sprinkle with cheese. Remove from the heat; cover and let stand for 2 minutes or until the cheese is melted. **Yield:** 4 servings.

Editor's Note: The milk and butter listed on the potato package are not used in this recipe.

Honey Pork and Peppers

I'm always trying out new recipes on my husband and son. This easy, quick and delicious one is a keeper—a nice change from pork roast or pork chops.
—Carol Heim, Nokesville, Virginia

> 1-1/2 **pounds boneless pork, cut into 1-inch cubes**
> 2 **tablespoons vegetable oil**
> 1 **envelope (.87 ounce) brown gravy mix**
> 1 **cup water**
> 1/4 **cup honey**
> 3 **tablespoons soy sauce**
> 2 **tablespoons red wine vinegar**
> 1/2 **teaspoon ground ginger**
> 1/8 **teaspoon garlic powder**
> 1 **medium onion, cut into wedges**
> 1 **medium sweet red pepper, cut into 1-inch pieces**
> 1 **medium green pepper, cut into 1-inch pieces**
> **Hot cooked rice**

In a large skillet over medium heat, cook pork in oil until browned, about 15 minutes. Combine gravy mix, water, honey, soy sauce, vinegar, ginger and garlic powder; add to the pork. Cover and simmer for 20 minutes, stirring occasionally. Add onion and peppers; cook 5-10 minutes longer. Serve over rice. **Yield:** 4-6 servings.

milk; bring to a boil. Cook and stir for 1 minute. Stir in cheese just until melted. Pour over potato mixture. Cover and bake at 350° for 30 minutes or until bubbly. **Yield:** 8 servings.

HAM 'N' POTATOES AU GRATIN

(Pictured above)

The comforting flavor of ham and potatoes can't be beat. This is a nice recipe to share at covered dish dinners. It's a meal in itself.
—Leila Long, Rock Hill, South Carolina

1/4 cup chopped green onions
1/4 cup chopped green pepper
  2 tablespoons butter, *divided*
  3 cups diced peeled potatoes, cooked
  1 pound fully cooked ham, cubed
1/4 cup mayonnaise
  1 tablespoon all-purpose flour
1/8 teaspoon pepper
3/4 cup milk
  1 cup (4 ounces) shredded cheddar cheese

In a skillet, saute the onions and green pepper in 1 tablespoon butter until tender. Combine the onions and pepper with the potatoes, ham and mayonnaise; pour into an ungreased 11-in. x 7-in. x 2-in. baking dish.

In a saucepan, melt remaining butter. Stir in flour and pepper until smooth. Gradually add

CHILI CHOPS

These pork chops have Southwest flair and are a definite favorite at our house. I like to serve them over rice along with fresh-from-the-oven corn bread.
—Thelma Lee Peedin, Newport News, Virginia

  6 pork chops (1/2 inch thick)
  2 tablespoons vegetable oil
1/2 teaspoon salt
1/8 teaspoon pepper
  1 can (10-3/4 ounces) condensed tomato soup, undiluted
  1 can (15-1/2 ounces) kidney beans, rinsed and drained
1/2 cup sliced onion
  1 tablespoon chili powder
1/2 teaspoon garlic powder
  6 green pepper rings

In a large ovenproof skillet, brown chops in oil; drain. Remove the chops; sprinkle with salt and pepper. Combine soup, beans, onion, chili powder and garlic powder in the same skillet. Arrange chops over the soup mixture. Cover and bake at 325° for 35 minutes or until the chops are tender. Top each with a green pepper ring. Bake, uncovered, 10 minutes more. **Yield:** 6 servings.

"There is no such thing as society. There are individual men and women, and there are families."
—Margaret Thatcher

Asparagus Spaghetti Pie

(Pictured at right)

I've taken this cheesy ham dish to several luncheons and received many compliments. The pie looks special and tastes that way, too.
—Lorraine Danz, Lancaster, Pennsylvania

CRUST:
- 2 eggs
- 1 package (7 ounces) spaghetti, cooked and drained
- 1/2 cup grated Parmesan cheese
- 2 tablespoons butter, melted

FILLING:
- 1 cup cubed fully cooked ham
- 1 package (8 ounces) frozen asparagus spears, thawed and cut into 1-inch pieces
- 1 jar (4-1/2 ounces) sliced mushrooms, drained
- 1-1/2 cups (6 ounces) shredded Swiss cheese
- 2 eggs
- 1/2 cup sour cream
- 1 teaspoon dill weed
- 1 teaspoon minced chives

In a large bowl, beat eggs; add the spaghetti, Parmesan cheese and butter; mix well. Press onto the bottom and up the sides of a greased 10-in. pie plate. Combine ham, asparagus and mushrooms; spoon into crust. Sprinkle with Swiss cheese. Beat eggs, sour cream, dill and chives; pour over cheese. Bake at 350° for 35-40 minutes or until crust is set and center is lightly browned. Let stand for 10 minutes before serving. **Yield:** 6-8 servings.

Curried Rice Ham Rolls

My mother gave me this recipe, which had been handed down to her. She prepared these hearty ham rolls for church socials, and they were a huge success every time.
—Pamela Witte, Hastings, Nebraska

- 1/2 cup chopped onion
- 2 tablespoons butter

- 4 cups cooked brown *or* long grain rice
- 1 tablespoon dried parsley flakes
- 1 teaspoon salt
- 1/2 teaspoon curry powder
- 12 slices deli ham (1/8 inch thick)
- 4 hard-cooked eggs, sliced

CURRY SAUCE:
- 1/4 cup butter
- 2 tablespoons cornstarch
- 1/4 teaspoon curry powder
- 1/4 teaspoon salt
- 2 cups milk, *divided*

In a skillet, saute onion in butter until tender, about 3 minutes. In a large bowl, combine rice, parsley, salt, curry powder and onion; mix well. Spoon about 1/3 cup down the center of each ham slice; roll up. Secure with toothpicks if desired. Place rolls seam side down in a greased 13-in. x 9-in. x 2-in. baking pan. Arrange hard-cooked eggs on top.

For sauce, melt butter in a saucepan. Combine cornstarch, curry powder, salt and 1/3 cup milk; mix well. Gradually stir into butter. Add remaining milk; bring to a boil, stirring constantly. Cook and stir for 2 minutes. Pour over the ham rolls. Cover and bake at 375° for 25 minutes. Uncover and bake for 10 minutes. **Yield:** 6 servings.

The Lloyds

Chapter seven

From coast to coast, families have savored the

catch of the day by preparing favorite fish and

seafood recipes from their collections. Whether your

catch comes from a family angler or a market, you'll

reel in compliments with the taste-tempting

tuna, salmon, shrimp and more in this chapter.

New England Fish Bake
(Recipe on page 147)

♥Fish & Seafood

1/2 teaspoon dill weed
1/4 teaspoon pepper
6 to 8 large tomatoes

Combine the first nine ingredients in a bowl; set aside. In a small bowl, combine mayonnaise, lemon juice, salt, dill and pepper; mix well. Pour over rice mixture; toss gently. Cover and chill for at least 1 hour.

Just before serving, cut a thin slice from the top of each tomato, or scallop the top with a sharp knife. Scoop out pulp and discard, leaving a 1/2-in.-thick shell. Fill each tomato with about 1/2 cup of salad. Serve immediately. **Yield:** 6-8 servings.

SEAFOOD-STUFFED TOMATOES

(Pictured above)

A tempting combination of tiny shrimp, crabmeat, hard-cooked eggs and rice makes a cool, hearty salad perfect for warm days. Our daughter likes to prepare this salad for company. It's so easy to fix.
—Gwen Landry, Jennings, Louisiana

2 cups cooked rice
1 cup cooked salad shrimp
2 cans (6 ounces *each*) crabmeat, rinsed, drained and cartilage removed
4 hard-cooked eggs, chopped
1/2 cup chopped celery
1/2 cup chopped green pepper
1/4 cup chopped onion
1/4 cup chopped dill pickle
1 jar (2 ounces) chopped pimientos, drained
3/4 cup mayonnaise
2 tablespoons lemon juice
1 teaspoon salt

TUNA BURGERS

I gave Mom's original recipe a boost by adding onion and green pepper to these delightfully different tuna sandwiches. The filling has a great fresh taste.
—Nancy Selig, Lunenburg, Nova Scotia

6 hard-cooked eggs, chopped
2 cans (6 ounces *each*) tuna, drained and flaked
1 cup (4 ounces) shredded sharp cheddar cheese
1/2 cup chopped green pepper
1/2 cup chopped onion
3/4 teaspoon garlic salt
3/4 teaspoon pepper
1 cup mayonnaise
8 kaiser rolls, split

In a bowl, combine eggs and tuna. Add the cheese, green pepper, onion, garlic salt and pepper; mix well. Stir in the mayonnaise. Spoon about 1/2 cup onto each roll; wrap individually in heavy-duty foil. Bake at 400° for 15 minutes or until heated through. **Yield:** 8 servings.

Salmon Quesadillas

(Pictured below)

I like simple recipes that get me out of the kitchen fast, so my husband and I can spend more time with our two sons. These super-quick wedges are always a hit…and a tasty change of pace from salmon patties.
—Heidi Main, Anchorage, Alaska

- 2 garlic cloves, minced
- 1 teaspoon vegetable oil
- 1 can (14-3/4 ounces) salmon, drained, bones and skin removed
- 1 to 2 teaspoons dried basil
- 1/2 teaspoon pepper
- 1 tablespoon butter, softened
- 4 flour tortillas (8 inches)
- 2 cups (8 ounces) shredded mozzarella cheese

Guacamole *or* salsa

In a skillet, saute garlic in oil until tender. Stir in salmon, basil and pepper. Cook over medium heat until heated through. Meanwhile, spread butter over one side of each tortilla. Place tortillas, buttered side down, on a griddle. Sprinkle each with 1/2 cup mozzarella cheese. Spread 1/2 cup of salmon mixture over half of each tortilla. Fold over the filling and cook on low for 1-2 minutes on each side or until the cheese is melted. Cut each into three wedges; serve with guacamole or salsa. **Yield:** 4 servings.

New England Fish Bake

(Pictured on page 145)

I've lived in Rhode Island for over 35 years and love the fresh seafood dishes served here. This is a favorite of mine. My mother-in-law gave me the recipe.
—Norma DesRoches, Warwick, Rhode Island

- 4 medium potatoes, peeled
- 1 teaspoon all-purpose flour
- 1 small onion, sliced into rings
- 1/2 teaspoon salt
- 1/4 teaspoon pepper
- 3/4 cup milk, *divided*
- 1-1/2 pounds cod fillets *or* freshwater fish (trout, catfish *or* pike)
- 3 tablespoons grated Parmesan cheese, optional
- 2 tablespoons minced fresh parsley *or* 2 teaspoons dried parsley flakes
- 1/4 teaspoon paprika

Place potatoes in a saucepan and cover with water; bring to a boil. Cook until almost tender; drain. Slice 1/8 in. thick; place in a greased shallow 2-qt. baking dish. Sprinkle with flour. Top with onion; sprinkle with salt and pepper.

Pour half of the milk over potatoes. Place fish on top; pour remaining milk over fish. Sprinkle with Parmesan cheese if desired. Cover and bake at 375° for 20-30 minutes or until fish flakes easily with a fork. Sprinkle with parsley and paprika. **Yield:** 3-4 servings.

ITALIAN-STYLE WALLEYE

(Pictured at right)

Herbs and melted cheese dress up fillets in this recipe. When I want a quick fish dinner, this is the recipe I turn to most often.
—Cathy Lueschen, Columbus, Nebraska

4 to 6 walleye fillets (about 1-1/2 pounds)
1 can (15 ounces) tomato sauce
2 tablespoons chopped fresh parsley
1 teaspoon Italian seasoning
1/2 teaspoon dried basil
1/4 teaspoon salt
1/8 teaspoon pepper
1 cup (4 ounces) shredded mozzarella cheese

Place walleye in a greased shallow 3-qt. or 13-in. x 9-in. x 2-in. baking dish. Combine tomato sauce, parsley, Italian seasoning, basil, salt and pepper; pour over the fish. Bake, uncovered, at 350° for 15 minutes. Sprinkle with mozzarella cheese. Bake 5-10 minutes longer or until fish flakes easily with a fork. **Yield:** 4-6 servings.

CATFISH JAMBALAYA

(Pictured at right)

My family owns a catfish processing plant. We have plenty of catfish recipes, but this colorful and zippy main dish ranks as one of our all-time favorites.
—Mrs. Bill Saul, Macon, Mississippi

2 cups chopped onion
1/2 cup chopped celery
1/2 cup chopped green pepper
2 garlic cloves, minced
1/4 cup butter
1 can (10 ounces) diced tomatoes and green chilies, undrained
1 cup sliced fresh mushrooms
1/4 teaspoon cayenne pepper
1/2 teaspoon salt
1 pound catfish fillets, cubed
Hot cooked rice, optional
Sliced green onions, optional

In a saucepan over medium-high heat, saute onion, celery, green pepper and garlic in butter until tender, about 10 minutes. Add tomatoes, mushrooms, cayenne and salt; bring to a boil. Add catfish. Reduce heat; cover and simmer until the fish flakes easily with a fork, about 10 minutes. If desired, serve with hot rice and top with sliced green onions. **Yield:** 4 servings.

CRACKER-COATED FRIED PERCH

(Pictured at right)

Your favorite fisherman would be proud to find his catch fried with this golden coating. I've gotten raves each time I've made this fish. It's a quick-and-easy recipe that delivers fantastic flavor.
—Dennis Dornfeldt, Sheboygan, Wisconsin

2 eggs
1/2 cup milk
2 cups butter-flavored cracker crumbs
1/2 teaspoon garlic salt
1/4 teaspoon dried oregano
1/4 teaspoon dried tarragon
1/4 teaspoon pepper
1 pound perch fillets
Vegetable oil

In a shallow bowl, beat eggs and milk. In another shallow bowl, combine cracker crumbs, garlic salt, oregano, tarragon and pepper. Dip the perch in egg mixture, then coat with crumbs. Heat oil in a skillet over medium heat. Fry fish for several minutes on each side or until it flakes easily with a fork. **Yield:** 4 servings.

Fish & Seafood

GINGERED HONEY SALMON

(Pictured below)

Ginger, garlic powder and green onion blend nicely in an easy marinade that gives pleasant flavor to this salmon. The marinade is versatile, too— we also like to use it when we're grilling chicken.
—Dan Strumberger, Farmington, Minnesota

1/3 **cup orange juice**
1/3 **cup soy sauce**
1/4 **cup honey**
  1 **green onion, chopped**
  1 **teaspoon ground ginger**
  1 **teaspoon garlic powder**
  1 **salmon fillet (1-1/2 pounds
      and 3/4 inch thick)**

Coat grill rack with nonstick cooking spray before starting the grill. In a bowl, combine the first six ingredients; mix well. Set aside 1/3 cup for basting; cover and refrigerate. Pour remaining marinade into a large resealable plastic bag or shallow glass container; add salmon and turn to coat. Seal or cover and refrigerate for 30 minutes, turning once or twice.

Drain and discard the marinade. Place the salmon skin side down on grill. Grill, covered, over

"The family is the cornerstone of our society."
—Lyndon Baines Johnson

medium-hot heat for 5 minutes. Baste with reserved marinade. Grill 10-15 minutes longer or until fish flakes easily with a fork, basting frequently. **Yield:** 4-6 servings.

INSTEAD OF FRYING FISH

My husband is an avid fisherman, and I've put this recipe to good use over the years. It has a crispy potato chip coating that bakes up toasty brown. The fillets also stay nice and moist.
—Sharon Funfsinn, Mendota, Illinois

  1 **pound walleye, perch *or* pike fillets**
1/4 **cup milk**
  1 **cup crushed potato chips**
1/4 **cup grated Parmesan cheese**
1/4 **teaspoon dried thyme**
  1 **tablespoon dry bread crumbs**
  2 **tablespoons butter, melted**

Cut fish into serving-size pieces. Place milk in a shallow bowl. In another shallow bowl, combine potato chips, Parmesan cheese and thyme. Dip fish in milk, then coat with the potato chip mixture.

Sprinkle a greased 8-in. square baking dish with bread crumbs. Place fish over crumbs; drizzle with butter. Bake, uncovered, at 500° for 12-14 minutes or until fish flakes easily with a fork. **Yield:** 4 servings.

Louisiana Gumbo

(Pictured above)

This recipe certainly reflects our area of the country. With sausage, ham and chicken in addition to the shrimp, this gumbo is really a meal in itself. It's well worth the preparation.
—Wilton and Gloria Mason, Springhill, Louisiana

1 broiler/fryer chicken (3 to 3-1/2 pounds), cut up
2 quarts water
3/4 cup all-purpose flour
1/2 cup vegetable oil
1/2 cup sliced green onions
1/2 cup chopped onion
1/2 cup chopped green pepper
1/2 cup chopped sweet red pepper
1/2 cup chopped celery
2 garlic cloves, minced
1/2 pound fully cooked smoked sausage, cut into 1-inch cubes
1/2 pound fully cooked ham, cut into 3/4-inch cubes
1/2 pound fresh *or* frozen uncooked shrimp, peeled and deveined
1 cup cut fresh *or* frozen okra (3/4-inch pieces)
1 can (15 ounces) kidney beans, rinsed and drained
1/2 teaspoon salt
1/4 teaspoon pepper
1/4 teaspoon hot pepper sauce

Place the chicken and water in a Dutch oven; bring to a boil. Skim fat. Reduce heat; cover and simmer 30-45 minutes or until chicken is tender. Remove chicken; cool. Reserve 6 cups broth. Remove chicken from bones; cut into bite-size pieces.

In a 4-qt. kettle, mix flour and oil until smooth; cook and stir over medium-low heat until browned, 2-3 minutes. Stir in onions, peppers, celery and garlic; cook for 5 minutes or until vegetables are tender. Stir in the sausage, ham and reserved broth and chicken; cover and simmer for 45 minutes.

Add the shrimp, okra, beans, salt, pepper and hot pepper sauce; cover and simmer 10 minutes longer or until shrimp is cooked. **Yield:** 12 servings.

Seafood Stuffing

For an easy and elegant side dish, I add canned crab and shrimp to boxed stuffing mix. When I served this to my mom as part of her birthday dinner, she said it was the best she had ever tasted.
—Marcy Thrall, Haddam Neck, Connecticut

1 package (6 ounces) instant chicken-flavored stuffing mix
1 can (6 ounces) crabmeat, drained and cartilage removed *or* 1 cup imitation crabmeat
1 can (6 ounces) small shrimp, rinsed and drained *or* 1 cup frozen small cooked shrimp
1 teaspoon lemon juice

Prepare stuffing according to package directions. Gently stir in crab, shrimp and lemon juice. Serve immediately. **Yield:** 4-6 servings.

1 teaspoon celery seed
1 teaspoon onion powder
Lettuce leaves and red onion rings, optional

Cook pasta according to package directions; rinse in cold water and drain. In a bowl, combine mayonnaise and sugar. Stir in the tuna, celery, onions, green pepper, carrot and parsley. Spoon into pasta shells; cover and refrigerate.

For the dressing, combine sour cream, sugar, vinegar, mayonnaise, celery seed and onion powder. Arrange lettuce, onion rings and stuffed pasta shells on a serving platter; drizzle with dressing. **Yield:** 5 servings.

TUNA-STUFFED JUMBO SHELLS

(Pictured above)

These light, fresh-tasting stuffed shells really star as part of a luncheon menu. I came up with this distinctive combination of ingredients by accident one day using leftovers from other recipes. It's a cool summer main dish.
—Phy Bresse, Lumberton, North Carolina

10 jumbo pasta shells
1/2 cup mayonnaise
2 tablespoons sugar
1 can (12 ounces) tuna, drained and flaked
1 cup diced celery
1/2 cup diced green onions
1/2 cup diced green pepper
1/2 cup shredded carrot
2 tablespoons minced fresh parsley
CREAMY CELERY DRESSING:
1/4 cup sour cream
1/4 cup sugar
1/4 cup cider vinegar
2 tablespoons mayonnaise

SHRIMP MONTEREY

For a special occasion or when company's coming, this delicious seafood dish makes a lasting impression. You'll be surprised at how fast you can prepare it. The mild sauce and Monterey Jack cheese nicely complement the shrimp. I serve it over pasta or rice.
—Jane Birch, Edison, New Jersey

2 garlic cloves, minced
2 tablespoons butter
2 pounds uncooked medium shrimp, peeled and deveined
1/2 cup white wine *or* chicken broth
2 cups (8 ounces) shredded Monterey Jack cheese
2 tablespoons minced fresh parsley

In a skillet over medium heat, saute garlic in butter for 1 minute. Add shrimp; cook for 4-5 minutes or until pink. Using a slotted spoon, transfer shrimp to a greased 11-in. x 7-in. x 2-in. baking dish; set aside and keep warm.

Add wine or chicken broth to the skillet; bring to a boil. Cook and stir for 5 minutes or until the sauce is reduced. Pour over the shrimp; top with shredded cheese and parsley. Bake, uncovered, at 350° for 10 minutes or until cheese is melted. **Yield:** 6 servings.

GOLDEN CATFISH FILLETS

(Pictured below)

These flavorful fillets cook up moist with an irresistible crisp, golden coating. Whether your fish comes from a nearby lake or the grocery store, this recipe makes a terrific summer meal.
—Tammy Moore-Worthington, Artesia, New Mexico

1 egg white
1 cup milk
1 cup cornmeal
3/4 teaspoon salt
1/4 teaspoon garlic powder
1/4 to 1/2 teaspoon cayenne pepper
1/8 teaspoon pepper
4 catfish fillets (8 ounces *each*)
Vegetable oil
Lemon *or* lime wedges, optional

In a shallow bowl, beat the egg white until foamy; add milk and mix well. In another shallow bowl, combine the cornmeal, salt, garlic powder, cayenne and pepper. Dip the fillets in milk mixture, then coat with cornmeal mixture. Heat 1/4 in. of oil in a large skillet; fry fish over medium-high for 3-4 minutes on each side or until it flakes easily with a fork. Garnish with lemon or lime if desired. **Yield:** 4 servings.

BAKED WALLEYE

We live very close to Lake Erie, which is nicknamed the "Walleye Capital of the World." I'm always looking for new recipes for this fish...I came up with this one on my own.
—Joyce Szymanski, Monroe, Michigan

3/4 cup chopped onion
3/4 cup chopped green pepper
3/4 cup chopped celery
  1 tablespoon dried parsley flakes
1/2 teaspoon garlic powder
1/2 teaspoon pepper
1/2 teaspoon seasoned salt
  1 cup V8 juice
  1 pound walleye fillets

In a saucepan, combine the first eight ingredients; bring to a boil. Reduce heat; simmer, uncovered, until vegetables are crisp-tender, stirring occasionally, about 5 minutes. Place fish in a greased 13-in. x 9-in. x 2-in. baking pan. Pour vegetable mixture over the fish. Cover and bake at 350° for 30 minutes or until fish flakes easily with a fork. **Yield:** 4 servings.

FISH AND VEGGIES PRIMAVERA

(Pictured above right)

The most time-consuming thing about this recipe is chopping the vegetables—and that takes just seconds. Broccoli, cauliflower and carrots perk up the seafood entree, which goes from oven to table in less than half an hour.
—Annette White, Whittier, California

  1 tablespoon butter, melted
  4 fresh *or* frozen orange roughy fillets
     (6 ounces *each*), thawed
  2 tablespoons lemon juice
Pinch pepper
  1 garlic clove, minced
  1 tablespoon olive oil
1-1/2 cups broccoli florets
  1 cup cauliflowerets
  1 cup julienned carrots
  1 cup sliced fresh mushrooms
1/2 cup sliced celery
1/4 teaspoon dried basil
1/4 teaspoon salt
1/4 cup grated Parmesan cheese

Place the butter in a 13-in. x 9-in. x 2-in. baking dish; add fish and turn to coat. Sprinkle with lemon juice and pepper. Bake, uncovered, at 450° for 5 minutes.

Meanwhile, in a large skillet over medium heat, saute garlic in oil. Add the next seven ingredients; stir-fry until the vegetables are crisp-tender, about 2-3 minutes. Spoon over the fish; sprinkle with Parmesan cheese. Bake, uncovered, at 450° for 3-5 minutes or until the fish flakes easily with a fork. **Yield:** 4 servings.

LEMONY SALMON PATTIES

Topped with a zippy white sauce, these little patties bake up golden brown in a muffin pan. They're impressive enough for company but easy enough that I can prepare them any time we like.
—Lorice Britt, Severn, North Carolina

1   can (14-3/4 ounces) pink salmon, drained, skin and bones removed
3/4 cup milk
1   cup soft bread crumbs
1   egg, beaten
1   tablespoon chopped fresh parsley
1   teaspoon minced onion
1/2 teaspoon Worcestershire sauce
1/4 teaspoon salt
1/8 teaspoon pepper

LEMON SAUCE:

2   tablespoons butter
4   teaspoons all-purpose flour
3/4 cup milk
2   tablespoons lemon juice
1/4 teaspoon salt
1/8 to 1/4 teaspoon cayenne pepper

Combine the first nine ingredients; mix well. Spoon into eight greased muffin cups, using 1/4 cup in each. Bake at 350° for 45 minutes or until browned.

Meanwhile, melt butter in a saucepan; stir in the flour to form a smooth paste. Gradually stir in milk; bring to a boil over medium heat, stirring constantly. Cook for 2 minutes or until thickened. Remove from the heat; stir in lemon juice, salt and cayenne. Serve over patties. **Yield:** 4 servings.

FISH STICK SUPPER

(Pictured at right)

Dill adds fresh flavor to this comforting combination of foods you likely keep in your freezer. When our children were growing up, they loved this meal.
—Ruth Andrewson, Leavenworth, Washington

1   package (12 ounces) frozen shredded hash brown potatoes, thawed
4   eggs
2   cups milk
1   tablespoon dried minced onion
1   tablespoon snipped fresh dill *or* 1 teaspoon dill weed
1-1/4 teaspoons seasoned salt
1/8 teaspoon pepper
1   cup (4 ounces) shredded cheddar cheese
1   package (12 ounces) frozen fish sticks (about 18)

Break apart hash browns with a fork; set aside. In a large bowl, beat eggs and milk. Add minced onion, dill, seasoned salt and pepper. Stir in hash browns and cheddar cheese. Transfer to a greased 11-in. x 7-in. x 2-in. baking dish; arrange fish sticks over the top.

Bake, uncovered, at 350° for 50 minutes or until top is golden brown and fish flakes with a fork. Let casserole stand for 5 minutes before cutting. **Yield:** 6 servings.

SALSA FISH

(Pictured above)

My family loves outdoor activities, especially fishing. I give their catch of the day some unexpected zip with salsa. It jazzes up these golden crumb-coated fillets and keeps them moist and tender.
—Diane Grajewski, North Branch, Michigan

   2 **pounds fish fillets (walleye, bass *or* perch)**
   1 **cup seasoned bread crumbs**
   1 **tablespoon vegetable oil**
1-1/2 **cups salsa**
   8 **ounces shredded *or* sliced mozzarella *or* provolone cheese**

Coat fish fillets in bread crumbs. In a skillet, brown fillets in oil. Arrange in a greased 13-in. x 9-in. x 2-in. baking dish. Top with salsa and cheese. Bake, uncovered, at 400° for 7-10 minutes or until fish flakes easily with a fork and cheese is melted. **Yield:** 6 servings.

"A family is a place where principles are hammered and honed on the anvil of everyday living."
—Charles Swindoll

SHRIMP MARINARA

This flavorful marinara sauce simmers for most of the day. Then shortly before mealtime, I add cooked shrimp, which merely require being heated through. Served over spaghetti, it makes a delicious dressed-up main dish.
—Sue Mackey, Galesburg, Illinois

    1 can (14-1/2 ounces) Italian diced
       tomatoes, undrained
    1 can (6 ounces) tomato paste
  1/2 to 1 cup water
    2 garlic cloves, minced
    2 tablespoons minced fresh parsley
    1 teaspoon salt
    1 teaspoon dried oregano
  1/2 teaspoon dried basil
  1/4 teaspoon pepper
    1 pound fresh *or* frozen shrimp, cooked,
       peeled and deveined
    1 pound spaghetti, cooked and drained
Shredded Parmesan cheese, optional

In a slow cooker, combine the first nine ingredients. Cover and cook on low for 3-4 hours. Stir in shrimp. Cover and cook 20 minutes longer or just until shrimp are heated through. Serve over spaghetti. Garnish with Parmesan cheese if desired. **Yield:** 6 servings.

BARBECUED ALASKAN SALMON

(Pictured below)

We eat salmon all summer long, and this is our favorite way to fix it. The mild sauce, which is brushed on as the fish grills, really enhances the taste and couldn't be simpler to prepare.
—Janis Smoke, King Salmon, Alaska

    2 tablespoons butter
    2 tablespoons brown sugar
    1 to 2 garlic cloves, minced
    1 tablespoon lemon juice
    2 teaspoons soy sauce
  1/2 teaspoon pepper
    4 salmon steaks (1 inch thick)

In a small saucepan, combine the first six ingredients. Cook and stir until sugar is dissolved. Meanwhile, grill salmon, covered, over medium-hot heat for 5 minutes. Turn salmon; baste with the butter sauce. Grill 7-9 minutes longer, turning and basting occasionally, or until the salmon flakes easily with a fork. **Yield:** 4 servings.

HERBED SHRIMP FETTUCCINE

(Pictured below)

Everyone will think you went all out when you serve this impressive seafood entree. You'll be amazed, though, at how easy and quick it is to fix. We've been enjoying this fettuccine for years.
—Marilyn Weaver, Sparks, Maryland

 6 ounces fettuccine *or* medium egg
　　noodles
 1 envelope herb and garlic soup mix
1-3/4 cups milk
 1 pound uncooked shrimp, peeled and
　　deveined
 2 cups broccoli florets
 1/4 cup grated Parmesan cheese

Cook fettuccine according to package directions. Meanwhile, combine soup mix and milk in a saucepan. Cook and stir over medium heat until smooth. Add shrimp and broccoli; simmer, uncovered, for 3-5 minutes or until shrimp are pink (do not boil). Drain pasta; toss with the shrimp mixture. Sprinkle with Parmesan cheese. **Yield:** 4 servings.

Family-Tested Tip

Finely crush butter-flavored crackers and use them to coat fish fillets before frying. If you'd like a little extra zip, add some seafood seasoning or salt-free seasoning blend to the crumbs.
—Anne Ralph, Roselle, New Jersey

BAKED FISH AND RICE

The first time I tried this meal-in-one dish, it was an instant hit at our house. Fish and rice are a tasty change of pace from traditional meat-and-potato fare.
—Jo Groth, Plainfield, Iowa

1-1/2 cups boiling chicken broth
 1/2 cup uncooked long grain rice
 1/4 teaspoon Italian seasoning
 1/4 teaspoon garlic powder
 1 package (10 ounces) frozen chopped
　　broccoli, thawed and drained
 1 tablespoon grated Parmesan cheese
 1 can (2.8 ounces) french-fried onions,
　　divided
 1 pound fresh *or* frozen fish fillets, thawed
Dash paprika
 1/2 cup shredded cheddar cheese

In a greased 11-in. x 7-in. x 2-in. baking dish, combine the broth, rice, Italian seasoning and garlic powder. Cover and bake at 375° for 10 minutes. Add the broccoli, Parmesan cheese and half of the onions. Top with fish fillets; sprinkle with paprika.

Cover and bake 20-25 minutes longer or until the fish flakes easily with a fork. Uncover; sprinkle with cheddar cheese and remaining onions. Return to the oven for 3 minutes or until cheese is melted. **Yield:** 4 servings.

LOW-FAT TARTAR SAUCE

(Pictured above)

I like to whip up a batch of this creamy tartar sauce whenever I plan to serve fish or seafood. Your family will be pleasantly surprised by the flavor of this healthier version.
—Laura Letobar, Livonia, Michigan

1/2 cup nonfat plain yogurt
1/4 cup fat-free mayonnaise
 1 tablespoon sweet pickle relish, drained
 2 teaspoons dried minced onion
 1 teaspoon dried parsley flakes
 1 teaspoon Dijon mustard
 2 drops hot pepper sauce

In a small bowl, combine all ingredients. Cover and refrigerate until serving. **Yield:** 1 cup.

LINDA'S LEMON FISH

(Pictured above)

I've made this recipe since I was a teenager. The zippy seasoning is great on almost any fish, but I prefer sole.
—Linda Gaido, New Brighton, Pennsylvania

 1 pound whitefish *or* sole fillets
1/4 cup lemon juice
 1 teaspoon olive oil
 1 to 2 teaspoons lemon-pepper seasoning
 1 small onion, thinly sliced
 1 teaspoon dried parsley flakes

Cut fish into serving-size pieces. Place in an ungreased 11-in. x 7-in. x 2-in. baking dish. Drizzle with lemon juice and oil; sprinkle with lemon-pepper. Arrange onion over fish; sprinkle with parsley. Cover and let stand for 5 minutes. Bake at 350° for 20 minutes or until fish flakes easily with a fork. **Yield:** 4 servings.

a greased 2-1/2-qt. baking dish. Combine saltines and butter; sprinkle over noodles.

Bake, uncovered, at 350° for 35-45 minutes or until heated through. If desired, sprinkle with paprika and garnish with tomato slices and thyme. **Yield:** 6 servings.

SEAFOOD RICE CASSEROLE

Cooking and creating new recipes are two of my favorite pastimes. My family loves rice and clams, so I decided to combine them in this recipe. It was a hit! This casserole is very filling and satisfying.
—Pat Wieghorst, Phillipsburg, New Jersey

  3 cups cooked long grain rice
1/3 cup chopped onion
  2 tablespoons chopped green chilies
  1 can (6-1/2 ounces) chopped clams, undrained
  1 can (5 ounces) evaporated milk
1/4 cup seasoned bread crumbs
1/2 cup shredded cheddar cheese

In a 1-1/2-qt. baking dish coated with nonstick cooking spray, combine rice, onion and chilies. In a bowl, combine clams and milk; pour over rice mixture. Sprinkle with crumbs and cheese. Bake, uncovered, at 350° for 45 minutes. **Yield:** 4 main-dish or 8 side-dish servings.

TUNA MUSHROOM CASSEROLE

(Pictured above)

I usually serve this casserole when I'm short on time and we need something hearty and comforting.
—Connie Moore, Medway, Ohio

  1 package (12 ounces) wide noodles, cooked and drained
  2 cans (6 ounces *each*) tuna, drained
  1 can (4 ounces) mushroom stems and pieces, drained
  1 can (10-3/4 ounces) condensed cream of mushroom soup, undiluted
1-1/3 cups milk
1/2 teaspoon salt
1/4 teaspoon pepper
1/2 cup crushed saltines
  3 tablespoons butter, melted
Paprika, tomato slices and fresh thyme, optional

In a large bowl, combine noodles, tuna and mushrooms. Combine the soup, milk, salt and pepper; pour over noodle mixture and mix well. Pour into

HERBED ORANGE ROUGHY

The simple seasonings in this quick-and-easy recipe enhance the pleasant, mild flavor of orange roughy. But this is also a wonderful way to prepare fillets of red snapper, catfish and trout.
—Sue Kroening, Mattoon, Illinois

  2 tablespoons lemon juice
  1 tablespoon butter, melted
1/2 teaspoon dried thyme
1/2 teaspoon grated lemon peel

1/4 teaspoon salt
1/4 teaspoon paprika
1/8 teaspoon garlic powder
  4 orange roughy, red snapper, catfish *or* trout fillets (6 ounces *each*)

In a small bowl, combine the first seven ingredients; dip fillets. Grill, covered, over medium-hot heat for 10 minutes or until fish flakes easily with a fork. **Yield:** 4 servings.

CLAM FRITTERS

(Pictured at right)

We had clam fritters every time we went to Rhode Island. This recipe reminds us of those trips and brings back that memorable taste whenever we want it.
—Cecelia Wilson, Rockville, Connecticut

2/3 cup all-purpose flour
  1 teaspoon baking powder
1/4 teaspoon salt
1/8 teaspoon pepper
  1 can (6-1/2 ounces) minced clams
  1 egg
  3 tablespoons milk
1/3 cup diced onion
Oil for deep-fat frying
Tartar sauce *and/or* lemon wedges, optional

In a bowl, combine flour, baking powder, salt and pepper; set aside. Drain clams, reserving 2 tablespoons juice; set clams aside. In a small bowl, beat egg, milk and reserved clam juice; stir into dry ingredients just until moistened. Add the clams and onion.

In an electric skillet or deep-fat fryer, heat oil to 375°. Drop the batter by tablespoonfuls into oil. Fry for 2-3 minutes, turning occasionally, until golden brown. Drain on paper towels. Serve fritters with tartar sauce and/or lemon wedges if desired. **Yield:** 14-16 fritters.

SHRIMP SCAMPI

I frequently prepare this simple seafood entree that looks fancy enough for company or special occasions. I've been serving this delicious dish for years, and everyone likes it.
—Lori Watkins, Burien, Washington

  8 ounces angel hair pasta
1-3/4 cups chicken broth
  2 garlic cloves, minced
1/4 teaspoon lemon-pepper seasoning
1/4 cup chopped green onions, *divided*
1/4 cup minced fresh parsley, *divided*
  1 pound uncooked shrimp, peeled and deveined

Cook pasta according to package directions. Meanwhile, in a large saucepan, combine the broth, garlic, lemon-pepper and 3 tablespoons each green onions and parsley. Bring to a boil. Add shrimp; cook for 3-5 minutes or until shrimp turn pink. Drain pasta and place in a serving bowl. Top with shrimp mixture and remaining onions and parsley. **Yield:** 4 servings.

GARDEN FISH PACKETS

(Pictured above)

I frequently serve this flavorful combination of fish, vegetables and cheese over a bed of rice. It's quick to prepare, and the foil packets make cleanup a breeze. For a fun family activity, have everyone help assemble the packets.
—*Sally Davis, Warren, Pennsylvania*

3 tablespoons butter, melted
3 pounds frozen cod *or* haddock fillets, thawed
2 teaspoons seasoned salt
3/4 teaspoon lemon-pepper seasoning
2 medium tomatoes, thinly sliced
2 medium green peppers, thinly sliced
1/2 cup thinly sliced green onions
1/2 pound sliced fresh mushrooms
2 cups (8 ounces) shredded mozzarella cheese

Drizzle the butter over eight pieces of heavy-duty foil (about 18 in. x 12 in.). Cut fish into eight portions; place one portion on each piece of foil. Sprinkle with seasoned salt and lemon-pepper. Top with vegetables and cheese.

Loosely wrap foil around fish; seal top and sides. Place in two ungreased 15-in. x 10-in. x 1-in. baking pans. Bake at 350° for 23-25 minutes or until fish flakes easily with a fork. Carefully open foil; transfer fish and vegetables to serving plates. **Yield:** 8 servings.

FRIED FISH NUGGETS

(Pictured at left)

My family always requests these cheesy fish bites during our annual fishing trip in Canada. You can use most any leftover fish with tasty results.
—Lynn Negaard, Litchfield, Minnesota

2 eggs, beaten
1/2 cup dry bread crumbs
1/2 cup shredded cheddar cheese
1/4 cup finely chopped onion
1 garlic clove, minced
1-1/2 teaspoons minced fresh parsley
1/4 teaspoon dill weed
1/4 teaspoon pepper
1-1/2 cups flaked cooked fish
Oil for deep-fat frying
Tartar sauce, optional

In a bowl, combine the first eight ingredients; mix well. Stir in the fish. Roll into 1-in. balls. Heat oil in a deep-fat fryer to 375°. Fry fish nuggets for 2 minutes or until golden brown; drain on paper towels. Serve with tartar sauce if desired. **Yield:** about 2-1/2 dozen.

Editor's Note: To prepare with fresh fish, poach 3/4 pound fresh fish until it flakes easily with a fork. Prepare recipe as directed.

GONE FISHIN' CHOWDER

(Pictured above left)

My grandpa and his brother, who are twins, love to fish. For years, they've used cooked fish to make this colorful chowder. It's so good that when I entered it in our 4-H Food Show, I received a top award.
—Jasmina Kocurek, Palacios, Texas

4 bacon strips
1 cup chopped onion
1 teaspoon dried thyme

5 cups water
3 cups diced peeled potatoes
1-1/2 cups coarsely chopped carrots
1/2 cup chopped celery
2 teaspoons salt
1/8 to 1/4 teaspoon pepper
1 can (28 ounces) diced tomatoes, undrained
1 tablespoon dried parsley flakes
1-1/2 cups cubed cooked fish

In a Dutch oven or soup kettle over medium heat, cook bacon until crisp. Drain, reserving 1 teaspoon drippings. Crumble bacon and set aside. Saute onion and thyme in drippings.

Add water, potatoes, carrots, celery, salt and pepper. Cover and simmer for 20-25 minutes or until vegetables are tender. Add tomatoes, parsley and bacon; cook for 10 minutes. Add fish; heat through. **Yield:** 12 servings (about 3 quarts).

Editor's Note: To prepare with fresh fish, dice 3/4 pound fresh fish and add to chowder at the same time as the tomatoes. Cook for 10-15 minutes or until fish is opaque.

"The family is our refuge and springboard; nourished on it, we can advance to new horizons."
—Alex Haley

Chapter eight

Favorite family meals just aren't the same

without the standout side dishes everyone craves.

Best-loved baked beans for picnics…mashed potatoes

that are must-haves for the holidays…veggie casseroles

that delight every time…these accompaniments play

their own starring role in memorable menus.

Asparagus Mornay
(Recipe on page 167)

♥ Side Dishes

ROBBIE'S RED RICE

(Pictured below)

Upon my move to the Low Country of South Carolina, I was introduced to red rice, a traditional Deep South dish. I experimented with a recipe, and this is the result.
—Robbie Joyce, Moncks Corner, South Carolina

  1 package (12 ounces) bulk pork
      or turkey sausage
1-1/2 cups water
  1 cup uncooked long grain rice
  1 cup chopped onion
1/3 cup *each* chopped green, yellow and
      sweet red pepper
1/4 cup butter, melted
1/4 teaspoon pepper
  4 bacon strips, cooked and crumbled
1/2 teaspoon salt
  1 can (14-1/2 ounces) diced tomatoes,
      undrained

In a skillet, cook sausage until no longer pink; drain. Transfer to an ungreased 2-qt. casserole; stir in the water, rice, onion, peppers, butter and pep-

per. Add bacon and salt. Cover and bake at 350° for 45 minutes. Stir in tomatoes. Bake 15 minutes longer. **Yield:** 10 servings.

SWEET POTATO PUFF

For added convenience, you can prepare this sweet potato dish the night before and just pop it in the oven the next day. It's a joy to serve this delicious, fluffy casserole to my five children and their families when we get together for special occasions.
—Fay Miller, Denham Springs, Louisiana

  3 cups cold mashed sweet potatoes
      (without added milk or butter)
1/2 cup sugar
1/2 cup butter, melted
  2 eggs, beaten
1/3 cup milk
  1 teaspoon vanilla extract
1/2 cup flaked coconut
TOPPING:
1/2 cup packed brown sugar
1/2 cup chopped pecans
  2 tablespoons butter, melted
1/4 cup all-purpose flour

In a mixing bowl, beat sweet potatoes, sugar, butter, eggs, milk and vanilla until fluffy. Stir in coconut. Spoon into a greased 2-1/2-qt. baking dish. Combine topping ingredients until well blended; sprinkle over sweet potatoes. Bake, uncovered, at 350° for 35-40 minutes or until golden brown. **Yield:** 8 servings.

pepper in a shallow plate. Dip each tomato slice into egg, then into cornmeal mixture. In a medium skillet, heat oil over medium-high. Fry tomatoes, a few at a time, for 2 minutes per side or until golden brown. Drain on a paper towel-lined wire rack. Serve immediately. **Yield:** 4-6 servings.

ASPARAGUS MORNAY

(Pictured on page 165)

When I was growing up on my parents' dairy farm, we always had a large asparagus patch. I still love asparagus, but my husband and two children weren't that eager to eat it until I tried this recipe. Now even the toughest vegetable critics in our family enjoy these savory spears.
—Linda McKee, Big Prairie, Ohio

1-1/2 pounds fresh asparagus, trimmed
   1 tablespoon butter
   1 tablespoon all-purpose flour
   1 cup half-and-half cream
 1/2 teaspoon chicken bouillon granules
 1/8 teaspoon ground nutmeg
 1/8 teaspoon salt
 1/2 cup shredded Swiss cheese
   2 tablespoons crushed butter-flavored crackers

In a skillet, cook asparagus in a small amount of water until crisp-tender, about 6-8 minutes; drain. Arrange spears in the bottom of a greased 1-1/2-qt. baking dish; set aside and keep warm.

In a small saucepan, melt butter over low heat. Add flour; cook and stir for 1 minute. Whisk in the cream, chicken bouillon, nutmeg and salt; bring to a boil over medium heat. Cook and stir for 2 minutes. Remove from the heat; stir in Swiss cheese until melted.

Pour the sauce over the asparagus. Sprinkle with the cracker crumbs. Broil 6 in. from the heat for 3-5 minutes or until lightly browned. **Yield:** 4-6 servings.

GREEN TOMATOES PARMESAN

(Pictured above)

These fried tomatoes look so pretty and taste so good! If you follow the recipe directions, you should end up with firm tomatoes. It's a tried-and-true method.
—Clara Mifflin, Creal Springs, Illinois

   3 medium green tomatoes, sliced 1/4 inch thick
Salt
 1/4 cup cornmeal
 1/4 cup grated Parmesan cheese
   2 tablespoons all-purpose flour
 3/4 teaspoon garlic salt
 1/2 teaspoon dried oregano
 1/8 teaspoon pepper
   1 egg, beaten
 1/4 cup vegetable oil

Lightly sprinkle tomatoes with salt; drain on paper towels for 30-60 minutes. Meanwhile, combine cornmeal, Parmesan, flour, garlic salt, oregano and

BAKED CORNMEAL DUMPLINGS

(Pictured below)

These big, golden dumplings are delicious with stew or any type of dinner with gravy. When it comes to a comforting, home-style side dish, they can't be beat. I sprinkle a little parsley on top for color.
—Grace Yaskovic, Branchville, New Jersey

2/3 cup all-purpose flour
2/3 cup cornmeal
   3 tablespoons grated Parmesan cheese
   2 teaspoons baking powder
   1 tablespoon minced fresh parsley *or* 1
        teaspoon dried parsley flakes
1/4 teaspoon salt
1/2 cup milk
1/4 cup vegetable oil
   1 quart chicken broth
Additional minced fresh parsley, optional

In a bowl, combine the first six ingredients. Combine milk and oil; stir into dry ingredients. Bring broth to a boil; carefully transfer to a 2-1/2-qt. round baking dish. Drop batter in six mounds onto broth.

Cover and bake at 400° for 20-25 minutes or until a toothpick inserted in a dumpling comes out clean (do not lift the cover while baking). Garnish with parsley if desired. **Yield:** 6 servings.

Cheddar Tomato Dumplings

(Pictured below left)

Simmered in tomato sauce, these fluffy dumplings with cheddar cheese in the dough make a satisfying side dish as well as a delicious, meatless main course.
—Marie Hattrup, The Dalles, Oregon

- 2 tablespoons finely chopped onion
- 1 tablespoon finely chopped green pepper
- 2 tablespoons vegetable oil
- 2 tablespoons all-purpose flour
- 1 can (28 ounces) diced tomatoes, undrained
- 1 tablespoon minced celery leaves
- 1 teaspoon sugar
- 1/2 teaspoon salt
- 1/4 teaspoon pepper

DUMPLINGS:
- 1 cup all-purpose flour
- 2 teaspoons baking powder
- 1/2 teaspoon salt
- 2 tablespoons shortening
- 1/2 cup shredded cheddar cheese
- 1/2 cup milk

In a large skillet, saute onion and green pepper in oil until tender. Add flour; stir well. Gradually blend in tomatoes. Add celery leaves, sugar, salt and pepper; bring to a boil over medium heat. Cook and stir for 2 minutes. Reduce heat; cover and simmer for 5 minutes.

Meanwhile, for dumplings, combine flour, baking powder and salt in a bowl; cut in shortening until crumbly. Add cheddar cheese. Stir in milk just until moistened.

Drop batter by tablespoonfuls onto simmering tomato sauce. Cover and simmer for 20 minutes or until a toothpick inserted in a dumpling comes out clean (do not lift the cover while simmering). **Yield:** 4-5 servings.

Spinach Dumplings

(Pictured below far left)

I've been making these green dumplings—called gnocchi verdi in Italian—since the 1970s. They are a great accompaniment to almost any meal.
—Gail Sykora, Menomonee Falls, Wisconsin

- 1 tablespoon finely chopped onion
- 6 tablespoons butter
- 3 packages (10 ounces *each*) frozen chopped spinach, thawed and drained
- 1 cup ricotta cheese
- 1-1/2 cups all-purpose flour, *divided*
- 1/2 cup grated Parmesan cheese
- 3/4 teaspoon garlic salt
- 2 eggs, beaten
- 3 quarts water
- 3 tablespoons chicken bouillon granules

TOPPING:
- 1/4 cup butter, melted
- 1/2 cup grated Parmesan cheese

In a skillet, saute onion in butter until tender. Add spinach; cook and stir over medium heat until liquid has evaporated, about 5 minutes. Stir in ricotta; cook and stir for 3 minutes. Transfer to a large bowl. Add 3/4 cup flour, Parmesan and garlic salt. Cool for 5 minutes.

Stir in the eggs; mix well. Place the remaining flour in a bowl. Drop the batter by tablespoonfuls into the flour; roll gently to coat and shape each into an oval.

In a large saucepan, bring water and bouillon to a boil. Reduce heat. Add a third of the dumplings at a time; simmer, uncovered, for 8-10 minutes or until a toothpick inserted in a dumpling comes out clean. Remove with a slotted spoon; keep warm. Drizzle with butter; sprinkle with Parmesan. **Yield:** 12 servings.

TANGY GREEN BEAN CASSEROLE

Here's a bean dish that my family requests often. It's easy to prepare and makes a wonderful addition to a buffet supper or potluck dinner.
—Judy Rush, Newport, Rhode Island

2 pounds fresh green beans, cut into 1-1/2-inch pieces
2 tablespoons finely chopped onion
2 tablespoons olive oil
1 tablespoon vinegar
1 garlic clove, minced
1/2 teaspoon salt
1/4 teaspoon pepper
2 tablespoons dry bread crumbs
2 tablespoons grated Parmesan cheese
1 tablespoon butter, melted

In a saucepan, cover beans with water. Cook until crisp-tender; drain. Add the onion, oil, vinegar, garlic, salt and pepper; toss to coat. Transfer to an ungreased 2-qt. baking dish. Toss bread crumbs, cheese and butter; sprinkle over bean mixture. Bake, uncovered, at 350° for 20-25 minutes or until golden brown. **Yield:** 6-8 servings.

TOMATOES WITH PARSLEY PESTO

(Pictured above)

You'll love the summery flavor of this pretty salad. It's a snap to whip up the pesto in the blender, then pour it over ripe tomato wedges.
—Donna Hackman, Huddleston, Virginia

1 cup packed fresh parsley
1/4 cup snipped fresh chives
1 garlic clove
1/4 teaspoon salt
Dash pepper
3 tablespoons olive oil
2 tablespoons red wine vinegar
3 medium tomatoes, cut into wedges

In a blender or food processor, combine parsley, chives, garlic, salt and pepper. Cover and process until finely chopped. Add oil and vinegar; mix well. Transfer to a bowl; cover and refrigerate. When ready to serve, add tomatoes and gently toss to coat. **Yield:** 6 servings.

"One's family is the most important thing in life."
—Robert C. Byrd

CRANBERRY-STUFFED ACORN SQUASH

This recipe showcases a few of autumn's best foods. Cranberries combine with chopped apple, diced orange and walnuts for a pretty, fresh-tasting filling. Baked in squash, it's an extra-special side dish that can fit right into a Thanksgiving Day feast.
—Jim Ulberg, Elk Rapids, Michigan

    4   medium acorn squash
    1   cup fresh *or* frozen cranberries, coarsely
        chopped
    1   medium tart apple, coarsely chopped
    1   medium orange, peeled and diced
  2/3   cup packed brown sugar
  1/4   cup chopped walnuts
  1/4   cup butter, melted
    1   teaspoon grated orange peel
Pinch salt

Cut squash in half; discard seeds. Place squash, cut side down, in a 15-in. x 10-in. x 1-in. baking pan. Fill pan with hot water to a depth of 1/2 in. Bake, uncovered, at 350° for 30 minutes.

Meanwhile, combine cranberries, apple, orange, brown sugar, walnuts, butter and orange peel. Drain water from pan; turn squash cut side up. Sprinkle with salt. Stuff with the cranberry mixture. Bake 25 minutes longer or until squash is tender. **Yield:** 8 servings.

BLACK BEANS AND RICE

(Pictured at right)

I often serve this quick skillet side dish to delighted guests. Chock-full of beans, rice, peppers and cheddar cheese, it pleases everyone and is hearty enough to present as a meatless main course.
—Bonnie Baumgardner, Sylva, North Carolina

    1   medium onion, chopped
    1   medium green pepper, chopped
    1   medium sweet red pepper, chopped
    1   garlic clove, minced
  1/2   teaspoon dried basil
  1/4   teaspoon pepper
    1   tablespoon tomato sauce
    1   can (15 ounces) black beans, rinsed and
        drained
    1   cup cooked long grain rice
    1   tablespoon red wine vinegar
  1/4   cup shredded cheddar cheese

In a nonstick skillet that has been coated with non-stick cooking spray, saute the onion, green and red peppers, garlic, basil and pepper until tender. Stir in tomato sauce. Add beans, rice and vinegar; heat through. Transfer to a serving dish; sprinkle with cheese. **Yield:** 4 servings.

MAKE-AHEAD POTATOES

(Pictured below)

There's no need to slave away making mashed potatoes at the last minute, not when this creamy, comforting potato side dish is so handy to prepare well in advance. Plus, it's an easy dish for people to serve themselves and it looks so appealing on a buffet.
—Margaret Twitched, Danbury, Iowa

 10 **large potatoes, peeled and quartered**
  1 **cup (8 ounces) sour cream**
  1 **package (8 ounces) cream cheese, softened**
  6 **tablespoons butter,** *divided*
  2 **tablespoons dried minced onion**
 1/2 **to 1 teaspoon salt**
Paprika

Place potatoes in a Dutch oven or large kettle; cover with water and bring to a boil. Reduce heat; cover and cook for 20-25 minutes or until potatoes are tender.

Drain potatoes and place in a bowl; mash. Add sour cream, cream cheese, 4 tablespoons butter, onion and salt; stir until smooth and the cream cheese and butter are melted. Spread in a greased 13-in. x 9-in. x 2-in. baking dish.

Melt the remaining butter; drizzle over the potatoes. Sprinkle with paprika. Refrigerate or bake immediately, covered, at 350° for 40 minutes; uncover and bake 20 minutes longer. If potatoes are made ahead and refrigerated, let stand at room temperature for 30 minutes before baking. **Yield:** 12 servings.

BARLEY AND CORN CASSEROLE

This hearty and colorful casserole goes well with a variety of main courses, from pork and chicken to fish. For convenience, this dish can be prepared ahead and refrigerated until mealtime. After it's been in the oven a while, I simply stir in the last two ingredients and finish baking it.
—Diane Molberg, Emerald Park, Saskatchewan

  3 **garlic cloves, minced**
  1 **cup chopped onion**
 2/3 **cup chopped carrots**
  1 **tablespoon vegetable oil**
  3 **cups chicken broth**
  1 **cup medium pearl barley**
 1/4 **teaspoon salt**
 1/8 **teaspoon pepper**
  2 **cups frozen corn, thawed**
 1/2 **cup chopped fresh parsley**

In a skillet over medium heat, saute garlic, onion and carrots in oil until tender. Transfer to a greased 2-qt. baking dish; add chicken broth, barley, salt and pepper. Mix well. Cover and bake at 350° for 1 hour.

Stir in corn and parsley. Cover and bake 10-15 minutes more or until barley is tender and corn is heated through. **Yield:** 12 servings.

PEPPY PARMESAN PASTA

(Pictured above)

When my husband and I needed to round out dinner in a hurry, we came up with this flavorful pasta dish.
—*Debbie Horst, Phoenix, Arizona*

8 ounces angel hair pasta
1 large tomato, chopped
1 package (3 ounces) sliced pepperoni
1 can (2-1/4 ounces) sliced ripe olives, drained
1/4 cup grated Parmesan cheese
3 tablespoons olive oil
1/2 teaspoon salt *or* salt-free seasoning blend, optional
1/4 teaspoon garlic powder

Cook pasta according to package directions. Meanwhile, in a serving bowl, combine the tomato, pepperoni, olives, Parmesan cheese, oil, salt if desired and garlic powder. Drain pasta; add to the tomato mixture and toss to coat. **Yield:** 4 servings.

> ### Family-Tested Tips
>
> Before freezing tomato-based foods in plastic storage containers, coat the containers with nonstick cooking spray to keep them free of stains.
> —*Betty Checkett, St. Louis, Missouri*
>
> For a deliciously different side dish, stir a can of peach pie filling into 2 pounds of cooked sliced carrots. It's so simple and refreshing.
> —*Gladys Gierl, Pittsburgh, Pennsylvania*

ZUCCHINI BAKE

This recipe dresses up my garden-fresh zucchini with mushrooms, onion, cheddar cheese and a hint of basil. Requiring just five ingredients, this dish is a snap to make. I let everyone season their own servings with salt and pepper at the table.
—Jacquelyn Smith, Carmel, Maine

2 cups sliced zucchini
1-1/2 cups sliced fresh mushrooms
1/4 cup sliced onion
1/2 cup shredded cheddar cheese
1/2 teaspoon dried basil

In a greased shallow 1-qt. baking dish, layer zucchini, mushrooms and onion. Sprinkle with cheese and basil. Cover and bake at 350° for 20 minutes. Uncover and bake 10 minutes longer or until vegetables are tender. **Yield:** 4 servings.

GRANDMOTHER'S CORN PUDDING

(Pictured above)

Corn pudding is a very popular side dish on Maryland's Eastern Shore. My grandmother always served this pudding for holidays and family reunions. Today, my family can't wait for special occasions, so I whip up this comforting dish at least once or twice a month to keep them happy!
—Susan Brown Langenstein, Salisbury, Maryland

4 eggs
1 cup milk
1 can (15 ounces) cream-style corn
1/2 cup sugar
5 slices day-old bread, crusts removed
1 tablespoon butter, softened

In a bowl, beat eggs and milk. Add corn and sugar; mix well. Cut bread into 1/2-in. cubes and place in a greased 9-in. square baking dish. Pour egg mixture over bread. Dot with butter. Bake, uncovered, at 350° for 50-60 minutes or until a knife inserted near the center comes out clean. **Yield:** 9 servings.

GARLIC ANGEL HAIR PASTA

I add the garlic cloves to these noodles as they cook. It gives me flavorful results fast, which is especially nice on busy weeknights or when I have dinner guests. This simple pasta dish is not only delicious, it's also easy on my grocery budget.
—Denise Baumert, Dalhart, Texas

8 ounces uncooked angel hair pasta
2 garlic cloves, peeled and halved
1/4 cup butter
1/4 cup grated Parmesan cheese
1 teaspoon snipped fresh *or* dried chives
1/2 teaspoon garlic salt, optional

Cook pasta according to package directions, adding garlic to the water. Drain; discard garlic. Place pasta in a serving bowl; add butter. Toss gently until butter is melted. Add Parmesan cheese, chives and garlic salt if desired; toss to coat. **Yield:** 8 servings.

Pesto Pepper Tortellini

This is a shortcut version of a rich, creamy pasta dish I sampled years ago. I've served this tortellini as both a special side dish and a meatless entree.
—Mickie Taft, Milwaukee, Wisconsin

  1 package (19 ounces) frozen cheese tortellini
1/2 cup julienned sweet red pepper
  3 garlic cloves, minced
1/2 cup butter
  2 cups heavy whipping cream
1/4 cup ground walnuts
  2 tablespoons minced fresh basil *or* 2 teaspoons dried basil
  1 tablespoon chopped green onion *or* chives

Prepare tortellini according to package directions. Meanwhile, in a skillet, saute red pepper and garlic in butter until pepper is crisp-tender. Stir in cream; cook for 8-10 minutes or until slightly thickened. Add walnuts, basil and onion; heat through. Drain tortellini; add to sauce and toss to coat. **Yield:** 4 servings.

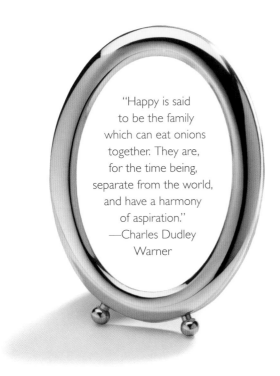

"Happy is said to be the family which can eat onions together. They are, for the time being, separate from the world, and have a harmony of aspiration."
—Charles Dudley Warner

Grilled Potato Fans

(Pictured above)

If you're looking for a change from plain baked potatoes, try these tender and buttery potato fans seasoned with oregano, garlic powder, celery and onion. To cut down on grilling time, I sometimes microwave the potatoes for 5-6 minutes before slicing them.
—Jennifer Black-Ortiz, San Jose, California

  6 medium baking potatoes
  2 medium onions, halved and thinly sliced
  6 tablespoons butter, cubed
1/4 cup finely chopped celery
  1 teaspoon salt
  1 teaspoon dried oregano
1/4 teaspoon garlic powder
1/4 teaspoon pepper

With a sharp knife, make cuts 1/2 in. apart in each potato, leaving slices attached at the bottom. Fan the potatoes slightly. Place each on a piece of heavy-duty foil (about 12 in. square). Insert onions and butter between potato slices. Sprinkle with celery, salt, oregano, garlic powder and pepper. Fold foil around potatoes and seal tightly. Grill, covered, over medium-hot heat for 40-45 minutes or until tender. **Yield:** 6 servings.

RICE CROQUETTES

(Pictured below)

This tasty side dish turned out to be very popular with my family. These golden croquettes are crisp and add some fun to a simple dinner like roast chicken and salad.
—Lucia Edwards, Cotati, California

1/2 cup chopped onion
  2 tablespoons butter
  1 cup uncooked long grain rice
2-1/4 cups chicken broth
  2 tablespoons chopped fresh parsley
  1 egg, lightly beaten
1/2 cup grated Parmesan cheese
  1 teaspoon dried basil
1/4 teaspoon pepper
1/2 cup dry bread crumbs
Vegetable oil
Additional fresh parsley, optional

In a large saucepan, saute onion in butter until tender. Add rice; saute for 3 minutes. Stir in broth and parsley; bring to a boil. Reduce heat; cover and simmer for 20 minutes. Cool for 30 minutes.

Stir in egg, cheese, basil and pepper. Moisten hands with water and shape 1/4 cupfuls into logs. Roll in crumbs. In an electric skillet, heat 1/4 in. of oil to 375°. Fry croquettes, a few at a time, for 3-4 minutes or until crisp and golden, turning often. Drain on paper towels. Garnish with parsley if desired. **Yield:** 16 croquettes.

CRANBERRY BAKED BEANS

(Pictured above)

I knew I'd found a winner when I got the idea to simmer beans in cranberry juice. The tartness of the juice is a nice subtle contrast to the sweet brown sugar and molasses in these baked beans. They're wonderful warm or cold.
—Wendie Osipowicz, New Britain, Connecticut

> 3 **cups dried navy beans**
> 5 **cups cranberry juice**
> 1/2 **pound lean salt pork *or* bacon, diced**
> 3/4 **cup chopped onion**
> 1/2 **cup ketchup**
> 1/4 **cup molasses**
> 5 **teaspoons dark brown sugar**
> 1-1/2 **teaspoons ground mustard**
> 1-1/2 **teaspoons salt**
> 1/8 **teaspoon ground ginger**

Place beans in a Dutch oven or soup kettle; add water to cover by 2 in. Bring to a boil; boil for 2 minutes. Remove from the heat; cover and let stand for 1 hour.

Drain beans and discard liquid. Return beans to Dutch oven. Add cranberry juice; bring to a boil. Reduce heat; cover and simmer for 1 hour or until the beans are almost tender.

Drain, reserving cranberry liquid. Place beans in a 2-1/2-qt. casserole or bean pot; add remaining ingredients and 1-1/2 cups of cranberry liquid. Cover and bake at 350° for 3 hours or until beans are tender and have reached desired consistency, stirring every 30 minutes. Add reserved cranberry liquid as needed. **Yield:** 10-12 servings.

SESAME GREEN BEANS

For me, the most time-consuming part of preparing this light side dish is picking the green beans in the garden. My family loves their fresh taste, and I love the fact that they're fast to fix!
—Jeanne Bennett, North Richland Hills, Texas

> 3/4 **pound fresh green beans**
> 1/2 **cup water**
> 1 **tablespoon butter**
> 1 **tablespoon soy sauce**
> 2 **teaspoons sesame seeds, toasted**

In a saucepan, bring beans and water to a boil; reduce heat to medium. Cover and cook for 10-15 minutes or until the beans are crisp-tender; drain. Add butter, soy sauce and sesame seeds; toss to coat. **Yield:** 6 servings.

FRUITED STUFFING BALLS

(Pictured at left)

This delightful dressing, shaped into individual servings, is a perfect addition to a traditional Thanksgiving dinner. We love the extra flavor it gets from apricots, raisins and crunchy pecans.
—Lucille Terry, Frankfort, Kentucky

- 2 cups diced celery
- 1/2 cup chopped onion
- 1/3 cup butter, melted
- 4 cups seasoned stuffing cubes
- 1 cup dried apricots, finely chopped
- 3/4 to 1 cup chicken broth
- 1/2 cup raisins
- 2 eggs, lightly beaten
- 1/4 cup chopped pecans
- 1 teaspoon rubbed sage
- 1 teaspoon salt
- 1/4 teaspoon pepper

In a large skillet, saute celery and onion in butter until tender. Remove from the heat. Add remaining ingredients; mix well. Shape into 12 balls. Place in a greased 13-in. x 9-in. x 2-in. baking dish. Bake, uncovered, at 375° for 20-25 minutes or until golden brown. **Yield:** 12 servings.

WILD RICE STUFFING

(Pictured at left)

Although it uses many of the same ingredients found in typical stuffings, this version has a bit of a twist because the wild rice provides a different texture.
—Edie DeSpain, Logan, Utah

- 2 cans (14-1/2 ounces *each*) chicken broth
- 1-1/2 cups water
- 2/3 cup uncooked wild rice
- 1/2 teaspoon salt
- 1/2 teaspoon dried thyme
- 4 medium carrots, sliced
- 2 celery ribs, chopped
- 1 medium onion, chopped
- 2 tablespoons vegetable oil
- 1/2 pound fresh mushrooms, sliced
- 1-1/2 cups uncooked long grain rice
- 1/4 cup minced fresh parsley

In a large saucepan, bring broth and water to a boil. Add the wild rice, salt and thyme. Reduce heat; cover and simmer for 30 minutes.

Meanwhile, in another saucepan, saute carrots, celery and onion in oil until almost tender. Add the mushrooms; saute 5 minutes longer. Add vegetables and long grain rice to wild rice. Cover and cook for 30-35 minutes or until rice is tender. Stir in parsley. **Yield:** 7 servings.

OVEN-ROASTED POTATO WEDGES

Rosemary lends a delicious, delicate flavor to these potato wedges. With homemade appeal, they're a great alternative to purchased French fries. People like these with everything from hamburgers to fish.
—Ellen Benninger, Stoneboro, Pennsylvania

- 4 unpeeled baking potatoes (2 pounds)
- 2 tablespoons olive oil
- 1 medium onion, chopped
- 2 garlic cloves, minced
- 1 tablespoon minced fresh rosemary *or* 1 teaspoon dried rosemary, crushed
- 1/2 teaspoon salt
- 1/4 teaspoon pepper

Cut potatoes lengthwise into wedges; place in a greased 13-in. x 9-in. x 2-in. baking pan. Drizzle with oil. Sprinkle with onion, garlic, rosemary, salt and pepper; stir to coat. Bake, uncovered, at 400° for 45-50 minutes or until tender, turning once. **Yield:** 8 servings.

APPLE-A-DAY CASSEROLE

(Pictured at right)

This sweet-tart casserole is a fun change of pace from traditional vegetable side dishes. It's quick to prepare if you use a food processor to slice the apples and carrots.
—Elizabeth Erwin, Syracuse, New York

- 6 medium tart apples, peeled and sliced
- 6 medium carrots, thinly sliced
- 1/2 cup orange juice
- 1/3 cup all-purpose flour
- 1/3 cup sugar
- 1/2 teaspoon ground nutmeg
- 2 tablespoons cold butter

Combine apples and carrots; place in a greased shallow 2-qt. baking dish. Drizzle with orange juice. Cover and bake at 350° for 40-45 minutes or until carrots are crisp-tender. In a bowl, combine the flour, sugar and nutmeg; cut in butter until crumbly. Sprinkle over apple mixture. Bake, uncovered, 10-15 minutes longer or until the carrots are tender. **Yield:** 6-8 servings.

ANYTIME CUCUMBER SLICES

These slices truly are great anytime. I can easily make a large batch to bring to a picnic or potluck.
—Jeanne Bunders, Wauzeka, Wisconsin

- 3 to 4 large cucumbers, sliced
- 2 medium onions, thinly sliced
- 3 tablespoons minced fresh dill *or* 1 tablespoon dill weed
- 1 cup sugar
- 1/2 cup vinegar
- 1/2 cup water
- 1 teaspoon salt

In a bowl, combine cucumbers, onions and dill. In a saucepan, combine sugar, vinegar, water and salt; bring to a boil. Pour over cucumber mixture. Cover and refrigerate for 3 hours or overnight. **Yield:** 6 cups.

"The ultimate economic and spiritual unit of any civilization is still the family."
—Clare Boothe Luce

BROCCOLI NOODLE SIDE DISH

When I want to round out a menu with pasta, this pleasing recipe is one I frequently rely on.
—Louise Saluti, Sandwich, Massachusetts

6 cups (8 ounces) uncooked wide noodles
3 to 4 garlic cloves, minced
1/4 cup olive oil
4 cups broccoli florets (about 1 pound)
1/2 pound fresh mushrooms, thinly sliced
1/2 teaspoon dried thyme
1/4 teaspoon pepper
1 teaspoon salt

Cook the noodles according to package directions. Meanwhile, in a skillet, saute minced garlic in oil until tender. Add broccoli; saute for 4 minutes or until crisp-tender. Add mushrooms, thyme, pepper and salt; saute for 2-3 minutes. Drain the noodles and add to the broccoli mixture. Stir gently over low heat until heated through. **Yield:** 8 servings.

ROSEMARY CARROTS

You'll really enjoy the bold rosemary flavor in each bite of this pretty side dish. The sliced carrots get added sweetness from a bit of brown sugar.
—Jacqueline Thompson Graves, Lawrenceville, Georgia

2-1/4 cups thinly sliced carrots
1/2 cup water
1 tablespoon snipped fresh *or* dried chives
1 tablespoon brown sugar
1 teaspoon chicken bouillon granules
1/2 teaspoon snipped fresh rosemary *or* pinch dried rosemary, crushed
1/8 teaspoon pepper

Place carrots and water in a saucepan; cover and cook over medium heat for 8-9 minutes or until crisp-tender. Drain, reserving 2 tablespoons cooking liquid. Transfer carrots to a serving bowl and keep warm. In the same pan, combine chives,

brown sugar, bouillon, rosemary, pepper and reserved cooking liquid. Bring to a boil; stir until bouillon is dissolved. Pour over the carrots and toss to coat. **Yield:** 4 servings.

HOT CURRIED FRUIT

(Pictured below)

This soothing side dish is made with a blend of handy canned fruits. It tastes especially good on chilly days as an alternative to cold fruit salads.
—Elizabeth Hunter, Prosperity, South Carolina

1 can (29 ounces) apricot halves, drained
1 can (29 ounces) pear halves, drained
1 can (29 ounces) peach halves, drained
1 can (20 ounces) pineapple chunks, drained
3/4 cup golden raisins
1/4 cup butter
1/2 cup packed brown sugar
1 teaspoon curry powder

In a 2-1/2-qt. casserole, combine fruit and raisins. Melt butter in a small saucepan; stir in brown sugar and curry powder. Cook and stir over low heat until sugar is dissolved. Pour over fruit mixture; mix gently. Cover and bake at 400° for 30 minutes or until heated through. **Yield:** 10-12 servings.

CORN 'N' BROCCOLI BAKE

This sweet, comforting side dish is a very creamy casserole that resembles corn pudding. I like that this bake doesn't require a lot of ingredients.
—Betty Sitzman, Wray, Colorado

  1 can (16 ounces) cream-style corn
  1 package (10 ounces) frozen chopped broccoli, thawed
1/2 cup crushed saltines, *divided*
  1 egg, beaten
  1 tablespoon dried minced onion
Dash pepper
  2 tablespoons butter, melted

In a bowl, combine the corn, broccoli, 1/4 cup of saltines, egg, onion and pepper. Place in a greased 1-1/2-qt. baking dish. Combine the butter and remaining saltines; sprinkle over top. Cover and bake at 350° for 45 minutes. **Yield:** 6 servings.

CARROT CASSEROLE

(Pictured above)

Each time I make this dish, people rave about how good it is. One friend told me, "I don't usually eat carrots, but this is delicious!" That made my day.
—Lois Hagen, Stevens Point, Wisconsin

  8 cups sliced carrots
  2 medium onions, sliced
  5 tablespoons butter, *divided*
  1 can (10-3/4 ounces) condensed cream of celery soup, undiluted
1/2 teaspoon salt
1/4 teaspoon pepper
  1 cup (4 ounces) shredded cheddar cheese
  1 cup seasoned croutons

Place carrots in a saucepan and cover with water; bring to a boil. Cook until crisp-tender. Meanwhile, in a skillet, saute onions in 3 tablespoons butter until tender. Stir in the soup, salt, pepper and cheddar cheese.

Drain carrots; add to the onion mixture. Pour into a greased 13-in. x 9-in. x 2-in. baking dish. Sprinkle with croutons. Melt remaining butter; drizzle over croutons. Bake, uncovered, at 350° for 20-25 minutes. **Yield:** 10-12 servings.

APPLE-CRANBERRY RELISH

This fresh ruby-colored relish is sweet and tangy, and the apples and celery give it a terrific crunch. At our house, it's a holiday menu mainstay since it's so pleasant with poultry and pork.
—Edith McFarland, Willits, California

  2 medium navel oranges
  2 bags (12 ounces *each*) fresh *or* frozen cranberries
  2 medium apples, peeled and cut into chunks
  2 celery ribs, cut into chunks
  3 cups sugar

Grate peel of oranges and set aside. Peel and discard white membrane. Separate orange into sections and place half in a food processor or blender. Add half of the cranberries, apples and celery. Process until coarsely chopped.

Transfer to a bowl; repeat with remaining oranges, cranberries, apples and celery. Stir in sugar and reserved orange peel. Cover and refrigerate overnight. **Yield:** 16 servings (8 cups).

Colorful Vegetable Casserole

With its eye-opening zippy flavor, horseradish really livens up this blend of cauliflower, broccoli and carrots. It's a great way to eat your vegetables!
—Precious Owens, Elizabethtown, Kentucky

3 cups cauliflowerets
3 cups sliced carrots
3 cups broccoli florets
1 cup mayonnaise
1/4 cup finely chopped onion
3 tablespoons prepared horseradish
1/4 teaspoon salt
1/8 teaspoon pepper
1/3 cup dry bread crumbs
2 tablespoons butter, melted
1/8 teaspoon paprika

Place cauliflower and carrots in a large saucepan; add a small amount of water. Cover and cook for 3 minutes. Add broccoli; cook 4-6 minutes longer or until all the vegetables are crisp-tender. Drain.

Combine mayonnaise, onion, horseradish, salt and pepper; add vegetables and mix well. Pour into a greased 2-qt. baking dish. Combine bread crumbs, butter and paprika; sprinkle over vegetables. Bake, uncovered, at 350° for 25-30 minutes or until heated through. **Yield:** 12-14 servings.

South Coast Hominy

(Pictured at right)

The first time I tasted this hominy dish, I couldn't eat enough. It's something my stepmother has prepared for a long time. Whenever I fix it for friends or family, there are never any leftovers.
—Leslie Hampel, Palmer, Texas

1/2 cup chopped onion
1/2 cup chopped green pepper
5 tablespoons butter, *divided*
3 tablespoons all-purpose flour
1 teaspoon salt
1/2 teaspoon ground mustard
Dash cayenne pepper
1-1/2 cups milk
1 cup (4 ounces) shredded cheddar cheese
1 can (15-1/2 ounces) white hominy, drained
1/2 cup sliced ripe olives, optional
1/2 cup dry bread crumbs

In a skillet, saute onion and green pepper in 3 tablespoons butter until tender. Add flour, salt, mustard and cayenne; cook and stir until smooth and bubbly, about 2 minutes. Gradually add milk; bring to a boil. Boil for 2 minutes, stirring constantly. Stir in cheese until melted.

Remove from the heat; add hominy and olives if desired. Pour into a greased 1-1/2-qt. baking dish. Melt remaining butter and toss with bread crumbs; sprinkle over hominy mixture. Bake, uncovered, at 375° for 30 minutes or until golden. **Yield:** 6-8 servings.

MOM'S EASY BEAN BAKE

My mom's baked beans are the best I've ever tasted. Family and friends expect me to bring a pot of these beans to gatherings…they've become my trademark.
—Sue Gronholz, Columbus, Wisconsin

2-1/2 cups dried great northern beans
     (about 1 pound)
  1 teaspoon salt
  1 pound sliced bacon, cooked and crumbled
  1 cup packed brown sugar
  3 tablespoons molasses
  3 small onions, chopped

Place beans and salt in a saucepan; cover with water. Bring to a boil; boil for 2 minutes. Remove from the heat; cover and let stand for 1 hour.

Drain, discarding liquid, and return beans to pan. Cover with fresh water; bring to a boil. Reduce heat; cover and simmer for 1 hour or until beans are tender.

Drain, reserving liquid. Combine beans, 1 cup liquid and the remaining ingredients in a greased 2-1/2-qt. baking dish. Cover and bake at 350° for 1-1/4 hours or until beans are tender, stirring occasionally (add additional reserved liquid if needed). **Yield:** 8-10 servings.

GRILLED CORN AND PEPPERS

(Pictured above)

Every Fourth of July, we invite friends to our houseboat for a cookout. We always have corn on the cob prepared this way, and everyone enjoys it. The onions and peppers add fantastic flavor to the sweet ears of corn.
—Cindy Williams, Fort Myers, Florida

  3 cups Italian salad dressing
  8 large ears fresh corn, husked and cleaned
  4 medium green peppers, julienned
  4 medium sweet red peppers, julienned
  2 medium red onions, sliced and separated into rings

Place salad dressing in a large resealable plastic bag or shallow glass container. Add corn, peppers and onions; turn to coat. Seal or cover and refrigerate for 30 minutes.

Drain and discard marinade. Place vegetables in a grill pan or disposable foil pan with holes punched in the bottom. Grill, covered, over medium heat for 25 minutes or until corn is tender, turning frequently. **Yield:** 8 servings.

MAPLE BAKED ONIONS

I created this side dish to make use of the great maple syrup we have here in Vermont. My family loves this recipe, and it's so easy to prepare.
—Donna Kurant, West Rutland, Vermont

  6 large sweet onions, sliced 1/2 inch thick
1/3 cup maple syrup
1/4 cup butter, melted

Layer onions in a greased 13-in. x 9-in. x 2-in. baking dish. Combine syrup and butter; pour over onions. Bake, uncovered, at 425° for 40-45 minutes or until tender. **Yield:** 8-10 servings.

THREE-RICE PILAF

(Pictured below)

My family's favorite rice recipe is this tempting medley of white, brown and wild rice. I prepare it as a side dish or a stuffing. In fall I add chopped dried apricots, and for the holidays I mix in dried cranberries.
—Ricki Bingham, Ogden, Utah

1/2 cup uncooked brown rice
1/2 cup finely chopped carrots
1/2 cup chopped onion
1/2 cup sliced fresh mushrooms
  2 tablespoons vegetable oil
1/2 cup uncooked wild rice
  3 cups chicken broth
1/4 teaspoon dried thyme
1/4 teaspoon dried rosemary, crushed
1/2 cup uncooked long grain rice
1/3 cup chopped dried apricots
  2 tablespoons minced green onions
1/4 teaspoon salt
1/8 teaspoon pepper
1/2 cup chopped pecans, toasted

In a large saucepan, saute brown rice, carrots, onion and mushrooms in oil for 10 minutes or until rice is golden. Add wild rice, broth, thyme and rosemary; bring to a boil. Reduce heat; cover and simmer for 25 minutes.

Stir in long grain rice; cover and simmer for 25 minutes or until liquid is absorbed and wild rice is tender. Remove from the heat; stir in apricots, green onions, salt and pepper. Cover and let stand for 5 minutes. Sprinkle with pecans just before serving. **Yield:** 8-10 servings.

BROCCOLI-HAZELNUT BAKE

(Pictured below)

Oregon's fertile Willamette Valley produces a lot of hazelnuts, and this is one of my favorite ways to use them. I came up with this vegetable side dish when I was doing some experimenting in the kitchen.
—Florence Snyder, Hillsboro, Oregon

    8 cups chopped fresh broccoli *or* 2 packages (10 ounces *each*) chopped frozen broccoli
    5 tablespoons butter, *divided*
    3 tablespoons all-purpose flour
1-1/2 cups milk
    2 teaspoons chicken bouillon granules
    1 cup herb-seasoned stuffing mix
  1/4 cup water
  2/3 cup chopped hazelnuts *or* filberts, toasted

Cook broccoli on the stove or in the microwave until crisp-tender. Meanwhile, in a saucepan over medium heat, melt 3 tablespoons butter. Stir in flour to form a smooth paste. Gradually add milk and chicken bouillon, stirring constantly. Cook and stir until thickened and bubbly; cook and stir 2 minutes longer.

Drain broccoli; add to sauce and mix well. Pour into a greased 9-in. square baking dish. In a bowl, combine the stuffing mix, water and nuts. Melt the remaining butter; pour over stuffing mixture and toss. Spoon over broccoli. Bake, uncovered, at 350° for 25-30 minutes. **Yield:** 6 servings.

MACARONI AU GRATIN

I always take along a good supply of this cheesy macaroni to parties…and more often than not, every last noodle is gobbled up. It's a comforting, homey baked dish that appeals to people of all ages. I like the fact that the recipe is easy to prepare, too.
—Jeannine Hopp, Menomonee Falls, Wisconsin

    1 package (7 ounces) macaroni
  1/4 cup butter
  1/4 cup all-purpose flour
    2 cups milk
    8 ounces process cheese (Velveeta), cubed
    1 tablespoon chopped onion
  1/2 teaspoon Worcestershire sauce
  1/2 teaspoon salt
  1/4 teaspoon pepper
  1/4 teaspoon ground mustard
    2 tablespoons seasoned bread crumbs

Cook macaroni according to package directions; drain. Place in a greased 2-qt. baking dish; set aside. In a saucepan, melt butter over medium heat. Stir in flour until well blended. Gradually add milk; bring to a boil. Cook and stir for 2 minutes; reduce heat. Add cheese, onion, Worcestershire sauce, salt, pepper and mustard; stir until cheese melts. Pour over macaroni and mix well. Sprinkle with bread crumbs. Bake, uncovered, at 375° for 30 minutes. **Yield:** 6 servings.

CREAMED CELERY AND PEAS

(Pictured above)

This special side dish never fails to draw people back for more. Celery and almonds provide great crunch.
—Dorothy Pritchett, Wills Point, Texas

  1/3 cup water
    2 cups sliced celery
    1 package (10 ounces) frozen peas
  1/2 cup sour cream
  1/2 teaspoon dried rosemary, crushed
  1/4 teaspoon salt
Dash garlic salt
    1 tablespoon chopped pimientos, drained
  1/4 cup slivered almonds, toasted

In a saucepan over medium heat, bring water to a boil. Add celery; cover and cook for 8 minutes. Add peas; return to a boil. Cover and cook for 2-3 minutes or until vegetables are tender; drain.

In a small bowl, combine sour cream, rosemary, salt and garlic salt; mix well. Toss vegetables with pimientos; place in a serving bowl. Top with sour cream mixture. Sprinkle with almonds. **Yield:** 6 servings.

ONION POTATO PIE

I jazzed up a basic potato pie recipe by adding sweet onions, for which our area is famous. I've used this pretty hash-brown bake not only as a side dish for dinner, but also as a savory option for brunch.
—Gwyn Frasco, Walla Walla, Washington

    8 cups frozen shredded hash brown potatoes, thawed
    6 tablespoons butter, *divided*
  3/4 teaspoon salt, *divided*
    1 cup diced sweet onion
  1/4 cup chopped sweet red pepper
    1 cup (4 ounces) shredded cheddar cheese
    3 eggs, lightly beaten
  1/3 cup milk

Gently squeeze potatoes to remove excess water. Melt 5 tablespoons butter; add to potatoes along with 1/2 teaspoon salt. Press in bottom and up sides of a greased 9-in. pie plate to form a crust. Bake at 425° for 25-30 minutes or until edges are browned. Cool to room temperature.

In a saucepan over medium heat, saute the onion and red pepper in remaining butter until tender, about 6-8 minutes. Spoon into crust; sprinkle with cheese. Combine the eggs, milk and remaining salt; pour over onion mixture.

Bake at 350° for 20-25 minutes or until a knife inserted near the center comes out clean. Let stand 5 minutes before serving. **Yield:** 6-8 servings.

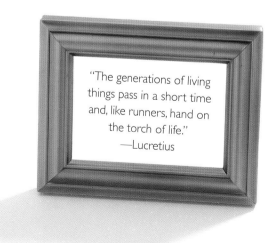

"The generations of living things pass in a short time and, like runners, hand on the torch of life."
—Lucretius

The
Lloyd
Family

Chapter nine

Nothing draws family members to the kitchen

faster than the irresistible aroma of freshly baked

yeast and quick breads, golden rolls and scrumptious

muffins. You'll find a delightful variety of all-time

favorites right here in this chapter. When these

from-the-oven goodies are part of your menu,

you won't need to ring the dinner bell!

Rhubarb Muffins
Whole Wheat Braids
Southern Banana Nut Bread
(Recipes on pages 190 and 191)

♥ Breads, Rolls & Muffins

SOUTHERN BANANA NUT BREAD

(Pictured on page 189)

This down-home banana bread recipe features pecans and bananas in both the bread and the topping. No one can resist a freshly baked slice.
—*Viva Forman, Tallahassee, Florida*

1/2 cup butter-flavored shortening
1-1/2 cups sugar
2 eggs
1 cup mashed ripe bananas (about 2 medium)
1 teaspoon vanilla extract
2 cups self-rising flour
1/2 cup buttermilk
3/4 cup chopped pecans
TOPPING:
1/4 to 1/3 cup mashed ripe bananas
1-1/4 cups confectioners' sugar
1 teaspoon lemon juice
Additional chopped pecans

In a mixing bowl, cream shortening and sugar; beat in eggs. Blend in bananas and vanilla. Add flour alternately with buttermilk. Fold in pecans. Pour into two greased 8-in. x 4-in. x 2-in. loaf pans. Bake at 350° for 45-55 minutes or until a toothpick inserted near the center comes out clean. Cool in pan for 10 minutes before removing to a wire rack; cool completely. For topping, combine bananas, confectioners' sugar and lemon juice; spread over loaves. Sprinkle with pecans. **Yield:** 2 loaves.

Editor's Note: As a substitute for each cup of self-rising flour, place 1-1/2 teaspoons baking powder and 1/2 teaspoon salt in a measuring cup; add all-purpose flour to equal 1 cup.

"We cannot destroy kindred: Our chains stretch a little sometimes, but they never break."
—Marquise de Sevigne

RHUBARB MUFFINS

(Pictured on page 189)

I had several rhubarb plants on our farm in Iowa. I'm now living on the East Coast, but I still love to make these moist, nutty muffins. I even submitted a batch of them for a 4-H bake sale here and won a ribbon.
—*Evelyn Winchester, Hilton, New York*

1 egg
1-1/4 cups packed brown sugar
1 cup buttermilk
1/2 cup vegetable oil
2 teaspoons vanilla extract
2-1/2 cups all-purpose flour
1 teaspoon baking soda
1 teaspoon baking powder
1/2 teaspoon salt
1-1/2 cups diced fresh rhubarb
1/2 cup chopped walnuts
TOPPING:
1/3 cup sugar
1 teaspoon ground cinnamon
1 teaspoon butter, melted

In a mixing bowl, beat egg. Add brown sugar, buttermilk, oil and vanilla; beat for 1 minute. Combine dry ingredients; stir into sugar mixture just until moistened. Fold in rhubarb and walnuts.

Fill greased or paper-lined muffin cups three-fourths full. Combine topping ingredients; sprinkle over muffins. Bake at 375° for 20-25 minutes or until a toothpick comes out clean. **Yield:** 1 dozen.

juice, water and oil; beat on low speed until moistened. Beat on high for 3 minutes. Stir in the pecans, apricots and remaining flour to form a stiff batter. Do not knead.

Grease two 8-in. x 4-in. x 2-in. loaf pans; sprinkle with cornmeal. Spoon batter into pans; sprinkle with cornmeal. Cover and let rise in a warm place until doubled, about 45 minutes.

Bake at 350° for 35-40 minutes or until golden brown. Immediately remove from pans to cool on wire racks. Slice and toast. **Yield:** 2 loaves.

WHOLE WHEAT BRAIDS

(Pictured on page 189)

There's nothing like fresh bread to complete a meal. I've had very good results with this recipe. Braiding the dough makes a pretty presentation.
—Suella Miller, LaGrange, Indiana

   3 **packages (1/4 ounce** *each***) active dry yeast**
   3 **cups warm water (110° to 115°)**
1/2 **cup sugar**
   3 **eggs**
1/3 **cup vegetable oil**
   1 **tablespoon salt**
   5 **cups whole wheat flour**
   4 **to 4-1/2 cups all-purpose flour**

In a mixing bowl, dissolve yeast in warm water. Add the sugar, eggs, oil, salt and whole wheat flour; beat until smooth. Add enough all-purpose flour to form a soft dough.

Turn onto a floured surface; knead until smooth and elastic, about 6-8 minutes. Place in a greased bowl, turning once to grease top. Cover and let rise in a warm place until doubled, about 1 hour.

Punch dough down. Divide into nine pieces; shape each piece into a 14-in. rope and braid three ropes together. Place in three greased 8-in. x 4-in. x 2-in. loaf pans. Cover and let rise until doubled, about 30 minutes. Bake at 350° for 40-45 minutes or until golden. Remove from pans to cool on wire racks. **Yield:** 3 loaves.

ENGLISH MUFFIN LOAVES

(Pictured above)

Slices of these fruit and nut loaves are a terrific breakfast on a cold day. I also like that they don't require kneading.
—Roberta Freedman, Mesilla Park, New Mexico

     5 **cups all-purpose flour,** *divided*
     2 **packages (1/4 ounce** *each***) active dry yeast**
     2 **tablespoons sugar**
     2 **teaspoons ground cinnamon**
     1 **teaspoon salt**
   1/4 **teaspoon baking soda**
1-1/2 **cups warm orange juice (120° to 130°)**
   1/2 **cup warm water (120° to 130°)**
   1/4 **cup vegetable oil**
   1/2 **cup chopped pecans**
   1/2 **cup chopped dried apricots**
Cornmeal

In a mixing bowl, combine 2 cups flour, yeast, sugar, cinnamon, salt and baking soda. Add orange

POPPY SEED KOLACHES

Preparing and sharing recipes I made as a boy are what keep me young at heart. And since I'm retired, I have plenty of time to bake traditional treats like this from scratch. It's a joy to serve these kolaches to our children, grandchildren and great-grandchildren.
—Carl Wanasek, Rogers, Arkansas

　1　package (1/4 ounce) active dry yeast
1/4　cup warm water (110° to 115°)
1/2　cup butter, melted
　1　cup milk
　1　egg plus 2 egg yolks
1/4　cup sugar
3/4　teaspoon salt
1/4　teaspoon ground mace
1/4　teaspoon grated lemon peel
　3　to 3-1/2 cups all-purpose flour
Additional melted butter
POPPY SEED FILLING:
3/4　cup poppy seeds
1/2　cup water
1/2　cup milk
1/4　cup raisins
1/2　cup sugar
　2　teaspoons butter
1/2　teaspoon vanilla extract
1/4　teaspoon ground cinnamon
1/4　cup graham cracker crumbs
Confectioners' sugar glaze, optional

In a mixing bowl, dissolve yeast in water. Add the next seven ingredients and 2 cups of flour; beat until smooth. Add enough remaining flour to form a soft dough. Turn onto a floured board; knead until smooth and elastic, about 6-8 minutes. Place in a greased bowl, turning once to grease top. Cover and let rise in a warm place until doubled, about 1 hour.

Punch dough down. Shape into walnut-size balls; roll each into a 2-1/2-in. circle. Place 2 in. apart on greased baking sheets; brush with butter. Cover and let rise until doubled, about 30 minutes.

Meanwhile, in a saucepan, bring poppy seeds and water to a boil; boil 1 minute or until thickened. Add milk and raisins; simmer for 10 minutes. Add sugar, butter, vanilla and cinnamon; simmer for 5 minutes. Remove from the heat; stir in the graham cracker crumbs.

Make a depression, about 1-1/2 in. in diameter, in the center of each roll; fill with 2 teaspoons of filling. Bake at 400° for 7-10 minutes or until golden brown. Cool on wire racks. Drizzle with glaze if desired. **Yield:** 3 dozen.

PEACHES AND CREAM MUFFINS

(Pictured at right)

In our house, muffins are a must for breakfast. These pretty ones feature a combination of fresh or frozen peaches and sour cream. The little golden bits of fruit taste so good in these not-too-sweet baked treats. Our daughters love them and request them often.
—Deanne Bagley, Bath, New York

　1　egg
1/2　cup milk *or* sour cream
1/4　cup vegetable oil
1-1/2　cups all-purpose flour
1/2　cup sugar
　2　teaspoons baking powder
1/2　teaspoon salt
　1　cup chopped fresh *or* frozen peaches, thawed

In a bowl, beat egg; add milk and oil. Combine flour, sugar, baking powder and salt; stir into the egg mixture just until moistened. Stir in the peaches. Fill greased or paper-lined muffin cups three-fourths full. Bake at 400° for 20-25 minutes or until a toothpick inserted in a muffin comes out clean. Cool for 5 minutes before removing from pan to a wire rack. **Yield:** 10 muffins.

BLUEBERRY MINI MUFFINS

(Pictured above)

These bite-size muffins are popular in our family. They're especially nice for potlucks since they leave enough room on your plate for all the other dishes you want to sample.
—Suzanne Fredette, Littleton, Massachusetts

1 cup butter, softened
2 cups sugar
5 eggs
1 cup buttermilk
2 teaspoons vanilla extract
5 cups all-purpose flour
1 teaspoon baking soda
1 teaspoon baking powder
3/4 teaspoon salt
3 cups fresh *or* frozen blueberries
Additional sugar, optional

In a mixing bowl, cream butter and sugar. Add eggs, buttermilk and vanilla; mix well. Combine flour, baking soda, baking powder and salt; stir into the creamed mixture just until moistened. Fold in blueberries (batter will be thick).

Fill greased or paper-lined miniature muffin cups with about a tablespoon of batter. Sprinkle with sugar if desired. Bake at 400° for 10-15 minutes or until a toothpick comes out clean. Cool for 5 minutes before removing from the pan to a wire rack. **Yield:** 7 dozen.

CRANBERRY NUT BREAD

(Pictured below)

I created this recipe years ago by combining a couple of recipes from my collection. There's a big burst of tart cranberry and lots of crunchy nuts in every piece. People also like the delicious hint of orange.
—Dawn Lowenstein, Hatboro, Pennsylvania

    2 cups all-purpose flour
    1 cup sugar
1-1/2 teaspoons baking powder
    1 teaspoon salt
  1/2 teaspoon baking soda
  1/4 cup butter
    1 egg
  3/4 cup orange juice
    1 tablespoon grated orange peel
1-1/2 cups fresh *or* frozen cranberries
  1/2 cup chopped walnuts

In a bowl, combine flour, sugar, baking powder, salt and baking soda. Cut in butter until mixture resembles coarse crumbs. Beat egg, orange juice and orange peel; stir into the dry ingredients just until blended. Add the cranberries and walnuts.

Spoon batter into a greased and floured 8-in. x 4-in. x 2-in. loaf pan. Bake at 350° for 65-70 minutes or until a toothpick inserted near the center comes out clean. Cool in pan 10 minutes before removing the bread to a wire rack to cool completely. **Yield:** 1 loaf.

PINEAPPLE ZUCCHINI BREAD

The tangy pineapple in this recipe gives a yummy twist to traditional zucchini bread. Freshly baked slices are irresistible treats for breakfast or any time of day. Because the recipe makes two loaves, it's perfect to use for gift-giving during the holiday season when you want an edible gift for someone special.
—Sharon Lafferty, Partlow, Virginia

    2 eggs
    2 cups sugar
    1 cup vegetable oil
    2 teaspoons vanilla extract
    3 cups all-purpose flour
    1 teaspoon salt
  1/2 teaspoon baking powder
  1/2 teaspoon baking soda
    2 teaspoons ground cinnamon
1-1/2 teaspoons ground nutmeg
    2 cups shredded zucchini
    1 can (8 ounces) crushed pineapple, undrained

In a mixing bowl, beat eggs, sugar, oil and vanilla. Combine dry ingredients; stir into egg mixture just until moistened. Fold in zucchini and pineapple. Pour into two greased 8-in. x 4-in. x 2-in. loaf pans.

Bake at 350° for 60-70 minutes or until a toothpick inserted near the center comes out clean. Cool in pans 10 minutes before removing to a wire rack. **Yield:** 2 loaves.

POPPY SEED MINI MUFFINS

(Pictured at right)

These moist muffins may be small, but they're always a big hit on a brunch buffet, as a quick snack or even packed inside a brown-bag lunch. Everyone loves the combination of poppy seeds and lemon. It's a good thing this recipe makes a large batch!
—*Kathryn Anderson, Casper, Wyoming*

  2 cups all-purpose flour
3/4 cup sugar
  1 teaspoon baking powder
  1 teaspoon baking soda
1/4 teaspoon salt
  1 cup (8 ounces) sour cream
1/2 cup vegetable oil
  2 eggs
  2 tablespoons poppy seeds
  2 tablespoons milk
1/2 teaspoon vanilla extract
1/2 teaspoon lemon extract

In a large bowl, combine the flour, sugar, baking powder, baking soda and salt; set aside. Combine remaining ingredients; mix well. Stir into dry ingredients just until moistened. Fill greased or paper-lined mini-muffin cups two-thirds full. Bake at 400° for 12-15 minutes or until a toothpick comes out clean. Cool in pan 10 minutes before removing to a wire rack. **Yield:** about 3-1/2 dozen.

WHEAT YEAST ROLLS

These wonderful, golden rolls are light and have a delicate flavor. They're also versatile—it seems I can pair them with just about any main dish and end up with a great meal. It's nice to have a simple and inexpensive recipe that adds homemade appeal to menus.
—*Peggy Starkweather, Gardiner, Montana*

  1 package (1/4 ounce) active dry yeast
  1 cup warm water (110° to 115°)
1/3 cup vegetable oil
  3 tablespoons sugar
  1 teaspoon salt
1-1/2 cups whole wheat flour
1-1/2 to 2 cups all-purpose flour

In a mixing bowl, dissolve yeast in water. Add oil, sugar, salt and whole wheat flour; beat until smooth. Add enough all-purpose flour to form a soft dough.

Turn onto a floured surface; knead until smooth and elastic, about 6-8 minutes. Place in a greased bowl; turn once to grease top. Cover and let rise in a warm place until doubled, about 1 hour.

Punch down; divide into 12 pieces. Shape into rolls; place 3 in. apart on greased baking sheets. Cover; let rise until doubled, about 30 minutes. Bake at 375° for 15-20 minutes or until golden. Cool on wire racks. **Yield:** 1 dozen.

Family-Tested Tip

To keep chopped nuts from sinking to the bottom of your quick breads and cakes, try shaking them in flour before adding them to the batter.
—*Dorothy Vanis, Ulysses, Nebraska*

Breads, Rolls & Muffins

CHRISTMAS BREAD

(Pictured at left)

Fruitcake is a traditional Christmas treat, but my family and friends prefer this slightly sweet bread. It's so pretty drizzled with vanilla icing and dotted with festive red and green candied fruit. I like to sprinkle extra fruit on top for added appeal.
—Betty Jean McLaughlin, La Vista, Nebraska

  1 package (1/4 ounce) active dry yeast
3/4 cup warm water (110° to 115°)
3/4 cup evaporated milk
1/3 cup sugar
1/3 cup shortening
1/2 teaspoon salt
  2 eggs
  4 to 4-1/2 cups all-purpose flour, *divided*
  1 cup chopped mixed candied fruit
  1 cup confectioners' sugar
  1 to 2 tablespoons milk
1/4 teaspoon vanilla extract
Additional candied fruit, optional

In a mixing bowl, dissolve yeast in water. Add evaporated milk, sugar, shortening, salt, eggs and 2 cups of flour; beat until smooth. Stir in mixed candied fruit and enough remaining flour to form a soft dough (do not knead). Place in a greased bowl. Cover and let rise in a warm place until doubled, about 1-1/4 hours.

Punch dough down. Turn onto a floured surface; knead 3-4 minutes. Pat evenly into a greased 10-in. tube pan. Cover and let rise in a warm place until nearly doubled, about 45 minutes.

Bake at 375° for 30-35 minutes or until golden brown. Remove from pan to cool on a wire rack. Combine confectioners' sugar, milk and vanilla; drizzle over bread. Garnish with additional candied fruit if desired. **Yield:** 1 loaf.

CRANBERRY EGGNOG BRAID

(Pictured at left)

Whether at Thanksgiving, Christmas or New Year's, this is a wonderful party bread. It always attracts attention with its beautiful braid shape and ruby-red cranberries.
—Mary Lindow, Florence, Wisconsin

    3 to 3-1/2 cups all-purpose flour, *divided*
  1/4 cup sugar
  1/2 teaspoon salt
    1 package (1/4 ounce) active dry yeast
  1/2 teaspoon ground nutmeg
1-1/4 cups eggnog
  1/4 cup butter
  1/2 cup dried cranberries
GLAZE:
    1 cup confectioners' sugar
    1 to 2 tablespoons eggnog
  1/4 teaspoon vanilla extract
Dash nutmeg

In a mixing bowl, combine 1-1/2 cups of flour, sugar, salt, yeast and nutmeg; set aside. In a saucepan, heat eggnog and butter to 120°-130° (the butter does not need to melt); add to flour mixture. Beat on low until moistened; beat on medium for 3 minutes.

Stir in cranberries and enough remaining flour to make a soft dough. Turn onto a floured surface; knead until smooth and elastic, about 6-8 minutes. Place in a greased bowl, turning once to grease top. Cover and let rise in a warm place until doubled, about 1 hour.

Punch dough down; divide into thirds. Shape each third into a 16-in. rope. Braid ropes on a greased baking sheet; seal ends. Cover and let rise until nearly doubled, about 30 minutes.

Bake at 350° for 25-30 minutes or until golden. Immediately remove from pan to a wire rack to cool completely. Combine the first three glaze ingredients; drizzle over braid. Dust with nutmeg. **Yield:** 1 loaf.

Editor's Note: This recipe was tested with commercially prepared eggnog.

SAUSAGE CORN BREAD

(Pictured at right)

Corn bread is a staple here in the South. I added sausage and cheddar cheese to a corn bread recipe and came up with this satisfying dish.
—Annie South, Tishomingo, Mississippi

- 1 pound bulk pork sausage
- 1 large onion, chopped
- 1-1/2 cups cornmeal
- 1/4 cup all-purpose flour
- 2-1/4 teaspoons baking powder
- 3/4 teaspoon salt
- 1 can (14-3/4 ounces) cream-style corn
- 3/4 cup milk
- 2 eggs
- 1/4 cup vegetable oil
- 2 cups (8 ounces) shredded sharp cheddar cheese

In a skillet, cook the sausage and onion over medium heat until meat is no longer pink and onion is tender; drain. In a bowl, combine cornmeal, flour, baking powder and salt. Add the corn, milk, eggs and oil. Pour half into a greased 10-in. ovenproof iron skillet. Sprinkle with the sausage mixture and cheese. Spread remaining cornmeal mixture on top. Bake at 425° for 45-50 minutes or until a toothpick inserted in the corn bread comes out clean. **Yield:** 8-10 servings.

THREE-GRAIN MUFFINS

This recipe combines oats, two breakfast cereals and buttermilk to create delicious, moist muffins.
—Dorothy Collins, Winnsboro, Texas

- 2 cups quick-cooking oats
- 2 cups crushed Shredded Wheat (about 4 large)
- 2 cups All-Bran
- 1 quart buttermilk
- 1 cup boiling water
- 1 cup vegetable oil
- 4 eggs, beaten
- 2-1/4 cups packed brown sugar
- 5 cups all-purpose flour
- 5 teaspoons baking soda
- 1 teaspoon salt

In a large bowl, combine oats, Shredded Wheat and bran. Add buttermilk, water, oil and eggs; stir for 1 minute. Stir in sugar. Combine flour, baking soda and salt; add to cereal mixture and stir well. Fill greased or paper-lined muffin cups two-thirds full. Bake at 400° for 18-20 minutes or until a toothpick comes out clean. Cool 10 minutes; remove from pans to wire racks. **Yield:** 4 dozen.

Editor's Note: Muffin batter can be stored in the refrigerator for up to 1 week.

Family-Tested Tip

For Christmas, shape your favorite cinnamon rolls into a festive tree or wreath. Tint the icing and top the rolls with candied red and green cherries.
—Judi Haydu, Bloomington, Illinois

MOTHER'S CINNAMON ROLLS

(Pictured below right)

I'm a busy wife, mother and nurse, but I love to cook and bake whenever I have the chance. It's a thrill to serve these scrumptious homemade rolls to my family and guests. For quicker preparation when time's short, just substitute frozen bread dough.
—Deanitta Clemmons, Brownsville, Indiana

- 2 packages (1/4 ounce *each*) active dry yeast
- 1/2 cup warm water (110° to 115°)
- 1-1/2 cups warm milk (110° to 115°)
- 1/2 cup butter, softened
- 1/2 cup sugar
- 1 teaspoon salt
- 2 eggs
- 6 to 6-1/2 cups all-purpose flour

FILLING:
- 1/4 cup butter, softened
- 1/2 cup sugar
- 4 teaspoons ground cinnamon
- 1/2 cup raisins, optional
- 1/2 cup chopped walnuts, optional

ICING:
- 2 cups confectioners' sugar
- 2 to 3 tablespoons milk
- 1 teaspoon vanilla extract

In a mixing bowl, dissolve the yeast in water; let stand for 5 minutes. Add the milk, butter, sugar, salt, eggs and 2 cups flour; beat on low for 3 minutes. Stir in enough of the remaining flour to form a soft dough.

Turn the dough onto a floured surface; knead until smooth and elastic, about 6-8 minutes. Place in a greased bowl, turning once to grease top. Cover and let rise in a warm place until doubled, about 1 hour.

Punch dough down; divide in half. Turn onto a lightly floured surface; roll out each half into a 12-in. x 8-in. rectangle. Spread with butter. Combine remaining filling ingredients; sprinkle over butter. Roll up from a long side; pinch seam to seal. Cut into 12 slices; place with cut side down in a greased 13-in. x 9-in. x 2-in. baking pan. Cover and let rise until doubled, about 30 minutes.

Bake at 350° for 25-30 minutes or until golden brown. Cool in pan on a wire rack. Combine the icing ingredients and drizzle over the warm rolls. **Yield:** 2 dozen.

Editor's Note: Two loaves of frozen bread dough may be used with this filling and icing.

per side or until golden brown. Drain on paper towels. Roll in sugar if desired. Serve immediately. **Yield:** 3 to 3-1/2 dozen.

DROP DOUGHNUTS

(Pictured above)

For over 30 years, I've been using extra mashed potatoes to make these light, fluffy doughnuts. They're surprisingly easy to prepare—I just mix together the dough and drop portions of it into hot oil. For an added touch of sweetness, roll them in sugar before serving.
—*Marilyn Kleinfall, Elk Grove Village, Illinois*

1/2 cup mashed potatoes (mashed with milk and butter)
1/4 cup sugar
  1 egg, beaten
1/2 cup sour cream
1/2 teaspoon vanilla extract
1-1/2 cups all-purpose flour
1/2 teaspoon baking soda
1/4 teaspoon baking powder
Oil for deep-fat frying
Additional sugar *or* confectioners' sugar, optional

In a bowl, combine potatoes, sugar, egg, sour cream and vanilla. Combine dry ingredients; stir into potato mixture. Heat oil in an electric skillet or deep-fat fryer to 375°. Drop dough by teaspoonfuls, 5 to 6 at a time, into hot oil. Fry for 1 minute

APPLE PINWHEELS

I swirl convenient crescent roll dough with a spiced apple filling for homemade appeal. The apple flavor is simply wonderful. When I have extra time, I drizzle the rolls with a confectioners' sugar glaze.
—*Christine Campos, Scottsdale, Arizona*

1/3 cup water
1/3 cup butter
1-1/3 cups sugar, *divided*
  2 tubes (8 ounces *each*) refrigerated crescent rolls
  3 cups finely chopped peeled tart apples
  1 teaspoon apple pie spice

In a saucepan, combine water, butter and 1 cup sugar; cook over medium heat until the butter is melted and the sugar is dissolved. Set aside.

Unroll crescent roll dough into one long rectangle; seal seams and perforations. Combine the apples, apple pie spice and remaining sugar; sprinkle over dough to within 1 in. of edges. Roll up, jelly-roll style, starting with a long side. Cut into 1-in. rolls; place in a greased 15-in. x 10-in. x 1-in. baking pan.

Pour reserved syrup over rolls. Bake at 350° for 40-45 minutes or until golden brown. Serve warm. **Yield:** 2 dozen.

HERBED GARLIC TOAST

My wife and I grow over 300 different herbs and sell both fresh and dried varieties. We love how they make meals more interesting, and we use them in many recipes…including this tasty toast.
—*Bruce Shomler, Paso Robles, California*

1/4 cup minced fresh parsley
  3 tablespoons minced fresh basil

3 tablespoons minced fresh thyme
1 tablespoon chopped fresh mint
3 tablespoons olive oil
2 tablespoons red wine vinegar
1 tablespoon sugar
2 garlic cloves, minced
1/2 teaspoon salt
1/4 teaspoon pepper
1 loaf (1/2 pound) French bread

In a small bowl, combine the first 10 ingredients; let stand at room temperature for 30 minutes. Cut bread into 12 slices; place in a single layer on an ungreased baking sheet. Bake at 350° for 5 minutes or until lightly browned. Immediately top each slice with 2 teaspoonfuls of herb mixture. Serve hot. **Yield:** about 6 servings.

WALNUT-DATE QUICK BREAD

I can remember my Aunt Emma making this bread when I was a young girl, and I always liked a slice of it right from the oven. This recipe must be 60 or more years old. But it still tastes as good as ever!
—Yvonne Covey, Haver Hill, Massachusetts

1 cup chopped dates
1 cup boiling water
3 tablespoons butter, softened
1 cup packed brown sugar
1 egg
1-3/4 cups all-purpose flour
1 teaspoon baking soda
1/4 teaspoon salt
1 cup chopped walnuts

In a small bowl, combine the dates and water; let stand for 15 minutes (do not drain). In a mixing bowl, cream butter and brown sugar; add egg and mix well. Combine flour, baking soda and salt; add to the creamed mixture alternately with dates and liquid. Stir in walnuts.

Pour into a greased 8-in. x 4-in. x 2-in. loaf pan. Bake at 350° for 60-65 minutes or until a toothpick inserted near the center comes out clean. Cool on a wire rack. **Yield:** 1 loaf.

PECAN BITES

(Pictured above)

While these are delicious year-round, you could easily turn them into an edible Christmas gift. They look festive on a decorative tray wrapped in red or green cellophane or tucked into a giveaway cookie plate. And don't forget to include the recipe so your recipient can enjoy this treat over and over again!
—Pat Schrand, Enterprise, Alabama

1 cup packed brown sugar
1/2 cup all-purpose flour
1 cup chopped pecans
2/3 cup butter, melted
2 eggs, beaten

In a bowl, combine brown sugar, flour and pecans; set aside. Combine butter and eggs; mix well. Stir into flour mixture. Fill greased and floured miniature muffin cups two-thirds full. Bake at 350° for 22-25 minutes or until lightly browned. Remove immediately to cool on wire racks. **Yield:** about 2-1/2 dozen.

Editor's Note: This recipe uses only 1/2 cup flour.

FLAVORFUL HERB BREAD

(Pictured below)

Made in a bread machine, this loaf is one of my favorites because it has a wonderful texture and slices beautifully. The flavor of the herbs really comes through.
—Gerri Hamilton, Kingsville, Ontario

1 cup warm milk (70° to 80°)
1 egg
2 tablespoons butter, softened
1/4 cup dried minced onion
2 tablespoons sugar
1-1/2 teaspoons salt
2 tablespoons dried parsley flakes
1 teaspoon dried oregano
3-1/2 cups bread flour
2 teaspoons active dry yeast

In bread machine pan, place all ingredients in order suggested by manufacturer. Select the basic bread setting. Choose crust color and loaf size if available. Bake according to bread machine directions (check dough after 5 minutes of mixing; add 1 to 2 tablespoons of water or flour if needed). **Yield:** 1 loaf (2 pounds).

Editor's Note: Use of the timer feature is not recommended for this recipe.

CINNAMON CRESCENTS

(Pictured at right)

I've had the recipe for these crispy, cinnamon-sugar roll-ups for years. The crescents are so easy to make, and my family considers them a real treat.
—Emily Engel, Quill Lake, Saskatchewan

2-1/2 cups all-purpose flour
   1 teaspoon baking powder
   1 cup cold butter
 1/2 cup milk
   1 egg, beaten
   1 cup sugar
   4 teaspoons ground cinnamon

Combine flour and baking powder in a large bowl; cut in butter until crumbly. Stir in milk and egg. Divide dough into three portions; shape each portion into a ball.

Combine sugar and cinnamon; sprinkle a third over a pastry board or a surface. Roll one ball into a 12-in. circle; cut into 12 wedges. Roll up from wide edge. Repeat with remaining dough and cinnamon-sugar. Place rolls with point side down on lightly greased baking sheets; form into crescent shapes. Bake at 350° for 16-18 minutes or until lightly browned (do not overbake). **Yield:** 3 dozen.

REFRIGERATOR ROLLS

I like to make baked goods from scratch. These golden rolls are irresistible, and the dough can be made several days in advance. I've also used it as a substitute in recipes that call for frozen bread dough.
—Nick Welty, Smithville, Ohio

   2 packages (1/4 ounce *each*) active dry yeast
1-3/4 cups warm water (110° to 115°)
   2 eggs
 1/2 cup sugar
 1/4 cup butter, softened
   1 teaspoon salt
   6 cups all-purpose flour

In a mixing bowl, dissolve the yeast in water. Add the eggs, sugar, butter, salt and 3 cups of flour; beat until smooth. Add enough of the remaining flour to form a soft dough. Turn dough onto a floured surface and knead until smooth and elastic, about 6-8 minutes. Place in a greased bowl, turning once to grease the top. Cover and refrigerate for 2 hours or up to 2 days.

Punch dough down and divide in half; shape each portion into 12 rolls. Place in two greased 9-in. round baking pans. Cover and let rise until nearly doubled, about 30 minutes. Bake at 350° for 20 minutes or until golden brown. **Yield:** 2 dozen.

Family-Tested Tip

For an easy-to-prepare spread for breads or muffins, combine softened cream cheese, a small can of drained crushed pineapple, 3/4 cup of chopped walnuts and a little milk or pineapple juice.
—Dorothy Jasper, Washington, Missouri

HEARTY MORNING MUFFINS

(Pictured at right)

These yummy muffins are packed full of goodies, including chocolate chips and apricots. We like these bites for Sunday breakfast, but it's a good idea to double the recipe and keep some in the freezer for brown-bag lunches during the week.
—Elaine Kauffman, Tofield, Alberta

  2   cups whole wheat flour
  1   cup sugar
  2   teaspoons baking soda
  2   teaspoons ground cinnamon
  2   cups shredded carrots
1/3   cup chopped dried apricots
1/3   cup sunflower kernels
1/3   cup flaked coconut
1/3   cup semisweet chocolate chips
  1   medium ripe banana, mashed
  3   eggs
  1   cup vegetable oil
  2   teaspoons vanilla extract

In a mixing bowl, combine flour, sugar, baking soda and cinnamon. Add the carrots, apricots, sunflower kernels, coconut and chocolate chips. Stir in the banana. Beat eggs, oil and vanilla; stir into carrot mixture just until moistened.

Fill greased or paper-lined muffin cups two-thirds full. Bake at 375° for 18-22 minutes or until a toothpick comes out clean. Cool 5 minutes; remove from pans to wire racks. **Yield:** 1-1/2 dozen.

SUNSHINE MUFFINS

(Pictured at right)

I use two convenient mixes to create these sweet corn bread muffins. The yellow cake mix gives them a smoother texture than traditional corn bread.
—Linnea Rein, Topeka, Kansas

  2   eggs
1/2   cup water
1/3   cup milk
  2   tablespoons vegetable oil
  1   package (9 ounces) yellow cake mix
  1   package (8-1/2 ounces) corn
       bread/muffin mix

In a bowl, combine the eggs, water, milk and oil. Stir in mixes and mix well. Fill greased and floured muffin cups half full.

Bake at 350° for 18-22 minutes or until a toothpick comes out clean. Cool 5 minutes; remove from pans to wire racks. **Yield:** 14 muffins.

CHEDDAR CHIVE MUFFINS

(Pictured at right)

These savory muffins have been a favorite ever since I made the first batch years ago. The ingredients are ones I usually have on hand, so it's easy to whip up a dozen of these at the last minute to round out a meal or for an afternoon snack.
—Donna Royer, Largo, Florida

1-1/4   cups milk
  3/4   cup mashed potato flakes
    1   egg
  1/3   cup vegetable oil
    1   cup (4 ounces) shredded cheddar cheese
1-2/3   cups all-purpose flour
    3   tablespoons sugar
    2   tablespoons snipped chives
    1   tablespoon dried parsley flakes
    1   tablespoon baking powder
    1   teaspoon salt

In a saucepan, bring milk to a boil. Remove from the heat; stir in potato flakes. Let stand for 2 minutes. Whip with a fork until smooth; cool slightly. Beat in egg, oil and cheese. Combine remaining ingredients; stir into potato mixture just until moistened (batter will be thick).

Fill greased muffin cups three-fourths full. Bake at 400° for 20-25 minutes or until a toothpick comes out clean. Cool 5 minutes; remove from pan to a wire rack. Serve warm. **Yield:** 1 dozen.

SOUR CREAM 'N' CHIVE BISCUITS

(Pictured above)

I grow chives in my front yard and like to use them in as many recipes as I can. These moist, tender biscuits are delectable as well as attractive.
—*Lucille Proctor, Panguitch, Utah*

2 cups all-purpose flour
1 tablespoon baking powder
1/2 teaspoon salt
1/4 teaspoon baking soda
1/3 cup shortening
3/4 cup sour cream
1/4 cup milk
1/4 cup snipped fresh chives

In a bowl, combine dry ingredients. Cut in shortening until mixture resembles coarse crumbs. With a fork, stir in sour cream, milk and chives until the mixture forms a ball.

On a lightly floured surface, knead five to six times. Roll to 3/4-in. thickness; cut with a 2-in. biscuit cutter. Place on an ungreased baking sheet. Bake at 350° for 12-15 minutes or until golden brown. **Yield:** 12-15 biscuits.

CARAMEL PECAN ROLLS

Soft and sweet, these rolls will get a lip-smacking smile from everyone. They rise nice and high, hold their shape and have a gooey caramel sauce that's scrumptious. There's no better way to start the day!
—*Carolyn Buschkamp, Emmetsburg, Iowa*

2 cups milk
1/2 cup water
1/2 cup sugar
1/2 cup butter
1/3 cup cornmeal
2 teaspoons salt
7 to 7-1/2 cups all-purpose flour
2 packages (1/4 ounce *each*) active dry yeast
2 eggs
TOPPING:
2 cups packed brown sugar
1/2 cup butter
1/2 cup milk
1/2 to 1 cup chopped pecans
FILLING:
1/4 cup butter, softened
1/2 cup sugar
2 teaspoons ground cinnamon

In a saucepan, combine the first six ingredients; bring to a boil, stirring frequently. Set aside to cool to 120°-130°. In a mixing bowl, combine 2 cups flour and yeast. Add cooled cornmeal mixture; beat on low until smooth. Add eggs and 1 cup of flour; mix for 1 minute. Stir in enough remaining flour to form a soft dough.

Turn the dough onto a floured board; knead until smooth and elastic, about 6-8 minutes. Place in a greased bowl, turning once to grease top. Cover and let rise in a warm place until doubled, about 1 hour.

Combine the first three topping ingredients in a saucepan; bring to a boil, stirring occasionally. Pour into two greased 13-in. x 9-in. x 2-in. baking pans. Sprinkle with pecans; set aside.

Punch dough down; divide in half. Roll each

into a 12-in. x 15-in. rectangle; spread with butter. Combine sugar and cinnamon; sprinkle over butter. Roll up dough from one long side; pinch seams and turn ends under. Cut each roll into 12 slices. Place 12 slices, cut side down, in each baking pan. Cover and let rise in a warm place until nearly doubled, about 30 minutes. Bake at 375° for 20-25 minutes or until golden brown. Let cool 1 minute; invert onto a serving platter. **Yield:** 2 dozen.

"Family: A social unit where the father is concerned with parking space, the children with outer space and the mother with closet space."
—Evan Esar

HOT CROSS BUNS

(Pictured below)

This recipe came from my niece in Ballwin, Missouri, who's one of the best cooks I know. With their pretty icing design on top, these yummy buns always attract attention when I set a basket of them on the table. They've become an Easter morning tradition.
—Dorothy Pritchett, Wills Point, Texas

    2 **packages (1/4 ounce *each*) active dry yeast**
1/2 **cup warm water (110° to 115°)**
    1 **cup warm milk (110° to 115°)**
1/2 **cup sugar**
1/4 **cup butter, softened**
    1 **teaspoon vanilla extract**

    1 **teaspoon salt**
1/2 **teaspoon ground nutmeg**
6-1/2 to 7 **cups all-purpose flour**
    4 **eggs**
1/2 **cup dried currants**
1/2 **cup raisins**
GLAZE/ICING:
    2 **tablespoons water**
    1 **egg yolk**
    1 **cup confectioners' sugar**
    4 **teaspoons milk**
1/4 **teaspoon vanilla extract**

In a mixing bowl, dissolve yeast in water. Add milk, sugar, butter, vanilla, salt, nutmeg and 3 cups of flour; beat until smooth. Add eggs, one at a time, beating well after each. Stir in the currants, raisins and enough remaining flour to form a soft dough. Turn onto a floured board; knead until smooth and elastic, 6-8 minutes. Place in a greased bowl, turning once to grease top. Cover and let rise in a warm place until doubled, about 1 hour.

Punch dough down; shape into 30 balls. Place on greased baking sheets. Cut a cross on top of each roll with a sharp knife. Cover and let rise until doubled, about 30 minutes.

Beat water and egg yolk; brush over rolls. Bake at 375° for 12-15 minutes or until golden. Cool on wire racks. For the icing, combine sugar, milk and vanilla until smooth; drizzle over rolls. **Yield:** 2-1/2 dozen.

2 teaspoons ground cinnamon
1-1/4 teaspoons ground cloves
1-1/4 teaspoons ground nutmeg
1 teaspoon baking soda
1 teaspoon ground ginger
2 eggs
2 cups milk
1 cup maple syrup
2 tablespoons vegetable oil

In a large bowl, combine the first eight ingredients. In another bowl, combine the eggs, milk, syrup and oil. Stir into the dry ingredients just until moistened (batter will be thin). Pour into two greased 9-in. x 5-in. x 3-in. loaf pans.

Bake at 325° for 60-70 minutes or until a toothpick inserted near the center comes out clean. Cool for 10 minutes before removing from pans to wire racks. **Yield:** 2 loaves.

SWEET RASPBERRY MUFFINS

(Pictured at left)

I like to linger over a cup of coffee and a warm sweet treat on weekend mornings. These moist muffins are perfect because making them ties up so little time in the kitchen. I also serve them with holiday meals when I want something different.
—Teresa Raab, Tustin, Michigan

2 cups biscuit/baking mix
2 tablespoons sugar
1/4 cup cold butter
2/3 cup milk
1/4 cup raspberry jam
GLAZE:
1/2 cup confectioners' sugar
2 teaspoons warm water
1/4 teaspoon vanilla extract

In a bowl, combine biscuit mix and sugar. Cut in butter until the mixture resembles coarse crumbs. Stir in milk just until moistened (batter will be thick). Spoon about 1 tablespoon of batter into 12 paper-lined muffin cups. Top with 1 teaspoon rasp-

GINGERBREAD LOAF

(Pictured above)

Enjoy the old-fashioned appeal of gingerbread in a loaf with this recipe originally from Holland. The moist spicy bread smells delicious while it's baking…and slices are wonderful spread with cream cheese. This recipe makes two big loaves, so we have one to eat and one to freeze for later or to give away.
—Martina Biemond, Rosedale, British Columbia

4 cups all-purpose flour
2 cups sugar
4 teaspoons baking powder

berry jam. Spoon the remaining batter (about 1 tablespoon each) over jam.

Bake at 425° for 12-14 minutes or until lightly browned. Cool in pans for 5 minutes. Meanwhile, in a small bowl, combine glaze ingredients until smooth. Remove muffins to a wire rack. Drizzle with glaze. **Yield:** 1 dozen.

CRANBERRY SWEET ROLLS

(Pictured below)

Christmas morning will be sweeter than ever when you serve these festive rolls spread with a rich and creamy frosting. The tart cranberry filling is a nice change of pace from cinnamon rolls.
—Germaine Stank, Pound, Wisconsin

1-1/4 cups sugar, *divided*
  1/2 cup water
    2 cups cranberries
    1 teaspoon grated orange peel
    2 packages (1/4 ounce *each*) active dry yeast

  1/2 cup warm water (110° to 115°)
  1/2 cup butter, softened
  1/2 cup milk
    2 eggs
    1 teaspoon salt
    1 teaspoon ground cinnamon
  1/2 teaspoon ground nutmeg
4-1/2 to 5 cups all-purpose flour
Melted butter
CREAM CHEESE FROSTING:
    1 cup confectioners' sugar
  1/2 of a 3-ounce package cream cheese, softened
  1/4 cup butter, softened
  1/2 teaspoon vanilla extract
  1/2 teaspoon milk

In a saucepan, bring 3/4 cup sugar and water to a boil. Add cranberries; return to a boil. Boil, uncovered, for 20 minutes, stirring occasionally. Stir in orange peel; cover and chill.

In a mixing bowl, dissolve the yeast in warm water. Add the next six ingredients, the remaining sugar and 3 cups flour; beat until smooth. Add enough of the remaining flour to form a soft dough. Turn the dough onto a floured surface; knead until smooth and elastic, about 6-8 minutes. Place dough in a greased bowl, turning once to grease top. Cover and let rise in a warm place until doubled, about 1 hour.

Punch dough down. Roll into a 15-in. x 10-in. rectangle; brush with butter. Spread cranberry filling over dough to within 1 in. of edges. Roll up, jelly roll style, starting at a long side. Cut into 15 slices; place, cut side down, in a greased 13-in. x 9-in. x 2-in. baking pan. Cover and let rise until doubled, about 30 minutes.

Bake at 375° for 25-30 minutes or until golden brown. Cool in pan 5 minutes; remove to a wire rack to cool. Beat the cream cheese frosting ingredients until smooth; spread the frosting over the warm rolls. **Yield:** 15 servings.

PARMESAN HERB BREAD

(Pictured above)

*Wedges of this delicious, cheese-topped bread go great with spaghetti and other Italian dishes.
This loaf also tastes special when dressed up with one of the accompanying spreads.*
—Diane Hixon, Niceville, Florida

1-1/2 cups biscuit/baking mix
  1 egg, beaten
1/4 cup apple juice
1/4 cup milk
  1 tablespoon dried minced onion
  1 tablespoon sugar
1/2 teaspoon dried oregano
1/4 cup grated Parmesan cheese
HERB BUTTER:
1/2 cup butter, softened
  1 garlic clove, minced
  2 tablespoons minced fresh parsley *or* 2
    teaspoons dried parsley flakes
  1 teaspoon dried basil

TOMATO BUTTER:
1/2 cup butter, softened
  4 teaspoons tomato paste
Dash cayenne pepper

In a mixing bowl, combine the first seven ingredients just until blended. Spoon into a greased 9-in. round cake pan. Sprinkle with Parmesan cheese. Bake at 400° for 18-20 minutes or until golden brown.

In separate small mixing bowls, combine the herb butter and tomato butter ingredients; beat until smooth. Serve the butter with warm bread. **Yield:** 6-8 servings.

MILK-AND-HONEY WHITE BREAD

(Pictured below)

My dad has been a wheat farmer all his life, and my state is the wheat capital of the country, so this recipe represents both my region and family well. These loaves are wonderful for sandwiches or toasted and spread with jelly for breakfast.
—Kathy McCreary, Goddard, Kansas

      1   package (1/4 ounce) active dry yeast
2-1/2   cups warm milk (110° to 115°)
   1/3   cup honey
   1/4   cup butter, melted
      2   teaspoons salt
      8   to 8-1/2 cups all-purpose flour

In a large mixing bowl, dissolve yeast in warm milk. Add honey, butter, salt and 5 cups of flour; beat until smooth. Add enough remaining flour to form a soft dough. Turn onto a floured board; knead until smooth and elastic, about 6-8 minutes. Place in a greased bowl, turning once to grease top. Cover and let rise in a warm place until doubled, about 1 hour.

Punch dough down and shape into two loaves. Place in greased 9-in. x 5-in. x 3-in. loaf pans.

Cover and let rise until doubled, about 30 minutes. Bake at 375° for 30-35 minutes or until golden brown. Cover with foil if necessary to prevent over-browning. Remove from pans and cool on wire racks. **Yield:** 2 loaves.

ONION SANDWICH ROLLS

These tempting rolls have a mild onion flavor from handy dry soup mix. They're great with Italian meals, as sandwich rolls or as hamburger buns. Plus, they freeze well, so you can prepare them ahead and take them out when needed.
—Josie-Lynn Belmont, Woodbine, Georgia

      1   envelope onion soup mix
   1/2   cup boiling water
      1   tablespoon butter
3-1/2   to 4 cups all-purpose flour, *divided*
      2   packages (1/4 ounce *each*) quick-rise yeast
      1   tablespoon sugar
      1   cup warm water (120° to 130°)

In a bowl, combine the soup mix, boiling water and butter; cool to 120°-130°. In a mixing bowl, combine 1 cup flour, yeast and sugar. Add the warm water; beat until smooth. Stir in 1 cup flour. Beat in onion soup mixture and enough remaining flour to form a soft dough.

Turn the dough onto a floured surface; knead until smooth and elastic, about 6 minutes. Cover and let stand for 10 minutes. Divide dough into 12 portions and shape each into a ball. Place on greased baking sheets; flatten slightly.

Place two large shallow pans on the work surface; fill half full with boiling water. Place baking pans with rolls over water-filled pans. Cover and let rise for 15 minutes. Bake at 375° for 16-19 minutes or until golden brown. Remove from pans to a wire rack. **Yield:** 1 dozen.

clean. Cool in pans 10 minutes before removing to wire racks to cool completely. **Yield:** 5 miniature loaves.

Editor's Note: This bread may also be baked in two greased 8-in. x 4-in. x 2-in. loaf pans for 75-80 minutes.

GOLDEN RAISIN BUNS

These delightful buns will remind you of old-fashioned cream puffs with a mild lemon flavor. They look appealing on a platter and sure get snatched up quickly.
—Kathy Scott, Hemingford, Nebraska

    2   cups hot water, *divided*
    1/2 cup golden raisins
    1/2 cup butter
    1   teaspoon sugar
    1/4 teaspoon salt
    1   cup all-purpose flour
    4   eggs
ICING:
    1   tablespoon butter
    4 to 5 teaspoons half-and-half cream
    1   cup confectioners' sugar
    1/2 teaspoon lemon juice
    1/2 teaspoon vanilla extract

In a small bowl, pour 1 cup of water over raisins; let stand for 5 minutes. Drain; set raisins aside. In a large saucepan, bring butter, sugar, salt and remaining water to a boil. Add flour all at once; stir until a smooth ball forms. Remove from the heat; beat by hand for 2 minutes.

Add eggs, one at a time, beating well after each addition. Beat until mixture is well blended, about 3 minutes. Stir in the raisins. Drop by tablespoonfuls 2 in. apart onto greased baking sheets. Bake at 375° for 30-35 minutes or until golden brown. Transfer to a wire rack.

For the icing, melt the butter in a small saucepan; stir in the cream. Remove from the heat; add the sugar, lemon juice and vanilla. Spread on the buns while still warm. Serve buns warm if desired. **Yield:** 20 servings.

DELICIOUS PUMPKIN BREAD

(Pictured above)

An enticing aroma wafts through my house when this tender cake-like bread is in the oven. During the holiday season, I like to bake extra loaves to give as gifts to my family members and friends.
—Linda Burnett, Stanton, California

    5   eggs
1-1/4 cups vegetable oil
    1   can (15 ounces) solid-pack pumpkin
    2   cups all-purpose flour
    2   cups sugar
    2   packages (3 ounces *each*) cook-and-serve vanilla pudding mix
    1   teaspoon baking soda
    1   teaspoon ground cinnamon
    1/2 teaspoon salt

In a mixing bowl, beat the eggs. Add oil and pumpkin; beat until smooth. Combine remaining ingredients; gradually beat into pumpkin mixture. Pour batter into five greased 5-in. x 2-1/2-in. x 2-in. loaf pans. Bake at 325° for 50-55 minutes or until a toothpick inserted near the center comes out

BREAKFAST SCONES

(Pictured below)

Don't let the name of these scones fool you…they're great to serve around the clock.
—Kate Carpenter, Callahan, Florida

 2 cups all-purpose flour
 1 cup whole wheat flour
1/2 cup packed brown sugar
 1 tablespoon baking powder
1/2 teaspoon baking soda
3/4 cup butter
 1 cup buttermilk

In a bowl, combine flours, brown sugar, baking powder and baking soda. Cut in butter until mixture resembles coarse crumbs. Stir in buttermilk until a soft dough forms. Turn onto a lightly floured board and knead gently 10-12 times or until no longer sticky.

Divide dough in half; gently pat or roll each half into an 8-in. circle 1/2 in. thick. Cut each circle into eight wedges. Separate wedges and place on an ungreased baking sheet. Bake at 400° for 15-18 minutes. **Yield:** 16 scones.

VERY BERRY SPREAD

(Pictured at left)

Two kinds of berries make this jam deliciously different. I always keep some of this spread on hand to enjoy not only for breakfast, but also as a treat during the day.
—Irene Hagel, Choiceland, Saskatchewan

 5 cups fresh *or* frozen raspberries
 3 cups fresh *or* frozen blueberries
 1 tablespoon lemon juice
 1 tablespoon grated lemon peel
 1 package (1-3/4 ounces) powdered fruit pectin
 6 cups sugar

In a large kettle, combine the berries, lemon juice, lemon peel and pectin. Bring to a full rolling boil over high heat, stirring constantly. Stir in sugar; return to a full rolling boil. Boil for 1 minute, stirring constantly.

Remove from the heat; skim off any foam. Pour hot into hot jars, leaving 1/4-in. headspace. Adjust caps. Process for 10 minutes in a boiling-water bath. **Yield:** about 8 half-pints.

Family-Tested Tip

Give pumpkin bread a yummy twist by replacing the raisins with butterscotch or chocolate chips.
—Star Strahle, Copperopolis, California

Chapter ten

Everyone will save room for dessert

when these tempting treats are waiting at the

end of a meal. You're sure to delight your loved

ones with any of these scrumptious sweets…from

golden fruit cobblers and ice cream confections

to comforting puddings and tantalizing tarts.

Lemon Whirligigs with Raspberries
(Recipe on page 216)

❤ Desserts
& Treats

APRICOT RICE CUSTARD

(Pictured below)

This creamy custard drizzled with apricot sauce makes a comforting dessert or a refreshingly different breakfast.
—Elizabeth Montgomery, Taylorville, Illinois

> 1 cup uncooked long grain rice
> 3 cups milk
> 1/2 cup sugar
> 1/2 teaspoon salt
> 2 eggs, lightly beaten
> 1/2 teaspoon vanilla extract
> 1/4 teaspoon almond extract

Dash ground cinnamon
SAUCE:

> 1 can (8-1/2 ounces) apricot halves
> 1 can (8 ounces) crushed pineapple, undrained
> 1/3 cup packed brown sugar
> 2 tablespoons lemon juice
> 1 tablespoon cornstarch

In a large saucepan, cook rice according to package directions. Stir in milk, sugar and salt; bring to a boil. Reduce heat to low. Stir 1/2 cup into eggs; return all to the pan. Cook and stir for 15 minutes or until mixture coats a spoon (do not boil). Remove from heat; stir in extracts and cinnamon.

For sauce, drain apricot syrup into a saucepan. Chop apricots; add to syrup. Stir in remaining sauce ingredients; bring to a boil. Boil for 2 minutes, stirring occasionally. Serve sauce and custard warm or chilled. **Yield:** 8-10 servings.

LEMON WHIRLIGIGS WITH RASPBERRIES

(Pictured on page 215)

Golden whirligigs with a tart lemon flavor float on a raspberry sauce in this dessert. I love serving it to guests. My children also like it made with blackberries.
—Vicki Ayres, Wappingers Falls, New York

> 2/3 cup sugar
> 2 tablespoons cornstarch
> 1/4 teaspoon ground cinnamon
> 1/8 teaspoon ground nutmeg
> 1/8 teaspoon salt
> 1 cup water
> 3 cups fresh raspberries

WHIRLIGIGS:

> 1 cup all-purpose flour
> 2 teaspoons baking powder
> 1/2 teaspoon salt
> 3 tablespoons shortening
> 1 egg, lightly beaten
> 2 tablespoons half-and-half cream
> 1/4 cup sugar
> 2 tablespoons butter, melted
> 1 teaspoon grated lemon peel

Heavy whipping cream and additional raspberries, optional

In a saucepan, combine sugar, cornstarch, cinnamon, nutmeg and salt. Gradually add water; bring to a boil. Reduce heat to medium; cook and stir until sauce thickens, about 5 minutes. Place raspberries in an ungreased 1-1/2-qt. shallow baking dish; pour hot sauce over top. Bake at 400° for 10 minutes; remove from oven and set aside.

For whirligigs, combine the first three ingredi-

APPLE DUMPLING DESSERT

(Pictured at left)

This delicious dessert has a nice bonus—no bites of dry crust without filling. The layers have plenty of apple pieces and are sweetened with a yummy syrup.
—Janet Weaver, Wooster, Ohio

PASTRY:
- 4 cups all-purpose flour
- 2 teaspoons salt
- 1-1/3 cups shortening
- 8 to 9 tablespoons cold water

FILLING:
- 8 cups chopped peeled tart apples
- 1/4 cup sugar
- 3/4 teaspoon ground cinnamon

SYRUP:
- 2 cups water
- 1 cup packed brown sugar

Whipped topping *or* vanilla ice cream, optional
Mint leaves, optional

In a bowl, combine flour and salt; cut in shortening until the mixture resembles coarse crumbs. Sprinkle with water, 1 tablespoon at a time, and toss with a fork until dough can be formed into a ball. Divide dough into four parts.

On a lightly floured surface, roll one part of the dough to fit the bottom of an ungreased 13-in. x 9-in. x 2-in. baking dish. Place in dish; top with a third of the apples. Combine sugar and cinnamon; sprinkle a third over apples. Repeat layers of pastry, apples and cinnamon-sugar twice. Roll out the remaining dough to fit the top of dish and place on top. Using a sharp knife, cut 2-in. slits through all layers at once.

For syrup, bring water and sugar to a boil. Cook and stir until sugar is dissolved. Pour over top crust. Bake at 400° for 35-40 minutes or until browned and bubbly. Serve warm with whipped topping or ice cream if desired. Garnish with mint if desired. **Yield:** 12 servings.

ents in a bowl; cut in shortening until crumbly. Combine egg and cream; stir into dry ingredients to form a stiff dough. Shape into a ball; place on a lightly floured surface. Roll into a 12-in. x 6-in. rectangle. Combine sugar, butter and grated lemon peel; spread over dough. Roll up, jelly roll style, starting at a long side. Cut into 10 slices; pat each slice slightly to flatten.

Place whirligigs on top of berry mixture. Bake at 400° for 15 minutes or until whirligigs are golden. Garnish servings with cream and raspberries if desired. **Yield:** 10 servings.

Family-Tested Tips

Before putting peanut butter in a measuring cup, coat the inside with water or oil. The peanut butter will slide right out—no scraping needed.
—Charline Statler, San Diego, California

Heavy cream will whip faster if you put the bowl (make sure it's freezer-proof) and beaters in the freezer first to chill them.
—Mrs. Henry Reifenheiser, Henderson, Nevada

CRANBERRY ICE

(Pictured above)

This recipe dates back to 1931, but I think you'll agree the refreshing flavor is timeless. Since I was a child, I've enjoyed this dessert for many occasions, but especially around the holidays.
—*Eleanor Dunbar, Peoria, Illinois*

4 cups fresh *or* frozen cranberries
4 cups cold water, *divided*
1 package (3 ounces) lemon gelatin
2 cups boiling water
3 cups sugar
1/2 cup lemon juice
1/2 cup orange juice

In a saucepan, bring the cranberries and 2 cups cold water to a boil. Reduce heat; simmer for 5 minutes. Press through a strainer to remove the skins; set the juice aside and discard skins.

In a bowl, stir the gelatin, boiling water and sugar until dissolved. Add cranberry juice, lemon and orange juices and remaining cold water. Pour into a 13-in. x 9-in. x 2-in. pan. Cover and freeze until ice begins to form around the edges of the pan, about 1-1/2 hours; stir. Freeze until mushy, about 30 minutes. Spoon into a freezer container; cover and freeze. **Yield:** 20 servings.

ALMOND CRANBERRY TART

(Pictured at left)

Cranberries and currant jelly make a jewel-toned filling for the cookie-type crust in this dessert.
—Billie Moss, El Sobrante, California

1-1/4 cups sugar, *divided*
    1 cup finely chopped toasted slivered almonds
    1 cup all-purpose flour
1/2 cup butter
    1 egg
    1 teaspoon vanilla extract
    1 envelope unflavored gelatin
1/4 cup water
    1 package (12 ounces) fresh *or* frozen cranberries
1/2 cup red currant jelly
Whipped cream and additional chopped almonds, optional

In a bowl, combine 1/4 cup sugar, almonds and flour. Cut in the butter until crumbly. Beat egg and vanilla; add to flour mixture and stir until moistened. Cover and chill for 30 minutes.

Coat fingers with flour and press mixture into the bottom and 1-1/2 in. up the sides of a greased 9-in. springform pan. Bake at 350° for 25-30 minutes or until golden brown. Cool.

Meanwhile, soften gelatin in water; set aside. In a saucepan, cook cranberries, jelly and remaining sugar over medium-low heat until berries pop. Remove from the heat; stir in gelatin until dissolved. Cool; pour into crust. Chill at least 4 hours. Garnish with whipped cream and almonds if desired. **Yield:** 8-10 servings.

CRANBERRY NUT DESSERT

(Pictured above left)

When time's short, I reach for this easy recipe—it's like a pie that doesn't need a crust. The tart whole cranberries make it moist and delicious.
—Peggy Van Arsdale, Trenton, New Jersey

    1 cup all-purpose flour
    1 cup sugar
1/4 teaspoon salt
    2 cups fresh *or* frozen cranberries
1/2 cup chopped walnuts
1/2 cup butter, melted
    2 eggs, beaten
1/2 teaspoon almond extract
Whipped cream *or* ice cream, optional

In a bowl, combine the flour, sugar and salt. Add cranberries and nuts; toss to coat. Stir in the butter, eggs and extract (mixture will be very thick if using frozen berries). Spread mixture into a greased 9-in. pie plate.

Bake at 350° for 40 minutes or until a toothpick inserted near the center comes out clean. Serve warm with whipped cream or ice cream if desired. **Yield:** 8 servings.

EASY MINT CHIP ICE CREAM

A longtime family favorite, this mint-chocolate chip treat also delights the students in my home economics classes. You can whip up this easy homemade ice cream in just minutes before popping it in the freezer to set up overnight. What's best is, you don't need an ice cream freezer or any other special equipment.
—Cynthia Kolberg, Syracuse, Indiana

    1 can (14 ounces) sweetened condensed milk
    2 tablespoons water
1/4 to 1/2 teaspoon peppermint extract
    3 to 4 drops green food coloring
    2 cups heavy whipping cream, whipped
    1 cup (6 ounces) miniature semisweet chocolate chips

In a large bowl, combine milk, water, extract and food coloring. Fold in whipped cream and chocolate chips. Pour into a foil-lined 9-in. x 5-in. x 3-in. loaf pan. Cover and freeze for 6 hours or until firm. Lift out of the pan and remove foil; slice. **Yield:** 8 servings.

In a bowl, combine the graham cracker crumbs, brown sugar, 1/2 cup peanut butter and butter; spoon half into a 3-qt. bowl. In a mixing bowl, beat the cream cheese and sugar until smooth; fold in the whipped topping. Spread half over the crumb mixture in the bowl. Top with one can of apple pie filling.

Combine confectioners' sugar, cinnamon and remaining peanut butter until crumbly; sprinkle half over pie filling. Repeat layers. Refrigerate until serving. **Yield:** about 20 servings.

COCONUT CRUNCH DELIGHT

This tempting dessert is a terrific way to end a heavy meal. The nutty coconut crust and topping wonderfully complement the cool and creamy pudding layer.
—*Debby Chiorino, Oxnard, California*

1/2 cup butter, melted
1 cup all-purpose flour
1-1/4 cups flaked coconut
1/4 cup packed brown sugar
1 cup slivered almonds
1 package (3.4 ounces) instant vanilla pudding mix
1 package (3.4 ounces) instant coconut cream pudding mix
2-2/3 cups cold milk
2 cups whipped topping
Fresh strawberries, optional

In a bowl, combine the first five ingredients; press lightly into a greased 13-in. x 9-in. x 2-in. baking pan. Bake at 350° for 25-30 minutes or until golden brown, stirring every 10 minutes to form coarse crumbs. Cool.

Divide the crumb mixture in half; press half into the same baking pan. In a mixing bowl, beat the pudding mixes and milk. Fold in the whipped topping; spoon over the crust. Top with the remaining crumb mixture. Cover and refrigerate overnight. Garnish with fresh strawberries if desired. **Yield:** 12-16 servings.

PEANUT BUTTER APPLE DESSERT

(Pictured above)

My mom, who's well-known in our community for her cooking, shared the recipe for this yummy and impressive dessert. It's very popular with my husband. He made it for his men's Bible study group and ended up giving out the recipe!
—*Kim Spencer, Hickman, Nebraska*

1-1/2 cups graham cracker crumbs (about 24 squares)
1/2 cup packed brown sugar
1/2 cup plus 1/3 cup peanut butter, *divided*
1/4 cup butter, melted
1 package (8 ounces) cream cheese, softened
3/4 cup sugar
1 carton (16 ounces) frozen whipped topping, thawed
2 cans (21 ounces *each*) apple pie filling
3/4 cup confectioners' sugar
1 teaspoon ground cinnamon

ORANGE CHARLOTTE

(Pictured below)

Mom prepared this light and fluffy citrus dessert whenever Dad grilled outdoors. It gave our meals on sunny summer days a fresh-tasting finish…and always looked so beautiful with a garnish of mandarin oranges and bright red maraschino cherries.
—Sue Gronholz, Columbus, Wisconsin

  3 **envelopes unflavored gelatin**
3/4 **cup cold water**
3/4 **cup boiling water**
1-1/2 **cups orange juice**
  2 **tablespoons lemon juice**
1-1/2 **teaspoons grated orange peel**
1-1/2 **cups sugar,** *divided*
2-1/2 **cups heavy whipping cream**
1/2 **cup mandarin oranges**
  3 **maraschino cherries**

In a large bowl, combine gelatin and cold water; let stand for 10 minutes. Add boiling water; stir until gelatin dissolves. Add juices, orange peel and 3/4 cup sugar. Set bowl in ice water until mixture is syrupy, stirring occasionally. Meanwhile, whip cream until soft peaks form. Gradually add remaining sugar and beat until stiff peaks form.

When gelatin mixture begins to thicken, fold in whipped cream. Lightly coat a 9-in. springform pan with nonstick cooking spray. Pour mixture into pan; chill overnight. Just before serving, run a knife around the edge of pan to loosen. Remove sides of pan. Garnish with oranges and cherries. **Yield:** 10-12 servings.

APRICOT CHEESE KUGEL

This sweet noodle kugel is a fun dessert and a super addition to any brunch buffet. My family and friends scrape the pan clean. I got the recipe from my sister.
—Florence Palermo, Melrose Park, Illinois

  1 **package (16 ounces) wide egg noodles**
  1 **package (8 ounces) cream cheese, softened**
  1 **cup butter, softened**
1-1/2 **cups sugar**
1/2 **cup lemon juice**
 12 **eggs**
  1 **jar (18 ounces) apricot preserves**
1/2 **teaspoon ground cinnamon,** *divided*

Cook noodles according to package directions. Meanwhile, in a mixing bowl, beat cream cheese, butter and sugar until smooth; add lemon juice and mix well. Beat in eggs, one at a time. Drain and rinse noodles; add to egg mixture. Spoon half into an ungreased 13-in. x 9-in. x 2-in. baking dish. Top with half of the preserves; sprinkle with half of the cinnamon. Repeat layers.

Bake, uncovered, at 325° for 45 minutes or until golden brown and a knife inserted near the center comes out clean. Serve warm. **Yield:** 12-16 servings.

Editor's Note: Kugel may be reheated in the oven or microwave.

BLUEBERRY SLUMP

My mother-in-law used to make slump with wild blueberries and serve it warm with a pitcher of cream on the table. My husband and I have been eating it for over 65 years, but the recipe is even older!
—Eleanore Ebeling, Brewster, Minnesota

    3   cups fresh *or* frozen blueberries
  1/2   cup sugar
1-1/4   cups water
    1   teaspoon finely grated lemon peel
    1   tablespoon lemon juice
    1   cup all-purpose flour
    2   tablespoons sugar
    2   teaspoons baking powder
  1/2   teaspoon salt
    1   tablespoon butter
  1/2   cup milk
Cream *or* whipped cream, optional

In a large heavy saucepan, combine blueberries, sugar, water, lemon peel and juice; bring to a boil. Reduce heat and simmer, uncovered, for 5 minutes. Meanwhile, combine flour, sugar, baking powder and salt; cut in butter until mixture resembles coarse crumbs. Add milk quickly, mixing until dry ingredients are just moistened.

Drop the dough by spoonfuls into the simmering blueberries (makes six dumplings). Cover and cook over low heat for 10 minutes. Do not lift lid while simmering. Spoon the dumplings into individual serving bowls and spoon some sauce over each. Serve warm with cream or whipped cream if desired. **Yield:** 6 servings.

Family-Tested Tip

To make crumbs from graham crackers, place them in a shallow pan and use a potato masher to crush a small section of crackers at a time.
—*Rene Zummo, Waukesha, Wisconsin*

MOCHA FONDUE

(Pictured below)

People have such fun dipping pieces of pound cake, fresh strawberries and other fruit into this heavenly melted chocolate mixture. With a hint of coffee and cinnamon, it's an exquisite treat to serve at parties or other special events.
—Gloria Jarrett, Loveland, Ohio

    3   cups (18 ounces) milk chocolate chips
  1/2   cup heavy whipping cream
    1   tablespoon instant coffee granules
    2   tablespoons hot water
    1   teaspoon vanilla extract
  1/8   teaspoon ground cinnamon
    1   pound cake (16 ounces), cut into 1-inch cubes
Strawberries, kiwi *or* other fresh fruit

In a heavy saucepan, melt chocolate chips with cream over low heat, stirring constantly. Dissolve coffee in water; add to chocolate mixture with vanilla and cinnamon. Mix well. Serve warm, using cake pieces and fruit for dipping. **Yield:** 2 cups.

In a mixing bowl, cream butter and confectioners' sugar. Beat in the flour (mixture will be crumbly). Pat into the bottom of a greased 12-in. pizza pan. Bake at 300° for 25-28 minutes or until lightly browned. Cool.

In another mixing bowl, beat melted chips and cream. Add cream cheese and beat until smooth. Spread over crust. Chill for 30 minutes. Arrange berries over filling.

In a saucepan, combine pineapple juice, sugar, cornstarch and lemon juice; bring to a boil over medium heat. Boil for 2 minutes or until thickened, stirring constantly. Cool; brush over fruit. Chill 1 hour before serving. Store in the refrigerator. **Yield:** 12-16 servings.

WHITE CHOCOLATE MOUSSE

With blueberries, raspberries or strawberries, this elegant dessert is perfect for summertime. But you can layer the mousse with just about any fresh fruit you like.
—*Susan Herbert, Aurora, Illinois*

1　cup heavy whipping cream
2　tablespoons sugar
1　package (3 ounces) cream cheese, softened
3　squares (1 ounce *each*) white baking chocolate, melted
2　cups blueberries, raspberries *or* strawberries
Additional berries, optional

In a mixing bowl, beat cream until soft peaks form. Gradually add the sugar, beating until stiff peaks form; set aside. In another mixing bowl, beat cream cheese until fluffy. Add chocolate and beat until smooth. Fold in whipped cream.

Alternate layers of mousse and berries in parfait glasses, ending with mousse. Garnish with additional berries if desired. Serve immediately or refrigerate for up to 3 hours. **Yield:** 4-6 servings.

VANILLA CREAM FRUIT TART

(Pictured above)

It's well worth the effort to prepare this spectacular tart, which is best made and served the same day.
—*Susan Terzakis, Andover, Massachusetts*

3/4　cup butter, softened
1/2　cup confectioners' sugar
1-1/2　cups all-purpose flour
1　package (10 to 12 ounces) vanilla *or* white chips, melted and cooled
1/4　cup heavy whipping cream
1　package (8 ounces) cream cheese, softened
1　pint fresh strawberries, sliced
1　cup fresh blueberries
1　cup fresh raspberries
1/2　cup pineapple juice
1/4　cup sugar
1　tablespoon cornstarch
1/2　teaspoon lemon juice

MOCHA CHIP CHEESECAKE

(Pictured at right)

Two favorite flavors—coffee and chocolate—combine in this decadent treat. The chocolate crumb crust and sprinkling of chocolate chips contrast wonderfully with the creamy coffee filling. When you're offering slices of this cheesecake, few people can resist!
—Renee Gastineau, Seattle, Washington

CRUST:
   2 **cups chocolate wafer crumbs (about 32 wafers)**
 1/2 **cup sugar**
 1/2 **cup butter, melted**
FILLING:
   3 **packages (8 ounces *each*) cream cheese, softened**
   1 **cup sugar**
   3 **tablespoons all-purpose flour**
   4 **eggs**
 1/3 **cup heavy whipping cream**
   1 **tablespoon instant coffee granules**
   1 **teaspoon vanilla extract**
   1 **cup (6 ounces) miniature semisweet chocolate chips, *divided***

In a bowl, combine crumbs and sugar; stir in butter. Press onto the bottom and 2 in. up the sides of a greased 9-in. springform pan; set aside. In a mixing bowl, beat cream cheese and sugar until smooth. Add flour and beat well. Add eggs, beating on low speed just until combined.

In a small bowl, combine cream and coffee; let stand for 1 minute. Add to cream cheese mixture with vanilla; beat just until mixed. Stir in 3/4 cup chocolate chips. Pour into crust. Sprinkle with remaining chocolate chips.

Bake at 325° for 50-55 minutes or until center is almost set. Cool on a wire rack for 1 hour. Refrigerate overnight. Remove sides of pan. Let stand at room temperature for 30 minutes before slicing. **Yield:** 12-14 servings.

LUSCIOUS LEMON CHEESECAKE

(Pictured at right)

I'm always greeted with oohs and aahs when I bring out this exquisite dessert. It has a wonderful lemony flavor, silky texture and rich sour cream topping.
—Karen Jurack, Virginia Beach, Virginia

CRUST:
 1-1/4 **cups graham cracker crumbs (about 20 squares)**
  3/4 **cup finely chopped nuts**
  1/4 **cup sugar**
  1/3 **cup butter, melted**
FILLING:
    4 **packages (8 ounces *each*) cream cheese, softened**
 1-1/4 **cups sugar**
    4 **eggs**
    1 **tablespoon lemon juice**
    2 **teaspoons grated lemon peel**
    1 **teaspoon vanilla extract**
TOPPING:
    2 **cups (16 ounces) sour cream**
  1/4 **cup sugar**
    1 **teaspoon grated lemon peel**
    1 **teaspoon vanilla extract**

In a bowl, combine crumbs, nuts and sugar; stir in butter. Press onto the bottom of a greased 10-in. springform pan; set aside. In a mixing bowl, beat cream cheese and sugar until smooth. Add eggs, beating on low speed just until combined. Add lemon juice, peel and vanilla; beat just until blended. Pour into crust.

Bake at 350° for 55 minutes or until center is almost set. Remove from the oven; let stand for 5 minutes. Combine topping ingredients; spread over filling. Return to the oven for 5 minutes. Cool on a wire rack for 10 minutes.

Carefully run a knife around the edge of the pan to loosen; cool 1 hour longer. Refrigerate overnight. Remove the sides of pan. Let stand at room temperature for 30 minutes before slicing. **Yield:** 12-14 servings.

into a ball; cover and refrigerate overnight.

For filling, combine the bread crumbs and butter. Add apples, sugar, raisins, pecans and cinnamon; mix well and set aside. Divide dough into thirds; turn onto a floured board. Roll each into a 15-in. x 12-in. rectangle. Spoon filling evenly onto dough; spread to within 1 in. of edges. Roll up from one long side; pinch seams and ends to seal.

Carefully place each loaf seam side down on an ungreased baking sheet. Bake at 350° for 55-60 minutes or until light brown. Cool completely on wire racks. Dust with confectioners' sugar if desired. **Yield:** 3 loaves.

CHOCOLATE-FILLED CREAM PUFFS

Chocolate lovers always enjoy these pretty puffs, stuffed with a slightly sweet chocolate cream and drizzled with a chocolate glaze.
—Kathy Kittell, Lenexa, Kansas

  1 cup water
  6 tablespoons butter
  1 cup all-purpose flour
1/4 teaspoon salt
  4 eggs
FILLING:
  1 cup heavy whipping cream
1/2 cup confectioners' sugar
  2 tablespoons baking cocoa
GLAZE:
  1 square (1 ounce) unsweetened chocolate
  1 tablespoon butter
1/2 cup confectioners' sugar
  2 tablespoons water

In a saucepan over medium heat, bring water and butter to a boil. Add flour and salt all at once; stir until a smooth ball forms. Remove from the heat; let stand 5 minutes. Add eggs, one at a time, beating well after each. Beat until smooth.

Cover a baking sheet with foil; grease foil. Drop batter into six mounds onto foil. Bake at 400° for 15 minutes. Reduce heat to 350°; bake 30 minutes

APPLE STRUDEL

(Pictured above)

I frequently turn to this recipe during autumn. The aroma of this traditional dessert baking on a cool, crisp day is absolutely wonderful.
—Helen Lesh, Forsyth, Missouri

  1 cup cold butter
  2 cups all-purpose flour
  1 cup (8 ounces) sour cream
1/4 teaspoon salt
FILLING:
  2 cups dry bread crumbs
1/4 cup butter, melted
  4 medium baking apples, peeled and chopped
  2 cups sugar
  1 cup golden raisins
1/2 cup chopped pecans
  2 teaspoons ground cinnamon
Confectioners' sugar, optional

In a medium bowl, cut the butter into the flour until the mixture resembles coarse crumbs. Add the sour cream and salt; mix well. Shape the dough

longer. Remove puffs to a wire rack. Immediately cut a slit in each for steam to escape.

In a mixing bowl, beat cream until soft peaks form. Gradually add sugar and cocoa, beating until almost stiff. Split puffs and remove soft dough. Add filling; replace tops. Melt chocolate and butter; stir in sugar and water. Drizzle over puffs. Chill. **Yield:** 6 servings.

SWEET POTATO COBBLER

(Pictured at right)

My grandmother used to make the best sweet potato cobbler, but, like many cooks, she didn't follow a recipe. This one comes closest to recreating her wonderful dessert and brings back many fond memories.
—*Sherry Parker, Jacksonville, Alabama*

  2 pounds sweet potatoes, peeled and
     sliced 1/4 inch thick
3-1/2 cups water
1-1/2 cups sugar
  3 tablespoons all-purpose flour
1/2 teaspoon ground cinnamon
1/4 teaspoon ground nutmeg
1/4 teaspoon salt
3/4 cup butter, cubed
PASTRY:
  2 cups all-purpose flour
1/2 teaspoon salt
2/3 cup shortening
  5 to 6 tablespoons cold water
  2 tablespoons butter, melted
  4 teaspoons sugar
Whipped cream, optional

In a saucepan, cook potatoes in water until crisp-tender, about 10 minutes. Drain, reserving 1-1/2 cups cooking liquid. Layer potatoes in a greased 13-in. x 9-in. x 2-in. baking dish; add reserved liquid. Combine sugar, flour, cinnamon, nutmeg and salt; sprinkle over potatoes. Dot with butter.

For pastry, combine flour and salt; cut in shortening until mixture resembles coarse crumbs. Gradually add water, tossing with a fork until a ball forms. On a floured surface, roll pastry into a 13-in. x 9-in. rectangle. Place over filling; cut slits in top. Brush with butter; sprinkle with sugar. Bake at 400° for 30-35 minutes or until top is golden brown. Spoon into dishes; top with whipped cream if desired. **Yield:** 10-12 servings.

"Family life is the source of the greatest human happiness. This happiness is the simplest and least costly kind, and it cannot be purchased with money."
—Robert J. Havighurst

CARAMEL PEAR PUDDING

(Pictured at right)

Don't expect this old-fashioned dessert to last long. The delicate pears and irresistible caramel topping make it a winner whenever I serve it.
—Sharon Mensing, Greenfield, Iowa

1   cup all-purpose flour
2/3 cup sugar
1-1/2 teaspoons baking powder
1/2 teaspoon ground cinnamon
1/4 teaspoon salt
Pinch ground cloves
1/2 cup milk
4   medium pears, peeled and cut
    into 1/2-inch cubes
1/2 cup chopped pecans
3/4 cup packed brown sugar
1/4 cup butter
3/4 cup boiling water
Vanilla ice cream *or* whipped cream, optional

In a mixing bowl, combine the first six ingredients; beat in milk until smooth. Stir in pears and pecans. Spoon into an ungreased 2-qt. baking dish. In another bowl, combine brown sugar, butter and water; pour over batter. Bake, uncovered, at 375° for 45-50 minutes. Serve warm with ice cream or whipped cream if desired. **Yield:** 8 servings.

CHOCOLATE PEANUT DELIGHT

For this dessert I created, a brownie-like crust packed with nuts is topped with a peanut butter layer, whipped topping and more nuts. It was so well received that I made it for a restaurant where I used to work.
—Karen Kutruff, New Berlin, Pennsylvania

1   package (18-1/4 ounces) chocolate cake
    mix
1/2 cup butter, melted
1/4 cup milk
1   egg
1   cup chopped peanuts, *divided*

1   package (8 ounces) cream cheese,
    softened
1   cup peanut butter
1   cup confectioners' sugar
1   can (14 ounces) sweetened condensed
    milk
1-1/2 teaspoons vanilla extract
1   carton (16 ounces) frozen whipped
    topping, thawed, *divided*
1/2 cup semisweet chocolate chips
4-1/2 teaspoons butter
1/2 teaspoon vanilla extract

In a mixing bowl, combine dry cake mix, butter, milk and egg. Add 3/4 cup of peanuts. Spread into a greased 13-in. x 9-in. x 2-in. baking pan. Bake at 350° for 30 minutes or until a toothpick inserted near the center comes out clean. Cool on a wire rack.

In a mixing bowl, beat the cream cheese, peanut butter, sugar, condensed milk and vanilla until smooth. Fold in 3 cups whipped topping. Spread over the crust; top with the remaining whipped topping and peanuts.

In a microwave-safe bowl, heat chocolate chips and butter on high for 1 minute or until melted. Stir in vanilla until smooth; drizzle over the dessert. Refrigerate for 2-3 hours before cutting. **Yield:** 12-15 servings.

LIME CHIFFON DESSERT

This make-ahead recipe was given to me by an aunt many years ago. It called for lemon gelatin, but we like this dessert best with lime instead. My whole family thinks the light fluffy squares are great, especially on hot summer days.
—Joyce Key, Snellville, Georgia

1-1/2 cups crushed graham crackers
      (about 24 squares)
  1/3 cup sugar
  1/2 cup butter, melted
FILLING:
    1 package (3 ounces) lime gelatin
    1 cup boiling water
    2 packages (one 8 ounces, one 3 ounces) cream cheese, softened
    1 cup sugar
    1 teaspoon vanilla extract
    1 carton (16 ounces) frozen whipped topping, thawed

Combine the first three ingredients; set aside 2 tablespoons for topping. Press remaining crumbs onto the bottom of an ungreased 13-in. x 9-in. x 2-in. baking dish; set aside. In a bowl, dissolve gelatin in boiling water; cool.

In a mixing bowl, beat cream cheese and sugar. Add vanilla; mix well. Slowly add gelatin until combined. Fold in whipped topping. Spoon over crust; sprinkle with reserved crumbs. Cover and refrigerate for 3 hours or until set. **Yield:** 12-15 servings.

COLORADO PEACH COBBLER

(Pictured at right)

I've served this dessert for family and special guests many times over the years. I've used other fruits that are in season, but we prefer peaches. There's nothing better than a dish of this warm cobbler topped with a big scoop of vanilla ice cream.
—Clara Hinman, Flagler, Colorado

    1 cup sugar
    2 tablespoons all-purpose flour
  1/4 teaspoon ground nutmeg
    4 cups sliced peeled fresh peaches
TOPPING:
    1 cup sugar
    1 cup all-purpose flour
    1 teaspoon baking powder
    1 teaspoon salt
  1/3 cup cold butter
    1 egg, beaten
Ice cream, optional

In a bowl, combine sugar, flour and nutmeg. Add peaches; stir to coat. Pour into a greased 11-in. x 7-in. x 2-in. baking pan. For topping, combine sugar, flour, baking powder and salt; cut in the butter until the mixture resembles fine crumbs. Stir in egg. Spoon over peaches.

Bake at 375° for 35-40 minutes or until filling is bubbly and topping is golden. Serve hot or cold with ice cream if desired. **Yield:** 8-10 servings.

CRANBERRY GRAHAM SQUARES

(Pictured below)

With layers of pudding and whipped topping, this dessert is refreshingly creamy. Plus, it can be prepared in advance, so it's perfect for entertaining during the busy holiday season.
—H. Stevenson, Davidson, Saskatchewan

  2 **cups graham cracker crumbs**
  2 **tablespoons plus 3/4 cup sugar,** *divided*
1/8 **teaspoon salt**
1/2 **cup plus 1 tablespoon butter, melted,**
    divided
  1 **package (3 ounces) cook-and-serve**
    vanilla pudding mix
1-1/2 **cups cranberries**
3/4 **cup raisins**
3/4 **cup water**
  2 **teaspoons cornstarch**
1-1/2 **teaspoons cold water**
  1 **envelope whipped topping mix**

In a bowl, combine cracker crumbs, 2 tablespoons sugar, salt and 1/2 cup butter; set 1/2 cup aside. Press remaining crumbs into an ungreased 9-in. square baking pan. Chill. Meanwhile, cook pudding according to package directions; cool for 5 minutes. Spread over crust. Chill.

In a saucepan over medium heat, cook cranberries, raisins and water until berries pop, about 5-10 minutes. Stir in remaining sugar. Combine cornstarch and cold water until smooth; add to the cranberry mixture. Bring to a boil; cook and stir for 2 minutes. Remove from the heat; stir in remaining butter. Cool to room temperature.

Spread cranberry mixture over pudding layer. Prepare whipped topping according to package directions; spread over cranberry layer. Sprinkle with reserved crumbs. Chill for at least 6 hours. Store in the refrigerator. **Yield:** 9 servings.

CHERRY PECAN TORTE

(Pictured below left)

People are surprised when they hear that soda crackers are the "secret" ingredient in this meringue.
—Dolores Lueken, Ferdinand, Indiana

6 **egg whites**
1/2 **teaspoon cream of tartar**
2 **cups sugar**
2 **cups saltine crumbs**
3/4 **cup chopped pecans**
2 **teaspoons vanilla extract**
2 **cups heavy whipping cream, whipped**
1 **can (21 ounces) cherry pie filling**

In a mixing bowl, beat egg whites until foamy. Beat in cream of tartar. Gradually add sugar, 1 tablespoon at a time, beating on high until stiff peaks form. Fold in crumbs, pecans and vanilla. Spread into a greased 13-in. x 9-in. x 2-in. baking pan. Bake at 350° for 25 minutes. Cool completely. Spread whipped cream over top. Spoon pie filling over cream. Chill for at least 1 hour. **Yield:** 12-15 servings.

RICH TRUFFLE WEDGES

(Pictured above right)

This decadent, fudgy dessert has a big chocolate taste that's complemented by a tart raspberry sauce.
—Patricia Vatta, Norwood, Ontario

1/2 **cup butter**
6 **squares (1 ounce** *each***) semisweet chocolate, chopped**
3 **eggs**
2/3 **cup sugar**
1 **teaspoon vanilla extract**
1/4 **teaspoon salt**
2/3 **cup all-purpose flour**
GLAZE:
1/4 **cup butter**
2 **squares (1 ounce** *each***) semisweet chocolate**
2 **squares (1 ounce** *each***) unsweetened chocolate**
2 **teaspoons honey**
SAUCE:
2 **cups fresh** *or* **frozen unsweetened raspberries**
2 **tablespoons sugar**
Whipped cream, fresh raspberries and mint

In a microwave or double boiler, melt butter and chocolate; stir until smooth. Cool for 10 minutes. In a mixing bowl, beat the eggs, sugar, vanilla and salt until thick, about 4 minutes. Blend in chocolate mixture. Stir in flour; mix well. Pour into a greased and floured 9-in. springform pan. Bake at 350° for 25-30 minutes or until a toothpick inserted near the center comes out clean. Cool completely on a wire rack.

Combine the glaze ingredients in a small saucepan; cook and stir over low heat until melted and smooth. Cool slightly. Run a knife around the edge of the springform pan to loosen; remove cake to serving plate. Spread glaze over the top and sides; set aside.

For sauce, puree raspberries in a blender or food processor. Press through a sieve if desired; discard seeds. Stir in sugar; chill until serving. Spoon sauce over individual servings. Garnish with whipped cream, raspberries and mint. **Yield:** 12 servings.

CHOCOLATE AND FRUIT TRIFLE

(Pictured below)

With red and green fruit dressing up the cake and pudding layers, this trifle is perfect for Christmas.
—Angie Dierikx, State Center, Iowa

1 package (18-1/4 ounces) devil's food cake mix
1 can (14 ounces) sweetened condensed milk
1 cup cold water
1 package (3.4 ounces) instant vanilla pudding mix
2 cups heavy whipping cream, whipped
2 tablespoons orange juice
2 cups fresh strawberries, chopped
2 cups fresh raspberries
2 kiwifruit, peeled and chopped

Prepare cake batter according to package directions; pour into a greased 15-in. x 10-in. x 1-in. baking pan. Bake at 350° for 20 minutes or until a tooth-pick inserted near the center comes out clean. Cool completely on a wire rack. Crumble enough cake to measure 8 cups; set aside. (Save remaining cake for another use.)

In a mixing bowl, combine milk and water until smooth. Add pudding mix; beat on low speed for 2 minutes or until slightly thickened. Fold in the whipped cream. To assemble, spread 2-1/2 cups pudding mixture in a 4-qt. glass bowl. Top with half of the crumbled cake; sprinkle with 1 table-spoon orange juice. Arrange half of the berries and kiwi over cake.

Repeat pudding and cake layers; sprinkle with remaining orange juice. Top with remaining pudding mixture. Spoon remaining fruit around edge of bowl. Cover and refrigerate until serving. **Yield:** 12-16 servings.

"The family—that dear octopus from whose tentacles we never quite escape, nor, in our inmost hearts, ever quite wish to."
—Dodie Smith

CHERRY BERRIES ON A CLOUD

Whenever I serve this elegant dessert, I'm sure to be asked for the recipe. The base truly is as light as air.
—Darlene Alexander, Nekoosa, Wisconsin

6 egg whites
1/2 teaspoon cream of tartar
1/4 teaspoon salt
1-3/4 cups sugar

FILLING:

- 2 packages (3 ounces *each*) cream cheese, softened
- 1 cup sugar
- 1 teaspoon vanilla extract
- 2 cups heavy whipping cream, whipped
- 2 cups miniature marshmallows

TOPPING:

- 1 can (21 ounces) cherry pie filling
- 2 cups sliced fresh strawberries
- 1 teaspoon lemon juice

In a mixing bowl, beat egg whites, cream of tartar and salt until foamy. Gradually add sugar, 1 table-spoon at a time, beating on high until stiff peaks form (do not underbeat). Spread evenly in a greased 13-in. x 9-in. x 2-in. baking pan. Bake at 275° for 1 hour; turn off oven (do not open door). Let cool in oven overnight or for at least 12 hours.

Beat cream cheese, sugar and vanilla until smooth; gently fold in whipped cream and marsh-mallows. Spread over meringue. Chill for 4 hours. Cut into 16 pieces. Combine topping ingredients; spoon 1/4 cup over each serving. **Yield:** 16 servings.

Frozen Mocha Marbled Loaf

(Pictured above right)

This showstopping marbled dessert seems fancy, but it's really simple to prepare ahead of time and pop in the freezer. Frosty slices have a creamy blend of chocolate and coffee that's delightful any time of year.
—Cheryl Martinetto, Grand Rapids, Minnesota

- 2 cups finely crushed chocolate cream-filled sandwich cookies (about 22 cookies)
- 3 tablespoons butter, melted
- 1 package (8 ounces) cream cheese, softened
- 1 can (14 ounces) sweetened condensed milk

- 1 teaspoon vanilla extract
- 2 cups heavy whipping cream, whipped
- 2 tablespoons instant coffee granules
- 1 tablespoon hot water
- 1/2 cup chocolate syrup

Line a 9-in. x 5-in. x 3-in. loaf pan with foil. In a bowl, combine the cookie crumbs and butter. Press firmly onto the bottom and 1-1/2 in. up the sides of prepared pan.

In a mixing bowl, beat cream cheese until light. Add milk and vanilla; mix well. Fold in whipped cream. Spoon half of the mixture into another bowl and set aside. Dissolve coffee in hot water; fold into remaining cream cheese mixture. Fold in chocolate syrup.

Spoon half of the chocolate mixture over crust. Top with half of the reserved cream cheese mixture. Repeat layers. Cut through layers with a knife to swirl the chocolate (the pan will be full). Cover and freeze for 6 hours or overnight. To serve, lift out of pan; remove foil. Cut into slices. **Yield:** 12 servings.

Family-Tested Tips

Allow ice cream desserts to sit at room temperature for 10 minutes before serving. They'll soften slightly, making them easier to cut.
—*Elaine Nivins, Ardrossan, Alberta*

When a bottle of corn syrup is getting low, it can take quite a while for the remaining syrup to pour out. To help speed up the process, try running the capped bottle under hot water.
—*Vivian Tolson, Westville, Indiana*

CARAMEL FRIED ICE CREAM

For birthday parties or outdoor barbecues, this is a hit. I sometimes substitute strawberry or Neapolitan for the vanilla ice cream.
—*Darlene Markel, Sublimity, Oregon*

  1 quart vanilla ice cream
1/4 cup heavy whipping cream
  2 teaspoons vanilla extract
  2 cups flaked coconut, finely chopped
  2 cups finely crushed cornflakes
1/2 teaspoon ground cinnamon
CARAMEL SAUCE:
  1 cup sugar
1/2 cup butter
1/2 cup evaporated milk
Oil for deep-fat frying

Using a 1/2-cup ice cream scoop, place eight scoops of ice cream on a baking sheet. Cover and freeze for 2 hours or until firm. In a bowl, combine whipping cream and vanilla. In another bowl, combine coconut, cornflakes and cinnamon.

Remove scoops of ice cream from freezer; wearing plastic gloves, shape the ice cream into balls. Dip balls into cream mixture, then roll in coconut mixture, making sure to coat entire surface. Place coated balls on a baking sheet. Cover and freeze at least 3 hours or until firm.

For the caramel sauce, heat sugar in a heavy

BLACKBERRY COBBLER

(Pictured above)

In summer, blackberries abound in fields and along country roads around here. It's fun to pick them, especially when we know this dessert will be the result.
—*Tina Hankins, Laconia, New Hampshire*

1/4 cup butter, softened
1/2 cup sugar
  1 cup all-purpose flour
  2 teaspoons baking powder
1/2 cup milk
  2 cups fresh *or* frozen blackberries
3/4 cup raspberry *or* apple juice
Ice cream *or* whipped cream, optional

In a mixing bowl, cream butter and sugar. Combine flour and baking powder; add to creamed mixture alternately with milk. Stir just until moistened. Pour into a greased 1-1/2-qt. baking pan. Sprinkle with blackberries. Pour juice over all.

Bake at 350° for 45-50 minutes or until golden brown. Serve warm; top with ice cream or cream if desired. **Yield:** 6-8 servings.

saucepan over medium heat until partially melted and golden, stirring occasionally. Add butter. Gradually add milk, stirring constantly. Cook and stir for 8 minutes or until sauce is thick and golden; keep warm.

Heat oil in an electric skillet or deep-fat fryer to 375°. Fry ice cream balls until golden, about 30 seconds. Drain on paper towels. Serve immediately with caramel sauce. **Yield:** 8 servings.

LADYFINGER CHEESECAKE

(Pictured below)

Raspberry, strawberry or cherry pie filling gives a festive appearance to this rich no-bake cheesecake. The elegant-looking dessert makes a dramatic presentation that prompts recipe requests.
—Irene Pitzer, Madison, Tennessee

- 2 packages (11.1 ounces *each*) no-bake cheesecake mix
- 2/3 cup butter, melted
- 1/4 cup sugar
- 1 package (3 ounces) ladyfingers (25 cookies)
- 1 package (8 ounces) cream cheese, softened
- 3 cups cold milk, *divided*
- 1 carton (12 ounces) frozen whipped topping, thawed

- 1 can (21 ounces) raspberry pie filling *or* flavor of your choice

In a bowl, combine contents of crust mix packages, butter and sugar. Press onto the bottom of an ungreased 10-in. springform pan. Arrange ladyfingers around edge of pan.

In a mixing bowl, beat cream cheese and 1/2 cup milk until smooth. Gradually beat in remaining milk. Add the contents of the filling mix packages; beat until smooth. Beat on medium for 3 minutes. Fold in whipped topping. Pour over crust. Cover and refrigerate for at least 1 hour. Top with pie filling. Remove the sides of pan before serving. **Yield:** 12 servings.

RHUBARB STRAWBERRY CRUNCH

Garden-fresh rhubarb is put to great use in this easy recipe. It's wonderful with ice cream.
—Barbara Foss, Waukesha, Wisconsin

- 1 cup all-purpose flour
- 1 cup packed brown sugar
- 3/4 cup quick-cooking oats
- 1 teaspoon ground cinnamon
- 1/2 cup butter
- 4 cups sliced fresh *or* frozen rhubarb
- 1 pint fresh strawberries, halved
- 1 cup sugar
- 2 tablespoons cornstarch
- 1 cup water
- 1 teaspoon vanilla extract

Vanilla ice cream, optional

In a bowl, combine the first four ingredients; cut in butter until crumbly. Press half into an ungreased 9-in. square baking pan. Combine rhubarb and strawberries; spoon over crust.

In a saucepan, combine sugar and cornstarch. Stir in the water and vanilla; bring to a boil over medium heat. Cook and stir for 2 minutes. Pour over fruit. Sprinkle with remaining crumb mixture. Bake at 350° for 1 hour. Serve with ice cream if desired. **Yield:** 9 servings.

Chapter eleven

Making a grand entrance into family feasts,

these sensational cakes and prize-worthy pies

prepared by family bakers have made eyes light up

for generations. Whether your family's tastes lean

toward a home-style apple pie or a frosted

layer cake, look here to find best-loved recipes.

Butter Pecan Cake
(Recipe on page 238)

♥ Cakes & Pies

Bake at 350° for 35-40 minutes or until a tooth-pick inserted near the center of cake comes out clean. Cool. **Yield:** 9 servings.

AUNT LILLIAN'S CRUMB CAKE

(Pictured above)

I was treated to my aunt's cake every weekend when we went to visit. She created this recipe back in the '40s.
—Rose Gearheard, Phoenix, Oregon

1/2	cup butter, softened
1	cup sugar
2	eggs
1	cup (8 ounces) sour cream
1	teaspoon vanilla extract
1-1/2	cups all-purpose flour
1	teaspoon baking soda
1/4	teaspoon salt

TOPPING:

1/2	cup sugar
1/4	cup chopped walnuts
2	tablespoons flaked coconut
2	teaspoons ground cinnamon

In a mixing bowl, cream the butter and sugar. Add eggs, one at a time, beating well after each addition. Add the sour cream and vanilla; mix well. Combine flour, baking soda and salt; add to the creamed mixture and mix well. Spread half into a greased 9-in. square baking pan.

Combine the topping ingredients; sprinkle half over the batter. Carefully spread the remaining batter on top; sprinkle with the remaining topping. Gently swirl topping through batter with a knife.

BUTTER PECAN CAKE

(Pictured on page 237)

This sweet, delicious cake is one that my family's enjoyed for many years. It's a special dessert we have on Thanksgiving and Christmas.
—Becky Miller, Tallahassee, Florida

2-2/3	cups chopped pecans
1-1/4	cups butter, softened, *divided*
2	cups sugar
4	eggs
3	cups all-purpose flour
2	teaspoons baking powder
1/2	teaspoon salt
1	cup milk
2	teaspoons vanilla extract

FROSTING:

1	cup butter, softened
8	to 8-1/2 cups confectioners' sugar
1	can (5 ounces) evaporated milk
2	teaspoons vanilla extract

Place pecans and 1/4 cup of butter in a baking pan. Bake at 350° for 20-25 minutes or until toasted, stirring frequently; set aside.

In a mixing bowl, cream sugar and remaining butter. Add eggs, one at a time, beating well after each addition. Combine flour, baking powder and salt; add to the creamed mixture alternately with milk. Stir in vanilla and 1-1/3 cups of toasted pecans.

Pour the batter into three greased and floured 9-in. round cake pans. Bake at 350° for 25-30 minutes. Cool the cakes for 10 minutes; remove from pans to cool on a wire rack.

For the frosting, cream butter and sugar in a mixing bowl. Add milk and vanilla; beat until smooth. Stir in the remaining toasted pecans. Spread frosting between layers and over top and sides of cake. **Yield:** 12-16 servings.

TRADITIONAL PUMPKIN PIE

(Pictured below)

I don't need to remind family members to save room for this pie. The filling is rich and custard-like, and the pastry recipe is one I've used for as long as I can remember.
—Gloria Warczak, Cedarburg, Wisconsin

  2 cups all-purpose flour
3/4 teaspoon salt
2/3 cup shortening
  4 to 6 tablespoons cold water
FILLING:
  6 eggs
  1 can (29 ounces) solid-pack pumpkin
  2 cups packed brown sugar
  2 teaspoons ground cinnamon
  1 teaspoon salt
1/2 teaspoon *each* ground cloves, nutmeg and ginger
  2 cups evaporated milk

In a bowl, combine flour and salt; cut in shortening until crumbly. Sprinkle with water, 1 tablespoon at a time, tossing with a fork until dough forms a ball. Divide dough in half. On a floured surface, roll out each portion to fit a 9-in. pie plate. Place pastry in plates; trim pastry (set the scraps aside if leaf cutouts are desired) and flute edges. Set shells aside.

For the filling, beat the eggs in a mixing bowl. Add the pumpkin, brown sugar, cinnamon, salt, cloves, nutmeg and ginger; beat just until smooth. Gradually stir in the milk. Pour the filling into the pastry shells. Bake at 450° for 10 minutes. Reduce heat to 350°; bake 40-45 minutes longer or until a knife inserted near the center comes out clean. Cool pies on wire racks.

If desired, cut pastry scraps with a 1-in. leaf-shaped cookie cutter; place on an ungreased baking sheet. Bake at 350° for 10-15 minutes or until lightly browned. Place on baked pies. **Yield:** 2 pies (6-8 servings each).

STRAWBERRY RHUBARB PIE

(Pictured on the front cover)

My niece tasted this pie at a family dinner and urged me to enter it in our hometown pie contest. She said it would win the Grand Prize, and she was right! I cook at our local nursing home, and everyone enjoys this recipe.
—Janice Schmidt, Baxter, Iowa

  2 tablespoons cornstarch
  1 cup sugar
  1 cup water
  1 cup sliced rhubarb
1/2 of a 3-ounce package strawberry-flavored gelatin
  2 pints fresh strawberries, halved
  1 pastry shell (9 inches), baked

In a medium saucepan, mix cornstarch and sugar. Stir in water until smooth. Add rhubarb; cook and stir until clear and thickened. Add gelatin and stir until dissolved. Cool. Pour about half of rhubarb sauce into pastry shell. Arrange berries over sauce; top with remaining sauce. Refrigerate 3-4 hours. **Yield:** 8 servings.

BLUEBERRY CREAM PIE

(Pictured at right)

Whenever I ask my family which pie they'd like me to make, everyone gives the same answer—Blueberry Cream Pie! It's their all-time favorite.
—Kim Erickson, Sturgis, Michigan

1-1/3 cups vanilla wafer crumbs
   2 tablespoons sugar
   5 tablespoons butter, melted
 1/2 teaspoon vanilla extract
FILLING:
 1/4 cup sugar
   3 tablespoons all-purpose flour
Pinch salt
   1 cup half-and-half cream
   3 egg yolks, beaten
   3 tablespoons butter
   1 teaspoon vanilla extract
   1 tablespoon confectioners' sugar
TOPPING:
   5 cups fresh blueberries, *divided*
 2/3 cup sugar
   1 tablespoon cornstarch

Combine the first four ingredients; press into the bottom and sides of an ungreased 9-in. pie pan. Bake at 350° for 8-10 minutes or until crust just begins to brown. Cool.

In a saucepan, combine sugar, flour and salt. Gradually whisk in cream; cook and stir over medium heat until thickened and bubbly. Cook and stir 2 minutes more. Gradually whisk half into egg yolks; return all to saucepan. Bring to a gentle boil; cook and stir 2 minutes. Remove from heat; stir in butter and vanilla until butter is melted. Cool 5 minutes, stirring occasionally. Pour into crust; sprinkle with confectioners' sugar. Chill 30 minutes or until set.

Meanwhile, crush 2 cups of blueberries in a medium saucepan; bring to a boil. Boil 2 minutes, stirring constantly. Press blueberries through a sieve; set aside 1 cup juice (add water if necessary). Discard pulp. In a saucepan, combine sugar and cornstarch. Gradually stir in blueberry juice; bring to a boil. Boil 2 minutes, stirring constantly. Remove from heat; cool 15 minutes. Gently stir in remaining blueberries; carefully spoon over filling. Chill 3 hours or until set. Store pie in the refrigerator. **Yield:** 6-8 servings.

BANANA CREAM PIE

Made from our farm-fresh dairy products, this pie was a sensational creamy treat any time that Mom served it. Her recipe is a real treasure, and I've never found one that tastes better.
—Bernice Morris, Marshfield, Missouri

3/4 cup sugar
1/3 cup all-purpose flour
1/4 teaspoon salt
  2 cups milk
  3 egg yolks, lightly beaten
  2 tablespoons butter
  1 teaspoon vanilla extract
  1 pastry shell (9 inches), baked
  3 medium firm bananas
Whipped cream and additional sliced bananas

In a saucepan, combine sugar, flour and salt; stir in milk and mix well. Cook and stir over medium-high heat until the mixture is thickened and bubbly. Cook and stir for 2 minutes longer. Remove from the heat. Stir a small amount into egg yolks; return all to saucepan. Bring to a gentle boil. Cook and stir for 2 minutes; remove from the heat. Add butter and vanilla; cool slightly.

Slice the bananas into pastry shell; pour filling over top. Cool on wire rack for 1 hour. Store in the refrigerator. Before serving, garnish with whipped cream and bananas. **Yield:** 6-8 servings.

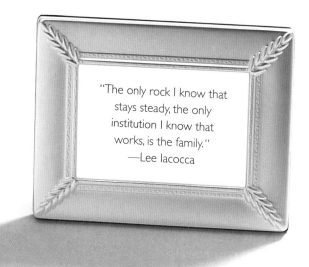

"The only rock I know that stays steady, the only institution I know that works, is the family."
—Lee Iacocca

POTLUCK APPLE PIE

(Pictured below right)

I experimented and came up with this scrumptious pie made in a jelly roll pan. It fed a large group and disappeared in a hurry.
—Alma Lynne Gravel, Trappe, Pennsylvania

2-1/4 **cups all-purpose flour,** *divided*
  1/4 **cup water**
Pinch salt
    1 **cup shortening**
FILLING:
  1/2 **cup maple syrup,** *divided*
    3 **pounds tart apples (8 to 9 medium), peeled and thinly sliced**
1-1/4 **cups sugar**
  1/4 **cup lemon juice**
    2 **teaspoons ground cinnamon**
    1 **teaspoon vanilla extract**
TOPPING:
    1 **cup all-purpose flour**
  1/2 **cup packed brown sugar**
  1/2 **cup cold butter**
    1 **cup chopped pecans**

In a small bowl, combine 1/4 cup flour and water until smooth; set aside. In a large bowl, combine salt and remaining flour; cut in shortening until mixture resembles coarse crumbs. Add reserved flour mixture; knead gently until dough forms a ball. Press dough onto the bottom and up the sides of an ungreased 15-in. x 10-in. x 1-in. baking pan.

Spread 1/4 cup syrup over crust. Arrange apples over syrup. Combine sugar, lemon juice, cinnamon, vanilla and remaining syrup; drizzle over apples. For topping, combine flour and sugar in a bowl; cut in butter until the mixture resembles coarse crumbs. Stir in pecans. Sprinkle over filling. Bake at 350° for 1 hour or until apples are tender. **Yield:** 18-24 servings.

Editor's Note: Pastry can be easily pressed into pan by placing a large sheet of plastic wrap on top of the dough.

CHERRY ALMOND PIE

(Pictured below)

I grew up in northern Michigan, where three generations of my family have been cherry producers. This traditional cherry pie makes a mouth-watering dessert.
—Ramona Pleva, Lincoln Park, New Jersey

    4 cups pitted canned *or* frozen tart red
      cherries
  3/4 cup sugar
    1 tablespoon butter
Pinch salt
  1/4 cup cornstarch
  1/3 cup cold water
  1/4 teaspoon almond extract
  1/4 teaspoon red food coloring, optional
Pastry for double-crust pie (9 inches)

Drain cherries, reserving 2/3 cup juice in a saucepan; discard remaining juice. To the juice, add cherries, sugar, butter and salt. In a small bowl, combine cornstarch and water until smooth; stir into cherry mixture. Bring to a boil over medium heat. Cook and stir for 2 minutes or until thickened and bubbly. Remove from the heat; stir in the almond extract and food coloring if desired. Cool.

Line a 9-in. pie plate with bottom pastry; add filling. Make a lattice crust. Trim, seal and flute edges. Bake at 375° for 45-50 minutes or until crust

is golden brown and filling is bubbly. Cool on a wire rack. **Yield:** 6-8 servings.

COCONUT ORANGE CUPCAKES

These yummy treats feature a delightful combination of coconut, mandarin oranges and vanilla chips.
—Donna Justin, Sparta, Wisconsin

    1 cup sugar
  2/3 cup vegetable oil
    2 eggs
    1 cup orange juice
    3 cups all-purpose flour
    1 tablespoon baking powder
    1 teaspoon baking soda
  3/4 teaspoon salt
    1 can (11 ounces) mandarin oranges,
      drained
    1 cup vanilla *or* white chips
TOPPING:
    1 cup flaked coconut
  1/3 cup sugar
    2 tablespoons butter, melted

In a mixing bowl, combine the sugar, oil, eggs and orange juice; mix well. Combine dry ingredients; stir into orange juice mixture just until moistened. Fold in the oranges and chips. Fill greased or paper-lined muffin cups two-thirds full. Combine topping ingredients; sprinkle over cupcakes. Bake at 375° for 15-20 minutes or until golden brown. **Yield:** 2 dozen.

Super Strawberry Shortcake

(Pictured above)

"Wow!" is what people say when I bring out this dessert. It's fun to serve and bursting with fabulous flavor.
—Renee Bisch, Wellesley, Ontario

1 quart fresh strawberries, sliced
1 to 2 tablespoons sugar
SHORTCAKE:
1-3/4 cups all-purpose flour
2 tablespoons sugar
1 tablespoon baking powder
1/2 teaspoon baking soda
1/2 teaspoon salt
1/4 cup cold butter
1 egg
3/4 cup sour cream
TOPPING:
1 cup heavy whipping cream
1 to 2 tablespoons sugar
1 teaspoon vanilla extract

Combine the strawberries and sugar; set aside. For shortcake, combine dry ingredients in a large bowl; cut in butter until crumbly. In a small bowl, beat egg; add sour cream. Stir into the crumb mixture just until moistened. Turn onto a floured board; knead 25 times or until smooth. Roll out into a 7-1/2-in. circle. Cut a 2-in. hole in center to form a ring. Place on a lightly greased baking sheet. Bake at 425° for 12-14 minutes or until golden. Remove from baking sheet; cool on a wire rack.

For topping, beat cream and sugar until stiff peaks form; stir in vanilla. Just before serving, split cake horizontally. Spoon juice from berries over bottom layer. Spoon half of berries over juice. Spread half of topping over berries. Add the top cake layer, remaining topping and berries. Cut into wedges. **Yield:** 8 servings.

LEMON SUPREME PIE

(Pictured at left)

A friend and I often visit a local restaurant for pie and coffee. When they stopped carrying our favorite dessert, I got busy and created this version, which we think tastes even better! The combination of cream cheese and tart lemon is wonderful.
—Jana Beckman, Wamego, Kansas

1 unbaked deep-dish pastry shell
(9 inches)
LEMON FILLING:
1-1/4 cups sugar, *divided*
6 tablespoons cornstarch
1/2 teaspoon salt
1-1/4 cups water
2 tablespoons butter
2 teaspoons grated lemon peel
4 to 5 drops yellow food coloring,
optional
1/2 cup fresh lemon juice
CREAM CHEESE FILLING:
2 packages (one 8 ounces, one 3 ounces)
cream cheese, softened
3/4 cup confectioners' sugar
1-1/2 cups whipped topping
1 tablespoon fresh lemon juice

Line the unpricked pastry shell with a double thickness of heavy-duty foil. Bake at 450° for 8 minutes. Remove the foil; bake 5 minutes longer. Cool on a wire rack.

In a saucepan, combine 3/4 cup sugar, cornstarch and salt. Stir in water; bring to a boil over medium-high heat. Reduce heat; add the remaining sugar. Cook and stir for 2 minutes or until thickened and bubbly. Remove from the heat; stir in butter, grated lemon peel and food coloring if desired. Gently stir in lemon juice (do not overmix). Cool to room temperature, about 1 hour. Do not stir.

In a mixing bowl, beat the cream cheese and sugar until smooth. Fold in whipped topping and lemon juice. Refrigerate 1/2 cup for garnish. Spread remaining cream cheese mixture into pastry shell; top with lemon filling. Chill overnight.

Place reserved cream cheese mixture in a pastry bag with a #21 star tip; pipe stars onto pie. Store in the refrigerator. **Yield:** 6-8 servings.

CHEDDAR PEAR PIE

(Pictured at left)

I take this pie to lots of different gatherings, and I make sure to bring copies of the recipe because people always ask for it. It's amusing to see some folks puzzling over what's in the filling—they expect apples but love the subtle flavor of the pears.
—Cynthia LaBree, Elmer, New Jersey

4 large ripe pears, peeled and thinly sliced
1/3 cup sugar
1 tablespoon cornstarch
1/8 teaspoon salt
1 unbaked pastry shell (9 inches)
TOPPING:
1/2 cup shredded cheddar cheese
1/2 cup all-purpose flour
1/4 cup butter, melted
1/4 cup sugar
1/4 teaspoon salt

In a bowl, combine pears, sugar, cornstarch and salt. Pour into pastry shell. Combine topping ingredients until crumbly; sprinkle over filling.

Bake at 425° for 25-35 minutes or until crust is golden and cheese is melted. Cool on a wire rack for 15-20 minutes. Serve warm. Store in the refrigerator. **Yield:** 6-8 servings.

CARROT LAYER CAKE

(Pictured below right)

My sister gave me this recipe for what she called "the ultimate carrot cake"…and it really lives up to the name. When people cut into it, they're bowled over by the moist, not-too-sweet cake that features an unexpected treat—a pecan filling. It's a dessert that turns any meal into a special occasion.
—Linda Van Holland, Innisfail, Alberta

FILLING:
- 1 cup sugar
- 2 tablespoons all-purpose flour
- 1/4 teaspoon salt
- 1 cup heavy whipping cream
- 1/2 cup butter
- 1 cup chopped pecans
- 1 teaspoon vanilla extract

CAKE:
- 1-1/4 cups vegetable oil
- 2 cups sugar
- 2 cups all-purpose flour
- 2 teaspoons ground cinnamon
- 2 teaspoons baking powder
- 1 teaspoon baking soda
- 1 teaspoon salt
- 4 eggs
- 4 cups finely shredded carrots
- 1 cup raisins
- 1 cup chopped pecans

FROSTING:
- 3/4 cup butter, softened
- 2 packages (3 ounces *each*) cream cheese, softened
- 1 teaspoon vanilla extract
- 3 cups confectioners' sugar

In a heavy saucepan, combine sugar, flour and salt. Stir in cream; add butter. Cook and stir over medium heat until the butter is melted; bring to a boil. Reduce heat. Simmer, uncovered, for 30 minutes, stirring occasionally. Stir in nuts and vanilla. Set aside to cool.

In a mixing bowl, beat oil and sugar for 1 minute. Combine flour, cinnamon, baking powder, baking soda and salt; add to the creamed mixture alternately with eggs. Mix well. Stir in carrots, raisins and nuts. Pour into three greased and floured 9-in. round baking pans. Bake at 350° for 35-40 minutes or until a toothpick inserted near the center comes out clean. Cool in pans 10 minutes; remove to wire racks and cool completely.

For the frosting, beat butter, cream cheese and vanilla until smooth. Gradually beat in sugar. Spread the filling between the cake layers. Frost the sides and top of cake. Store in the refrigerator. **Yield:** 16-20 servings.

Family-Tested Tip

To pack a piece of frosted sheet cake in a lunch box, slice the cake in half horizontally and make a sandwich with the frosting in the middle. You won't have to worry about it sticking to the plastic wrap.
—Carmelita Pile, Los Angeles, California

Pumpkin Cake Roll

(Pictured at right)

This lovely cake is delicious—especially if you like cream cheese and pumpkin. It tastes so good in fall and makes a fancy dessert for Thanksgiving, too.
—Elizabeth Montgomery, Taylorville, Illinois

- 3 eggs
- 1 cup sugar
- 2/3 cup cooked *or* canned pumpkin
- 1 teaspoon lemon juice
- 3/4 cup all-purpose flour
- 2 teaspoons ground cinnamon
- 1 teaspoon baking powder
- 1/2 teaspoon salt
- 1/4 teaspoon ground nutmeg
- 1 cup finely chopped walnuts

CREAM CHEESE FILLING:
- 2 packages (3 ounces *each*) cream cheese, softened
- 1 cup confectioners' sugar
- 1/4 cup butter, softened
- 1/2 teaspoon vanilla extract

Additional confectioners' sugar

In a mixing bowl, beat eggs on high for 5 minutes. Gradually beat in sugar until thick and lemon-colored. Add pumpkin and lemon juice. Combine flour, cinnamon, baking powder, salt and nutmeg; fold into pumpkin mixture.

Grease a 15-in. x 10-in. x 1-in. baking pan and line with waxed paper. Grease and flour the paper. Spread batter into pan; sprinkle with walnuts. Bake at 375° for 15 minutes or until cake springs back when lightly touched. Immediately turn out onto a linen towel dusted with confectioners' sugar. Peel off paper and roll cake up in towel, starting with a short end. Cool.

Meanwhile, in a mixing bowl, beat cream cheese, sugar, butter and vanilla until fluffy. Carefully unroll the cake. Spread the filling over cake to within 1 in. of edges. Roll up again. Cover and chill until serving. Dust with confectioners' sugar. **Yield:** 8-10 servings.

Coconut Pie

This old-fashioned dessert is easy to assemble, so it's one I rely on when dinnertime's fast approaching. I sometimes sprinkle slices with cinnamon or nutmeg.
— Virginia Krites, Cridersville, Ohio

- 2 cups milk
- 1 cup sugar
- 4 eggs
- 1/2 cup all-purpose flour
- 6 tablespoons butter
- 1 teaspoon vanilla extract
- 1/2 teaspoon salt
- 1 cup coconut

In a blender, combine the first seven ingredients. Cover and blend for 10 seconds; scrape sides. Blend another 10 seconds. Add coconut; blend for 2 seconds. Pour into a greased 10-in. pie plate.

Bake at 350° for 50-55 minutes or until a knife inserted near center comes out clean. Serve warm. **Yield:** 6 servings.

APRICOT TORTE

(Pictured above)

This elegant dessert is easy to make and so pretty. The chocolate buttercream really complements the apricot filling.
—Dorothy Pritchett, Wills Point, Texas

6 eggs, *separated*
1/2 cup plus 5 tablespoons sugar, *divided*
1 cup all-purpose flour
CHOCOLATE BUTTERCREAM:
  1/4 cup sugar
  3 eggs plus 2 egg yolks
  1 teaspoon vanilla extract
  1 teaspoon instant coffee granules
  2 squares (1 ounce *each*) semisweet
    chocolate
  1 cup butter, softened
APRICOT FILLING:
  2 cans (17 ounces *each*) apricot halves,
    drained
  1 cup apricot preserves
Chocolate curls

In a large mixing bowl, beat egg yolks and 1/2 cup sugar until thickened. In a small mixing bowl, beat egg whites until foamy. Gradually add remaining sugar, beating until stiff peaks form. Fold into yolk mixture. Gradually fold in flour. Divide batter between three greased and floured 9-in. round cake pans. Bake at 350° for 15 minutes or until golden. Cool in pans for 5 minutes; remove to wire racks to cool.

For buttercream, whisk sugar, eggs, yolks, vanilla and coffee in a saucepan. Add chocolate; cook and stir over low heat until thickened (do not boil). Cool completely. In a mixing bowl, cream butter. Gradually add the chocolate mixture; set aside.

Finely chop apricots; drain and place in a bowl. Stir in preserves; set aside. Split each cake into two horizontal layers; place one on a plate. Spread with 2/3 cup buttercream. Top with a cake layer and 2/3 cup apricot filling. Repeat layers twice. Cover and refrigerate 3 hours before serving. Garnish with chocolate curls. **Yield:** 12 servings.

CHERRY PUDDING CAKE

A cross between a cake and a cobbler, this dessert is one I've been making and sharing for over 30 years. Whenever I plan on bringing it to a potluck supper or other gathering, my family insists that I prepare an extra cake to leave at home!
—Brenda Parker, Kalamazoo, Michigan

    2 cups all-purpose flour
2-1/2 cups sugar, *divided*
    4 teaspoons baking powder
    1 cup milk
    2 tablespoons vegetable oil
    2 cans (14-1/2 ounces *each*) water-packed pitted tart red cherries, well drained
    2 to 3 drops red food coloring, optional
  1/8 teaspoon almond extract
Whipped cream *or* ice cream, optional

In a mixing bowl, combine flour, 1 cup of sugar, baking powder, milk and oil; pour into a greased shallow 3-qt. baking dish. In a bowl, combine cherries, food coloring if desired, extract and remaining sugar; spoon over batter.

Bake at 375° for 40-45 minutes or until a toothpick inserted in the cake portion comes out clean. Serve warm with whipped cream or ice cream if desired. **Yield:** 10-12 servings.

SPICED PINEAPPLE UPSIDE-DOWN CAKE

(Pictured at right)

I often bake this beautiful cake in my large iron skillet, but you can also use a 9 x 13 baking pan. I guarantee your family will enjoy this old-fashioned dessert.
—Jennifer Sergesketter, Newburgh, Indiana

1-1/3 cups butter, softened, *divided*
    1 cup packed brown sugar
    1 can (20 ounces) pineapple slices, drained
  10 to 12 maraschino cherries

  1/2 cup chopped pecans
1-1/2 cups sugar
    2 eggs
    1 teaspoon vanilla extract
    2 cups all-purpose flour
    2 teaspoons baking powder
  1/2 teaspoon baking soda
  1/2 teaspoon salt
  1/2 teaspoon ground cinnamon
  1/2 teaspoon ground nutmeg
    1 cup buttermilk

In a small saucepan, melt 2/3 cup of butter; stir in brown sugar. Spread in the bottom of an ungreased heavy 12-in. skillet or a 13-in. x 9-in. x 2-in. baking pan. Arrange pineapple in a single layer over sugar mixture; place a cherry in the center of each slice. Sprinkle with pecans and set aside.

In a mixing bowl, cream sugar and remaining butter. Beat in eggs and vanilla. Combine the dry ingredients; add alternately to batter with buttermilk, mixing well after each addition. Carefully pour over the pineapple.

Bake at 350° for 40 minutes for skillet (50-60 minutes for baking pan) or until a toothpick inserted near the center comes out clean. Immediately invert onto serving platter. **Yield:** 12 servings.

Bake at 425° for 10 minutes. Reduce heat to 350°; bake 50 minutes longer or until crust is golden brown and filling is bubbly. **Yield:** 6-8 servings.

PEANUT BUTTER CHOCOLATE CAKE

In our chocolate-loving house, this cake disappears very quickly! Cream cheese and peanut butter combine to create a finger-licking-good frosting.
—Dorcas Yoder, Weyers Cave, Virginia

  2 **cups all-purpose flour**
  2 **cups sugar**
2/3 **cup baking cocoa**
  2 **teaspoons baking soda**
  1 **teaspoon baking powder**
1/2 **teaspoon salt**
  2 **eggs**
  1 **cup milk**
2/3 **cup vegetable oil**
  1 **teaspoon vanilla extract**
  1 **cup brewed coffee, room temperature**
PEANUT BUTTER FROSTING:
  1 **package (3 ounces) cream cheese, softened**
1/4 **cup creamy peanut butter**
  2 **cups confectioners' sugar**
  2 **tablespoons milk**
1/2 **teaspoon vanilla extract**
Miniature semisweet chocolate chips, optional

In a mixing bowl, combine dry ingredients. Add eggs, milk, oil and vanilla; beat for 2 minutes. Stir in coffee (batter will be thin). Pour into a greased 13-in. x 9-in. x 2-in. baking pan. Bake at 350° for 35-40 minutes or until a toothpick inserted near the center comes out clean. Cool completely on a wire rack.

For frosting, beat the cream cheese and peanut butter in a mixing bowl until smooth. Beat in sugar, milk and vanilla. Spread over cake. Sprinkle with chocolate chips if desired. Store in the refrigerator. **Yield:** 12-16 servings.

CRANBERRY APPLE PIE

(Pictured above)

New England is a prime apple- and cranberry-growing region. This recipe combines those fruits in a heavenly pie that family and friends request time and again.
—Betty Winberg, Nashua, New Hampshire

  2 **cups sugar**
1/4 **cup cornstarch**
1/4 **cup orange juice**
1/2 **teaspoon ground cinnamon**
1/2 **teaspoon apple pie spice**
1/8 **teaspoon ground nutmeg**
1/4 **teaspoon lemon juice**
  4 **cups sliced peeled tart apples**
  2 **cups fresh *or* frozen cranberries**
Pastry for double-crust pie (9 inches)
  2 **tablespoons butter**

In a large bowl, combine the first seven ingredients. Add apples and cranberries; toss gently. Line a 9-in. pie plate with bottom pastry. Add filling; dot with butter. Roll the remaining pastry to fit top of pie. Cut vents in pastry, using a small apple cutter if desired. Place over filling; seal and flute the edges.

MAPLE PECAN PIE

(Pictured at right)

Our Vermont maple syrup can't be beat, and I like to use it in a variety of recipes. This maple-flavored pie is easy to make and one of my favorites.
—*Mildred Wescom, Belvidere, Vermont*

      3 eggs
  1/2 cup sugar
      1 cup maple syrup
      3 tablespoons butter, melted
  1/2 teaspoon vanilla extract
  1/4 teaspoon salt
      1 cup pecan halves
      1 unbaked pastry shell (9 inches)

In a bowl, whisk eggs and sugar until smooth. Add maple syrup, butter, vanilla, salt and pecans. Pour into pastry shell. Bake at 375° for 40-45 minutes or until a knife inserted near the center comes out clean. Cool on a wire rack for 1 hour. Store in the refrigerator. **Yield:** 8 servings.

LEMON POPPY SEED CAKE

I complete this luscious cake by brushing on sweetened lemon juice and dusting it with confectioners' sugar.
—*Brenda Wood, Egbert, Ontario*

      1 package (18-1/4 ounces) lemon cake mix
      1 package (3.4 ounces) instant lemon
          pudding mix
  3/4 cup warm water
  1/2 cup vegetable oil
      4 eggs
      1 teaspoon lemon extract
      1 teaspoon almond extract
  1/3 cup poppy seeds
  1/2 cup confectioners' sugar
Juice of 1 lemon
Additional confectioners' sugar, optional

In a mixing bowl, combine cake and pudding mixes. Add the water, oil, eggs and extracts. Beat for 30 seconds on low speed. Beat for 3 minutes on medium speed. Stir in poppy seeds. Pour into a greased 12-cup fluted tube pan.

Bake at 350° for 50-60 minutes or until a toothpick inserted near the center comes out clean. Cool in pan 10 minutes before inverting cake onto a serving plate. Combine the confectioners' sugar and lemon juice; brush over the warm cake. Cool. Dust with additional confectioners' sugar if desired. **Yield:** 12-16 servings.

"Call it a clan, call it a network, call it a tribe, call it a family. Whatever you call it, whoever you are, you need one."
—Jane Howard

creamed mixture and beat until smooth.

Pour batter into a greased 9-in. x 5-in. x 3-in. loaf pan. Push the apple slices vertically into batter, placing them close together. Bake at 300° for 1 hour and 40 minutes or until a toothpick inserted near the center comes out clean. Cool for 10 minutes on a wire rack. Remove from the pan. Serve warm. **Yield:** 10-12 servings.

SWEET POTATO PIE

I've been preparing this glazed pecan-topped pie for so long that I can't recall exactly when I started! My family absolutely loves the combination of ingredients in this old-fashioned dessert.
—Anita Ammerman, Albemarle, North Carolina

1-1/2 cups sugar
   2 tablespoons all-purpose flour
   1 can (5 ounces) evaporated milk
   1 egg, lightly beaten
   1 teaspoon vanilla extract
   2 cups mashed cooked sweet potatoes (about 3 potatoes)
   1 unbaked pastry shell (9 inches)
GLAZE:
  1/2 cup sugar
2-1/4 teaspoons all-purpose flour
   2 tablespoons butter, melted
   2 tablespoons evaporated milk
  1/4 cup pecan halves

In a bowl, combine sugar, flour, milk, egg and vanilla. Stir in the sweet potatoes. Pour into pastry shell. For glaze, combine the sugar, flour, butter and milk; drizzle over sweet potato mixture. Garnish with pecans. Cover edges of pastry loosely with foil.

Bake at 375° for 45 minutes. Remove foil; bake 15 minutes longer or until crust is golden brown and a knife inserted near the center comes out clean. **Yield:** 6-8 servings.

DUTCH APPLE CAKE

(Pictured above)

My husband and I came to Canada over 40 years ago from Holland. This traditional Dutch recipe is a family favorite and frequently goes along with me to potluck suppers and other get-togethers.
—Elizabeth Peters, Martintown, Ontario

   3 medium peeled tart apples, sliced 1/4 inch thick (3 cups)
   3 tablespoons plus 1 cup sugar, *divided*
   1 teaspoon ground cinnamon
2/3 cup butter, softened
   4 eggs
   1 teaspoon vanilla extract
   2 cups all-purpose flour
1/8 teaspoon salt

In a bowl, combine the apples, 3 tablespoons sugar and cinnamon; let stand for 1 hour. In a mixing bowl, cream butter and remaining sugar. Add eggs, one at a time, beating well after each. Add vanilla. Combine the flour and salt; gradually add to the

FRUITY BUNDT CAKE

(Pictured below)

Folks who typically don't care for traditional fruitcake will find this white bundt version irresistible. It has such wonderful flavor and holiday color.
—Blanche Whytsell, Arnoldsburg, West Virginia

  1 package (8 ounces) cream cheese, softened
  1 cup butter, softened
1-1/2 cups sugar
  4 eggs
1-1/2 teaspoons vanilla extract
2-1/4 cups cake flour, *divided*
1-1/2 teaspoons baking powder
  1 cup chopped pecans
1-1/2 cups chopped red and green candied cherries
GLAZE:
1-1/2 cups confectioners' sugar
  3 to 4 tablespoons milk
1/2 teaspoon vanilla extract
Pinch salt
Additional candied cherries

In a mixing bowl, beat cream cheese, butter and sugar until fluffy. Add eggs, one at a time, beating well after each addition. Add vanilla. Combine 2 cups of flour and baking powder; gradually beat in-to batter. Combine pecans, cherries and remaining flour; fold into batter. Pour into a greased and floured 10-in. fluted tube pan.

Bake at 325° for 1 hour or until a toothpick comes out clean. Cool 10 minutes; remove from pan to a wire rack to cool completely. Combine confectioners' sugar, milk, vanilla and salt; drizzle over cake. Garnish with cherries. **Yield:** 12-16 servings.

ALMOND MOCHA PIE

I received this recipe from an aunt years ago. The creamy chocolate pie—with a hint of coffee—is nice to have in the freezer for a quick reward on a hectic day.
—Edna Johnson, St. Croix Falls, Wisconsin

  1 teaspoon instant coffee granules
  2 tablespoons boiling water
  1 milk chocolate candy bar with almonds (7 ounces)
  1 carton (8 ounces) frozen whipped topping, thawed
  1 pastry shell (9 inches), baked
Chocolate curls and additional whipped topping, optional

In a small bowl, dissolve coffee in boiling water; set aside. In a microwave or saucepan, melt the candy bar; cool slightly. Fold in half of the whipped topping. Fold in coffee and remaining whipped topping. Pour into pastry shell; freeze.

Remove from the freezer 15 minutes before serving. Garnish with chocolate curls and additional whipped topping if desired. **Yield:** 6-8 servings.

Family-Tested Tip

When making a chocolate cake, coat the pan with baking cocoa instead of white flour. The cocoa works the same as flour but won't leave a white residue on the side of the cake.

—Deb Morrison, Skiatook, Oklahoma

CHOCOLATE ANGEL CAKE

(Pictured below)

*My dear mother-in-law taught me her specialty—
making the lightest of angel food cakes ever.*
—Joyce Shiffler, Manitou Springs, Colorado

1-1/2 cups confectioners' sugar
   1 cup cake flour
  1/4 cup baking cocoa
1-1/2 cups egg whites (about 10 eggs)
1-1/2 teaspoons cream of tartar
  1/2 teaspoon salt
   1 cup sugar
FROSTING:
1-1/2 cups heavy whipping cream
  1/2 cup sugar
  1/4 cup baking cocoa
  1/2 teaspoon salt
  1/2 teaspoon vanilla extract
Chocolate leaves *or* curls, optional

Sift together confectioners' sugar, flour and cocoa three times; set aside. In a mixing bowl, beat egg whites, cream of tartar and salt until soft peaks form. Add sugar, 2 tablespoons at a time, beating until stiff peaks form. Gradually fold in cocoa mixture, about a fourth at a time.

Spoon the batter into an ungreased 10-in. tube pan. Carefully run a metal spatula or knife through batter to remove air pockets. Bake on lowest oven rack at 375° for 35-40 minutes or until the top springs back when lightly touched and cracks feel dry. Immediately invert pan; cool completely. Run a knife around edges and center tube to loosen; remove cake.

In a mixing bowl, combine the first five frosting ingredients; cover and chill for 1 hour. Beat until stiff peaks form. Spread the frosting over the top and sides of the cake. Store in the refrigerator. Garnish with chocolate leaves or curls if desired. **Yield:** 12-16 servings.

HOT WATER GINGERBREAD

With a dollop of whipped topping, this nicely spiced, made-from-scratch cake is such a comforting and homey treat. It's also easy to prepare. The batter and yummy topping come together in a snap, and then I just pop it in the oven.
—Marjorie Green, South Haven, Michigan

   1 cup all-purpose flour
  1/2 cup sugar
   1 teaspoon salt
   1 teaspoon ground ginger
  1/2 teaspoon baking soda
   1 egg
  1/2 cup molasses
  1/2 cup hot water
   1 tablespoon butter, softened
TOPPING:
   2 tablespoons sugar
   2 teaspoons ground cinnamon
Whipped topping

Combine flour, sugar, salt, ginger and baking soda; set aside. In a mixing bowl, beat egg, molasses, water and butter until smooth. Gradually add dry ingredients; beat for 1 minute. Pour into a greased 8-in. square baking pan. Combine the sugar and cinnamon; sprinkle evenly over gingerbread.

Bake at 350° for 25 minutes or until a toothpick inserted near the center comes out clean. Cool completely before cutting. Top each square with whipped topping. **Yield:** 9 servings.

STRAWBERRY MERINGUE PIE

(Pictured above right)

This decadent dessert is simple, impressive-looking and perfect for just about any occasion.
—Kathleen Mercier, Orrington, Maine

1/3 **cup finely crushed saltines (about 12 crackers),** *divided*
3 **egg whites**
1/4 **teaspoon cream of tartar**
1/8 **teaspoon salt**
1 **cup sugar**
1 **teaspoon vanilla extract**
1/2 **cup chopped pecans, toasted**
1 **package (4 ounces) German sweet chocolate**
2 **tablespoons butter**
1 **cup heavy whipping cream**
2 **tablespoons confectioners' sugar**
4 **cups fresh strawberries, halved**

Sprinkle 2 tablespoons of cracker crumbs into a greased 9-in. pie plate. In a mixing bowl, beat egg whites, cream of tartar and salt until soft peaks form. Gradually add sugar and continue beating until stiff peaks form. Fold in vanilla, pecans and remaining cracker crumbs.

Spread meringue onto the bottom and up the sides of the prepared pan. Bake at 300° for 45 minutes. Turn off oven and do not open door; let cool in oven overnight.

In a small saucepan over low heat, melt choco-late and butter, stirring constantly. Drizzle over shell. Let stand at least 15 minutes or until set. Top with berries. Whip cream and confectioners' sugar until soft peaks form; spoon over berries. **Yield:** 6-8 servings.

PINEAPPLE LIME PIE

I've served this cool, refreshing citrus pie to family and guests many times over the years.
—Mrs. Herbert Fischer, Melbourne, Florida

1 **can (14 ounces) sweetened condensed milk**
1/2 **cup lime juice**
1 **can (8 ounces) crushed pineapple, drained**
2 **to 3 drops green food coloring, optional**
1 **pastry shell (9 inches), baked** *or* **1 graham cracker crust (9 inches)**
1 **cup heavy whipping cream**
2 **tablespoons sugar**
Shaved semisweet chocolate, optional

In a bowl, combine milk, lime juice and pineapple. Stir in food coloring if desired. Spoon into crust. In a small mixing bowl, beat cream until stiff peaks form; beat in sugar, 1 tablespoon at a time. Spoon over filling. Sprinkle with chocolate if desired. Chill for at least 8 hours. **Yield:** 6-8 servings.

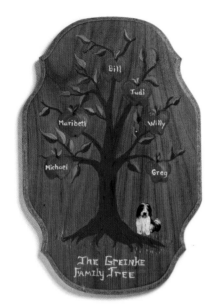

The Greinke Family Tree

Chapter twelve

Whether arranged on a Christmas goodie tray

or packed inside lunch sacks, favorite cookies

and candies are special treats for everyone in the

family. These winning recipes for luscious fudge,

classic cookies, crowd-pleasing brownies and more

are guaranteed to make sweet tooths smile.

Chunky Blond Brownies
(Recipe on page 258)

♥ Cookies & Candies

CHUNKY BLOND BROWNIES

(Pictured on page 257)

Every bite of these chewy blond brownies is packed with nuts and chunks of white and semisweet chocolate.
—*Rosemary Dreiske, Keldron, South Dakota*

1/2 cup butter, softened
3/4 cup sugar
3/4 cup packed brown sugar
  2 eggs
  2 teaspoons vanilla extract
1-1/2 cups all-purpose flour
  1 teaspoon baking powder
1/2 teaspoon salt
  1 cup vanilla *or* white chips
  1 cup semisweet chocolate chunks
  1 jar (3-1/2 ounces) macadamia nuts
    or 3/4 cup blanched almonds,
    chopped, *divided*

In a mixing bowl, cream butter and sugars. Add eggs and vanilla; mix well. Combine flour, baking powder and salt; add to creamed mixture and mix well. Stir in vanilla chips, chocolate chunks and 1/2 cup nuts.

Spoon into a greased 13-in. x 9-in. x 2-in. baking pan; spread to evenly cover bottom of pan. Sprinkle with the remaining nuts. Bake at 350° for 25-30 minutes or until golden brown. Cool on a wire rack. **Yield:** 2 dozen.

BLACK 'N' WHITE CHEESECAKE BARS

(Pictured at right)

Whenever it's my turn to make dessert for an event, I get requests for these scrumptious bars.
—*Bertille Cooper, St. Inigoes, Maryland*

2 cups (12 ounces) semisweet chocolate chips

1/2 cup butter
  2 cups graham cracker crumbs
  1 package (8 ounces) cream cheese, softened
  1 can (14 ounces) sweetened condensed milk
  1 egg
  1 teaspoon vanilla extract

In a double boiler or microwave, melt chocolate chips and butter, stirring occasionally. Stir in the graham cracker crumbs. Set aside 1/4 cup for topping. Press the remaining crumbs into an ungreased 13-in. x 9-in. x 2-in. baking pan.

In a mixing bowl, beat cream cheese until smooth. Gradually beat in milk, egg and vanilla. Pour over the crust. Sprinkle with the reserved crumbs. Bake at 325° for 25-30 minutes or until lightly browned. Cool. Refrigerate 3 hours or until completely chilled. Cut into bars. Store in the refrigerator. **Yield:** 4 dozen.

ORANGE CHOCOLATE MELTAWAYS

(Pictured at right)

The terrific combination of chocolate and orange makes these some of the best truffles I've ever tasted. I don't have a lot of time to cook, but when I do get in the kitchen, I like to try "fancy" recipes. In this case, "fancy" doesn't have to be difficult.
—Lori Kostecki, Wausau, Wisconsin

  1 package (11-1/2 ounces) milk chocolate chips
  1 cup (6 ounces) semisweet chocolate chips
3/4 cup heavy whipping cream
  1 teaspoon grated orange peel
2-1/2 teaspoons orange extract
1-1/2 cups finely chopped toasted pecans
COATING:
  1 cup (6 ounces) milk chocolate chips
  2 tablespoons shortening

Place chocolate chips in a mixing bowl; set aside. In a saucepan, bring cream and orange peel to a gentle boil; immediately pour over chips. Let stand for 1 minute; whisk until smooth. Add the extract. Cover and chill for 35 minutes or until mixture begins to thicken.

Beat for 10-15 seconds or just until the mixture lightens in color (do not overbeat). Spoon rounded teaspoonfuls of the mixture onto waxed paper-lined baking sheets. Cover and chill for 5 minutes. Gently shape into balls; roll half of the balls in chopped pecans.

In a microwave or double boiler, melt the chocolate and shortening; stir until smooth. Dip the remaining half of balls in the chocolate. Place on waxed paper to harden. Store in the refrigerator. **Yield:** 6 dozen.

PEANUT BUTTER 'N' JELLY COOKIES

This classic combination makes a great sandwich cookie. Both children and adults enjoy these treats.
—Margaret Wilson, Moreno Valley, California

1/2 cup shortening
1/2 cup peanut butter
1/2 cup sugar
1/2 cup packed brown sugar
  1 egg
1-1/4 cups all-purpose flour
3/4 teaspoon baking soda
1/2 teaspoon baking powder
1/4 teaspoon salt
Jam *or* jelly

In a mixing bowl, cream shortening, peanut butter and sugars. Beat in egg. Combine dry ingredients; gradually add to creamed mixture. Cover and chill for 1 hour. Roll into 1-in. balls; place 2 in. apart on greased baking sheets. Flatten slightly.

Bake at 375° for 10 minutes or until golden brown. Cool on wire racks. Spread jam on the bottom of half of the cookies; top with remaining cookies. **Yield:** about 4-1/2 dozen.

APPLE SNACK SQUARES

(Pictured above)

As soon as I was old enough to stand on a chair, I started cooking. This recipe came from my sister-in-law. The nutty squares get gobbled up quickly at our large family gatherings.
—Julia Quintrell, Sumerco, West Virginia

2	cups sugar
2	eggs
3/4	cup vegetable oil
2-1/2	cups self-rising flour
1	teaspoon ground cinnamon
3	cups diced peeled tart apples
1	cup chopped walnuts
3/4	cup butterscotch chips

In a bowl, combine sugar, eggs and oil; mix well. Stir in flour and cinnamon (batter will be thick). Stir in apples and nuts. Spread into a greased 13-in. x 9-in. x 2-in. baking pan. Sprinkle with chips. Bake at 350° for 35-40 minutes or until golden and a toothpick inserted near the center comes out clean. Cool before cutting. **Yield:** 2 dozen.

Editor's Note: As a substitute for *each* cup of self-rising flour, place 1-1/2 teaspoons of baking powder and 1/2 teaspoon of salt in a measuring cup. Add all-purpose flour to equal 1 cup.

FAVORITE CHOCOLATE COOKIES

These crispy cookies, studded with white chocolate, are my husband's absolute favorite. I often double the recipe and freeze half of the dough so I can bake a warm batch in a jiffy later.
—Selena Redel, Consort, Alberta

   1 cup butter, softened
1-1/2 cups sugar
   2 eggs
   2 teaspoons vanilla extract
   2 cups all-purpose flour
 2/3 cup baking cocoa
 3/4 teaspoon baking soda
 1/4 teaspoon salt
   1 package (10 to 12 ounces) vanilla *or* white chips
 1/2 cup chopped pecans, optional

In a mixing bowl, cream butter and sugar. Add the eggs, one at a time, beating well after each addition. Beat in vanilla. Combine the flour, cocoa, baking soda and salt; gradually add to creamed mixture. Stir in chips and pecans if desired.

Drop by tablespoonfuls 2 in. apart onto ungreased baking sheets. Bake at 350° for 10-12 minutes or until set. Remove to wire racks to cool. **Yield:** 4-1/2 dozen.

BANANA OATMEAL COOKIES

To help interest my kids in cooking, I started with this recipe from my childhood. My mom made these cookies when I was young. Now my children like them as much as I did, and we quadruple the recipe to serve our large family. You can't eat just one of these delicious goodies packed with chocolate and banana flavor.
—Jacqueline Wilson, Armstrong Creek, Wisconsin

1-1/2 cups all-purpose flour
   1 cup sugar
   1 teaspoon salt
 1/2 teaspoon baking soda
 1/2 teaspoon ground cinnamon
 1/4 teaspoon ground nutmeg
 3/4 cup butter, softened
   1 egg
   1 cup mashed ripe bananas (about 2)
1-3/4 cups quick-cooking oats
   1 cup (6 ounces) semisweet chocolate chips
 1/2 cup chopped walnuts

In a mixing bowl, combine the first six ingredients; beat in butter until mixture resembles coarse crumbs. Add egg, bananas and oats; mix well. Stir in chips and nuts.

Drop by tablespoonfuls onto greased baking sheets. Bake at 375° for 13-15 minutes or until golden brown. Cool on wire racks. **Yield:** 4 dozen.

"There is no doubt that it is around the family and the home that all the greatest virtues, the most dominating virtues of human society, are created, strengthened and maintained."
—Winston Churchill

into a greased 13-in. x 9-in. x 2-in. baking pan. Bake at 350° for 10 minutes.

Meanwhile, for filling, combine sugar and flour in a bowl. Whisk in cream and eggs. Stir in the rhubarb. Pour over crust. Bake at 350° for 40-45 minutes or until custard is set. Cool.

For topping, beat cream cheese, sugar and vanilla until smooth; fold in whipped cream. Spread over top. Cover and chill. Cut into bars. Store in the refrigerator. **Yield:** 3 dozen.

JUMBO MOLASSES COOKIES

These gigantic molasses cookies remind me of the wonderful ones my grandmother used to make years ago. At nearly 4 inches across, they're nicely spiced, delightfully chewy and bound to be noticed.
—Joan Stull, Titusville, Florida

   3 **cups butter-flavored shortening**
   4 **cups sugar**
   1 **cup molasses**
   4 **eggs**
   8 **cups all-purpose flour**
   2 **tablespoons plus 2 teaspoons baking soda**
   2 **teaspoons ground cinnamon**
   1 **teaspoon salt**
   1 **teaspoon ground cloves**
   1 **teaspoon ground ginger**
Additional sugar

In a large mixing bowl, cream shortening and sugar. Add molasses and eggs; mix well. Combine the flour, baking soda, cinnamon, salt, cloves and ginger; gradually add to creamed mixture. Cover and refrigerate for 1-2 hours.

Shape 1/4 cupfuls of dough into balls; roll in sugar. Place four cookies on a greased baking sheet at a time. Bake at 350° for 18-20 minutes or until edges are set. Remove to wire racks to cool. **Yield:** 3-1/2 dozen.

Editor's Note: In order to fit the ingredients in a large mixing bowl, prepare half of the recipe at a time.

RHUBARB CUSTARD BARS

(Pictured above)

Once people try these rich gooey bars, they often ask for the recipe. They love the shortbread-like crust, rhubarb filling and cream cheese topping.
—Shari Roach, South Milwaukee, Wisconsin

   2 **cups all-purpose flour**
1/4 **cup sugar**
   1 **cup cold butter**
FILLING:
   2 **cups sugar**
   7 **tablespoons all-purpose flour**
   1 **cup heavy whipping cream**
   3 **eggs, beaten**
   5 **cups finely chopped fresh *or* frozen rhubarb, thawed and drained**
TOPPING:
   2 **packages (3 ounces *each*) cream cheese, softened**
1/2 **cup sugar**
1/2 **teaspoon vanilla extract**
   1 **cup heavy whipping cream, whipped**

In a bowl, combine flour and sugar; cut in butter until the mixture resembles coarse crumbs. Press

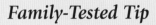

Family-Tested Tip

When making bar cookies such as oatmeal layer bars or marshmallow treats, use waxed paper to press the mixture into the pan. This produces an even layer and keeps your hands clean.

—*Laura Johnson, Largo, Florida*

1 cup butter, softened
1 cup sugar
1 cup confectioners' sugar
1 cup vegetable oil
2 eggs
1 teaspoon almond extract
3-1/2 cups all-purpose flour
1 cup whole wheat flour
1 teaspoon baking soda
1 teaspoon cream of tartar
1 teaspoon salt
2 cups chopped almonds
1 package (6 ounces) English toffee bits
Additional sugar

In a mixing bowl, cream butter and sugars. Add oil, eggs and extract; mix well. Combine flours, baking soda, cream of tartar and salt; gradually add to the creamed mixture. Stir in almonds and toffee bits.

Shape into 1-in. balls; roll in sugar. Place on ungreased baking sheets; flatten with a fork. Bake at 350° for 12-14 minutes or until lightly browned. **Yield:** about 12 dozen.

CASHEW BRITTLE

I like this quick-and-easy recipe because it doesn't require a candy thermometer. It also makes a great gift.
—Rhonda Glenn, Prince Frederick, Maryland

1 cup sugar
1/2 cup light corn syrup
1 to 1-1/2 cups salted cashew halves
1 teaspoon butter
1 teaspoon baking soda
1 teaspoon vanilla extract

In a microwave-safe bowl, combine the sugar and corn syrup. Microwave, uncovered, on high for 4 minutes; stir. Heat 3 minutes longer. Stir in cashews and butter. Microwave on high for 30-60 seconds or until mixture turns a light amber (mixture will be very hot). Quickly stir in baking soda and vanilla until light and foamy. Immediately pour onto a greased baking sheet and spread with a metal spatula. Chill for 20 minutes or until set; break into small pieces. Store in an airtight container. **Yield:** 3/4 pound.

Editor's Note: This recipe was tested in an 850-watt microwave.

TOFFEE ALMOND SANDIES

(Pictured at right)

Crisp and loaded with goodies, these are my husband's favorite cookies. I make them for our grandchildren, too.
—Alice Kahnk, Kennard, Nebraska

OAT-RAGEOUS CHOCOLATE CHIP COOKIES

(Pictured below)

My aunt gave me this recipe, which my family considers a real treat. We enjoy many different kinds of cookies, and this chock-full variety is like getting three of our favorites in one.
—Jaymie Noble, Kalamazoo, Michigan

1/2 cup butter, softened
1/2 cup creamy peanut butter
1/2 cup sugar
1/3 cup packed brown sugar
  1 egg
1/2 teaspoon vanilla extract
  1 cup all-purpose flour
1/2 cup quick-cooking oats
  1 teaspoon baking soda
1/4 teaspoon salt
  1 cup (6 ounces) semisweet chocolate
    chips

In a mixing bowl, cream butter, peanut butter and sugars; beat in egg and vanilla. Combine flour, oats, baking soda and salt. Add to the creamed mixture and mix well. Stir in chocolate chips. Drop by rounded teaspoonfuls onto ungreased baking sheets. Bake at 350° for 10-12 minutes or until lightly browned. **Yield:** about 3 dozen.

MOM'S BUTTERMILK COOKIES

This was my mother's recipe for comforting "cookie pillows," which may explain why they're such a wonderful bedtime snack. The tender treats are dressed up with thick frosting and a sprinkling of chopped walnuts.
—Jane Darling, Simi Valley, California

1/2 cup butter, softened
  1 cup sugar
  1 egg
  1 teaspoon vanilla extract
2-1/2 cups all-purpose flour
1/2 teaspoon baking soda
1/2 teaspoon salt
1/2 cup buttermilk
FROSTING:
  3 tablespoons butter, softened
3-1/2 cups confectioners' sugar
1/4 cup milk
  1 teaspoon vanilla extract
1/2 cup finely chopped walnuts, optional

In a mixing bowl, cream butter and sugar until light and fluffy. Beat in egg and vanilla. Combine flour, baking soda and salt; add to the creamed mixture alternately with buttermilk and mix well. Drop by rounded tablespoonfuls 2 in. apart onto greased baking sheets. Bake at 375° for 10-12 minutes or until edges are lightly browned. Remove to wire racks to cool.

For the frosting, combine butter, confectioners' sugar, milk and vanilla in a mixing bowl; beat until smooth. Frost the cookies; sprinkle with chopped walnuts if desired. **Yield:** 3 dozen.

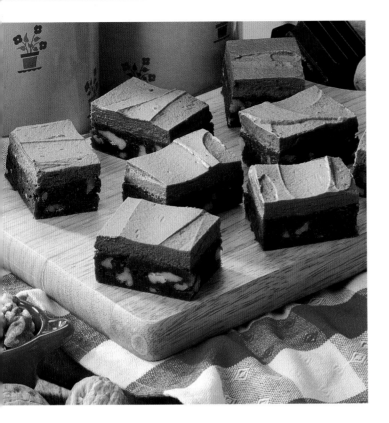

In a microwave or double boiler, melt chocolate and butter; cool for 10 minutes. Add sugar; mix well. Stir in eggs and vanilla. Add flour; mix well. Stir in walnuts.

Line a 13-in. x 9-in. x 2-in. baking pan with foil and grease the foil. Pour batter into pan. Bake at 350° for 25-30 minutes or until a toothpick inserted near the center comes out with moist crumbs (do not overbake). Cool completely.

For the topping, melt the chocolate chips, water and butter in a microwave or double boiler; stir until smooth. Cool to room temperature. Fold in whipped cream. Spread topping over the brownies. Chill before cutting. Store leftovers in the refrigerator. **Yield:** 3 dozen.

VERY CHOCOLATE BROWNIES

(Pictured above)

I think this may be the perfect brownie recipe. The mouth-watering bars are topped off with a fluffy chocolate-cream layer that's absolutely heavenly.
—Arlene Kay Butler, Ogden, Utah

   4 squares (1 ounce *each*) unsweetened chocolate
3/4 cup butter
   2 cups sugar
   3 eggs
   1 teaspoon vanilla extract
   1 cup all-purpose flour
   1 cup coarsely chopped walnuts
TOPPING:
   1 cup (6 ounces) semisweet chocolate chips
1/4 cup water
   2 tablespoons butter
   1 cup heavy whipping cream, whipped

LEMON BARS

This recipe is from my mother's file. I've been serving these wonderfully tangy bars for years. They're a nice addition to a platter of cookies when you want a variety of colors, shapes and flavors.
—Etta Soucy, Mesa, Arizona

   1 cup all-purpose flour
1/2 cup butter, softened
1/4 cup confectioners' sugar
FILLING:
   2 eggs
   1 cup sugar
   2 tablespoons all-purpose flour
1/2 teaspoon baking powder
   2 tablespoons lemon juice
   1 teaspoon grated lemon peel
Additional confectioners' sugar

Combine the first three ingredients; pat into an ungreased 8-in. square baking pan. Bake at 350° for 20 minutes. Meanwhile, beat eggs in a mixing bowl. Add sugar, flour, baking powder, lemon juice and peel; beat until frothy. Pour over the crust. Bake at 350° for 25 minutes or until light golden brown. Cool. Dust with confectioners' sugar. **Yield:** 9 servings.

ALMOND BUTTER CUTOUTS

(Pictured at right)

Ground almonds spread festive flavor throughout these cookies. My grandchildren love to dress them up with colored sugar or frosting. They're a nice change from traditional butter cookies.
—Edie DeSpain, Logan, Utah

1 cup butter, softened
1 cup sugar
2 egg yolks
1 teaspoon almond extract
2 cups all-purpose flour
1/2 teaspoon salt
1/2 teaspoon baking powder
1 cup ground almonds
Colored sugar and frosting, optional

In a mixing bowl, cream butter and sugar. Beat in egg yolks and extract. Combine flour, salt and baking powder; gradually add to creamed mixture. Stir in ground almonds. Cover and chill at least 2 hours.

Roll out on a lightly floured surface to 3/8-in. thickness. Cut with cookie cutters; place on ungreased baking sheets. Sprinkle with sugar if desired. Bake at 375° for 10-13 minutes or until the edges begin to brown. Cool on wire racks. Frost if desired. **Yield:** 3-4 dozen.

RASPBERRY SWIRLS

(Pictured at right)

My mother-in-law shared the recipe for these old-fashioned cookies. The swirls of raspberry jam give them a yummy Yuletide twist.
—Marcia Hostetter, Canton, New York

1 cup butter, softened
2 cups sugar
2 eggs
1 teaspoon vanilla extract
1/2 teaspoon lemon extract
3-3/4 cups all-purpose flour

2 teaspoons baking powder
1 teaspoon salt
1 jar (12 ounces) seedless raspberry jam
1 cup flaked coconut
1/2 cup chopped pecans

In a mixing bowl, cream the butter and sugar. Add the eggs and extracts; mix well. Combine the flour, baking powder and salt; add to creamed mixture and mix well. Cover and chill the dough for at least 2 hours.

Divide dough in half. On a lightly floured surface, roll each half into a 12-in. x 9-in. rectangle. Combine jam, coconut and pecans; spread over rectangles. Carefully roll up, starting with the long end, into a tight jelly roll. Wrap in plastic wrap. Refrigerate overnight or freeze for 2-3 hours.

Cut the roll into 1/4-in. slices; place on greased baking sheets. Bake at 375° for 10-12 minutes or until lightly browned. Cool cookies on wire racks. **Yield:** 8 dozen.

S'MORE CLUSTERS

Children love to help break up the chocolate bars and graham crackers for these irresistible treats. They taste just like s'mores but don't have the gooey mess.
—Kathy Schmittler, Sterling Heights, Michigan

6 milk chocolate candy bars (1.55 ounces *each*), broken into pieces
1-1/2 teaspoons vegetable oil
2 cups miniature marshmallows
8 whole graham crackers, broken into bite-size pieces

In a large microwave-safe bowl, toss chocolate and oil. Microwave, uncovered, at 50% power for 1-1/2 to 2 minutes or until chocolate is melted, stirring once. Stir in marshmallows and graham crackers. Spoon into paper-lined muffin cups (about 1/3 cup each). Refrigerate for 1 hour or until firm. **Yield:** 1 dozen.

Editor's Note: This recipe was tested in an 850-watt microwave.

PEPPERMINT KISSES

(Pictured at right)

These cookies really melt in your mouth. They're great when you don't want something rich and heavy.
—Lynn Bernstetter, Lake Elmo, Minnesota

  2 **egg whites**
1/8 **teaspoon salt**
1/8 **teaspoon cream of tartar**
1/2 **cup sugar**
  2 **peppermint candy canes (one green, one red), crushed**

In a mixing bowl, beat egg whites until foamy. Add salt and cream of tartar; beat until soft peaks form. Beat in sugar, 1 tablespoon at a time, until stiff and glossy. Spoon meringue into a pastry bag or a resealable plastic bag. If using a plastic bag, cut a 1-in. hole in a corner.

Squeeze 1-1/2-in. kisses of meringue onto ungreased foil-lined baking sheets. Sprinkle half with red crushed candy canes and half with green candy canes. Bake at 225° for 1-1/2 to 2 hours or until dry but not brown. Cool; remove from foil. Store in an airtight container. **Yield:** about 3 dozen.

GOODY-GOODY GUMDROPS

These homemade jewel-toned squares are softer than store-bought gumdrops. But their fantastic flavor has true old-fashioned flair people love.
—SueAnn Bunt, Painted Post, New York

  3 **envelopes unflavored gelatin**
1-1/4 **cups water,** *divided*
1-1/2 **cups sugar**
1/4 **to 1/2 teaspoon peppermint extract**
Green and red food coloring
Additional sugar

In a small bowl, sprinkle gelatin over 1/2 cup water; let stand for 5 minutes. In a saucepan, bring sugar and remaining water to a boil over medium heat, stirring constantly. Add the gelatin; reduce heat. Simmer and stir for 5 minutes. Remove from the heat and stir in extract.

Divide mixture into two bowls; add four drops green food coloring to one bowl and four drops red to the other. Pour into two greased 8-in. x 4-in. x 2-in. loaf pans. Chill 3 hours or until firm.

Loosen edges from pan with a knife; turn onto a sugared board. Cut into 1/2-in. cubes; roll in sugar. Let stand at room temperature, uncovered, for 3-4 hours, turning every hour so all sides dry. Cover and chill. **Yield:** about 1 pound.

Family-Tested Tip

Before starting a recipe that uses a candy thermometer, test your thermometer to ensure successful results. To test it, bring water to a boil—the thermometer should read 212°. Adjust your recipe temperature up or down based on your test.
—Jan Briggs, Greenfield, Wisconsin

FUDGY BUTTONS

Not all of Grandma's recipes are time-consuming—her fast fudge proves it! I'm carrying on her tasty tradition by making these treats for my family. They like the combination of chocolate and peanut butter.
—Ann August, Roscoe, Illinois

2 tablespoons butter
1-1/2 teaspoons baking cocoa
1/2 cup confectioners' sugar
1/2 teaspoon milk
2 tablespoons creamy peanut butter

In a small saucepan, melt the butter; remove from the heat. Add cocoa and mix well. Stir in sugar. Add milk and stir until smooth. Add peanut butter and mix well. Drop by teaspoonfuls onto waxed paper; flatten tops and shape into 1-in. patties. Refrigerate until serving. **Yield:** about 1-1/2 dozen.

SWEET TOOTH TREATS

(Pictured below)

I remember Mom would have these yummy snacks waiting for us kids when we got home from school. Now I whip up these homemade goodies for my husband and our two daughters.
—Tina Jacobs, Wantage, New Jersey

1 cup peanut butter
1/2 cup light corn syrup
1/2 cup confectioners' sugar
1/4 cup flaked coconut
2 cups Cheerios
1 cup (6 ounces) semisweet chocolate chips
1 tablespoon shortening

In a bowl, combine peanut butter, corn syrup, sugar and coconut until blended. Stir in cereal. Shape into 1-1/2-in. balls. In a small saucepan over medium heat, melt chocolate chips and shortening. Dip balls halfway into chocolate; place on waxed paper-lined baking sheets to harden. **Yield:** 2-1/2 dozen.

BLUEBERRY OAT BARS

Oats add crunch to the tasty crust and crumbly topping of these fruity bars. I often bake them for church parties.
—Deena Hubler, Jasper, Indiana

1-1/2 cups all-purpose flour
1-1/2 cups quick-cooking oats
1-1/2 cups sugar, *divided*
1/2 teaspoon baking soda
3/4 cup cold butter
2 cups fresh *or* frozen blueberries
2 tablespoons cornstarch
2 tablespoons lemon juice

In a bowl, combine flour, oats, 1 cup sugar and baking soda. Cut in butter until the mixture resembles coarse crumbs. Reserve 2 cups for topping. Press remaining crumb mixture into a greased 13-in. x 9-in. x 2-in. baking pan; set aside.

In a saucepan, combine blueberries, cornstarch, lemon juice and remaining sugar. Bring to a boil; boil for 2 minutes, stirring constantly. Spread evenly over the crust. Sprinkle with the reserved crumb mixture. Bake at 375° for 25 minutes or until lightly browned. Cool before cutting. **Yield:** 2-1/2 to 3 dozen.

CHOCOLATE MINT WAFERS

(Pictured above)

When my family starts munching on these chocolaty sandwich cookies with a cool mint filling, a batch never lasts very long.
—Annette Esau, Durham, Ontario

2/3 cup butter, softened
1/2 cup sugar
1/2 cup packed brown sugar
1/4 cup milk
  1 egg
  2 cups all-purpose flour
3/4 cup baking cocoa
  1 teaspoon baking powder
1/2 teaspoon baking soda
1/4 teaspoon salt
FILLING:
2-3/4 cups confectioners' sugar
1/4 cup half-and-half cream
1/4 teaspoon peppermint extract
1/4 teaspoon salt
Green food coloring

In a mixing bowl, cream butter and sugars. Add milk and egg; mix well. Combine dry ingredients; gradually add to creamed mixture and mix well. Cover and chill 2 hours or until firm. Roll chilled dough on a floured surface to 1/8-in. thickness. Cut with a 1-1/2-in. cookie cutter and place 1 in. apart on greased baking sheets.

Bake at 375° for 5-6 minutes or until edges are lightly browned. Remove to wire racks to cool completely. Combine filling ingredients; spread on half of the cookies and top with another cookie. **Yield:** about 7-1/2 dozen.

CINNAMON ROCK CANDY

(Pictured below right)

My mother made this hard cinnamon candy many times for us when we were kids. Now I fix it for my own family and give it as gifts at Christmas.
—Marganne Winter Oxley, Klamath Falls, Oregon

  1 cup water
3-3/4 cups sugar
1-1/4 cups light corn syrup
  1 teaspoon red liquid food coloring
  1 teaspoon cinnamon oil
1/3 cup confectioners' sugar

Line a 15-in. x 10-in. x 1-in. baking pan with foil; butter the foil and set aside. In a large heavy saucepan, combine water, sugar, corn syrup and food coloring. Bring to a boil over medium heat, stirring occasionally. Cover and cook for 3 minutes to dissolve sugar crystals.

Uncover; cook on medium-high heat, without stirring, until a candy thermometer reads 300° (hard-crack stage), about 25 minutes. Remove from the heat; stir in cinnamon oil (keep face away from mixture as odor is very strong). Immediately pour onto prepared pan. Cool completely, about 45 minutes.

Break the candy into pieces using the edge of a metal mallet. Sprinkle both sides of candy with confectioners' sugar. Store in airtight containers. **Yield:** about 2 pounds.

Editor's Note: Cinnamon oil can be found in some pharmacies or at kitchen and cake decorating supply stores.

SPRITZ COOKIES

(Pictured below)

These almond-flavored cookies are great for the holiday season. They can be left plain or decorated with colored sugar and frosting. In our house, it just wouldn't be Christmas without them.
—Tanya Hart, Muncie, Indiana

1	cup butter, softened
1/2	cup sugar
1/2	cup packed brown sugar
1	egg
1/2	teaspoon almond extract
1/2	teaspoon vanilla extract
2-1/2	cups all-purpose flour
1/4	teaspoon baking soda
1/4	teaspoon salt

Green and red colored sugar, chopped candied
  cherries and red frosting, optional

In a mixing bowl, cream the butter and sugars. Beat in the egg and extracts. Combine the flour, baking soda and salt; gradually add to the creamed mixture. Using a cookie press fitted with the disk of your choice, press dough 2 in. apart onto ungreased baking sheets. Sprinkle with colored sugar if desired. Bake at 375° for 7-9 minutes or until the edges just begin to brown. Immediately add cherries if desired, lightly pressing onto cookies. Cool on wire racks. Decorate with frosting if desired. **Yield:** about 7 dozen.

into two 10-in. logs. Discard the waxed paper. Wrap logs in plastic wrap and chill for 4 hours. Remove the plastic wrap. Cut the logs into 1/2-in. slices. Store in an airtight container in the refrigerator. **Yield:** about 4 dozen.

Editor's Note: This recipe was tested in an 850-watt microwave.

CARAMEL NUT CANDY

(Pictured above)

You can stir up a batch of these coconut-coated peanut caramel logs in no time because they're made in the microwave. Both of my sons-in-law rate these as their favorite homemade candies.
—*Adaline Crabtree, Silverdale, Washington*

28 caramels
1/4 cup butter
2 tablespoons half-and-half cream
1-1/2 cups confectioners' sugar
1 cup salted peanuts
2 cups miniature marshmallows
1 to 2 cups flaked coconut

Place caramels, butter and cream in a 2-qt. microwave-safe dish. Microwave, uncovered, on medium for 2 minutes; stir. Microwave 1-2 minutes more, stirring every minute, until smooth. Stir in sugar until smooth. Add peanuts. Gently fold in marshmallows.

Sprinkle the coconut in a 10-in. x 5-in. strip onto two sheets of waxed paper; spoon the caramel mixture down the center of coconut. Using the waxed paper, coat caramel with coconut and roll

CHOCOLATE COCONUT BARS

With a layer of coconut, these sweet chocolaty treats have a taste that's similar to a Mounds candy bar.
—*Sharon Skildum, Maple Grove, Minnesota*

2 cups graham cracker crumbs
1/2 cup butter, melted
1/4 cup sugar
2 cups flaked coconut
1 can (14 ounces) sweetened condensed milk
1/2 cup chopped pecans
1 plain chocolate candy bar (7 ounces)
2 tablespoons creamy peanut butter

Combine the crumbs, butter and sugar. Press into a greased 13-in. x 9-in. x 2-in. baking pan. Bake at 350° for 10 minutes. Meanwhile, in a bowl, combine coconut, milk and pecans; spread over the crust. Bake at 350° for 15 minutes; cool completely. In a small saucepan, melt the candy bar and peanut butter over low heat; spread over bars. Cool until set. **Yield:** about 3 dozen.

PEANUT BUTTER FUDGE

(Pictured at right)

My sister shared the recipe for this unbelievably easy confection. I prefer using creamy peanut butter, but the chunky style works just as well.
—Mrs. Kenneth Rummel, Linglestown, Pennsylvania

  2 cups sugar
1/2 cup milk
1-1/3 cups peanut butter
  1 jar (7 ounces) marshmallow creme

In a saucepan, bring sugar and milk to a boil; boil for 3 minutes. Add peanut butter and marshmallow creme; mix well. Quickly pour into a buttered 8-in. square pan; chill until set. Cut into squares. **Yield:** 3-4 dozen.

CRISP GINGERBREAD CUTOUTS

My grandsons started cooking by helping their grandpa mix up waffle and pancake batter. They also liked to make these nicely spiced cookies, which are fun to decorate with raisins and candies.
—Shelia Hanauer, Reidsville, North Carolina

1/2 cup shortening
1/2 cup sugar
1/2 cup molasses
  1 egg
2-1/4 cups all-purpose flour
1-1/2 teaspoons ground cinnamon
  1 teaspoon baking powder
  1 teaspoon ground ginger
  1 teaspoon ground cloves
1/2 teaspoon ground nutmeg
1/2 teaspoon baking soda
1/2 teaspoon salt
Raisins, halved
Red-hot candies

In a mixing bowl, cream shortening and sugar. Add molasses and egg; mix well. Combine dry ingredients; add to creamed mixture and mix well (dough will be soft). Cover and refrigerate for 1 hour.

On a lightly floured surface, roll dough to 1/8-in. thickness. Cut with a floured 2-1/2-in. gingerbread cookie cutter and place on greased baking sheets. Add raisins for eyes and red-hots for buttons. Bake at 350° for 8-10 minutes or until the edges are lightly browned. Remove to wire racks to cool. **Yield:** about 4-1/2 dozen.

"The family is the country of the heart."
—Giuseppe Mazzini

CARAMEL PEANUT BARS

(Pictured at right)

With chocolate, peanuts and caramel between golden oat and crumb layers, these bars are very popular. They taste like candy bars but have homemade goodness.
—Ardyce Piehl, Wisconsin Dells, Wisconsin

1-1/2 cups quick-cooking oats
1-1/2 cups all-purpose flour
1-1/4 cups packed brown sugar
  3/4 teaspoon baking soda
  1/4 teaspoon salt
  3/4 cup butter, melted
    1 package (14 ounces) caramels
  1/2 cup heavy whipping cream
1-1/2 cups (9 ounces) semisweet chocolate
     chips
  3/4 cup chopped peanuts

In a bowl, combine the first five ingredients; stir in butter. Set aside 1 cup for topping. Press the remaining mixture into a greased 13-in. x 9-in. x 2-in. baking pan. Bake at 350° for 10 minutes or until lightly browned.

Meanwhile, combine caramels and cream in a heavy saucepan or microwave-safe bowl. Cook over low heat or microwave until melted, stirring often. Sprinkle chocolate chips and peanuts over the crust; top with the caramel mixture. Sprinkle with reserved oat mixture. Bake for 15-20 minutes or until topping is golden brown. Cool completely before cutting. **Yield:** 3 dozen.

Family-Tested Tip

Make extra cookie dough, spoon dollops of it onto waxed paper and freeze them solid. Then put them in a freezer bag labeled with the recipe name, baking time and temperature. They can stay in the freezer for up to 4 months, and you can bake the cookies whenever you want a homemade treat.
—Maribeth Edwards, Follansbee, West Virginia

SOFT 'N' CHEWY CARAMELS

This candy was an absolute "must" at our house for Christmas when we were raising our four children. Now I enjoy making special confections like this for our grandchildren.
—Darlene Edinger, Turtle Lake, North Dakota

2 cups sugar
1 cup light corn syrup
2 cups half-and-half cream, *divided*
1 cup butter
1 teaspoon vanilla extract

Line a 13-in. x 9-in. x 2-in. pan with foil; butter the foil. Set aside. Combine sugar, corn syrup and 1 cup cream in a 5-qt. saucepan or Dutch oven; bring to a boil over medium heat, stirring constantly. Slowly stir in remaining cream. Cook over medium heat until a candy thermometer reads 250° (hardball stage), stirring frequently.

Remove from the heat; stir in butter and vanilla until well mixed, about 5 minutes. Pour into prepared pan. Cool. Remove foil from pan; cut candy into 1-in. squares. Wrap individually in waxed paper; twist ends. **Yield:** 9-10 dozen (2 pounds).

GOLDEN RAISIN COOKIES

Since my children are grown, I make these buttery cookies for the neighborhood kids. They say they know when I'm baking because the aroma carries out to the street.
—Isabel Podeszwa, Lakewood, New Jersey

          1 cup butter, softened
     1-1/2 cups sugar
          1 tablespoon lemon juice
          2 eggs
     3-1/2 cups all-purpose flour
     1-1/2 teaspoons cream of tartar
     1-1/2 teaspoons baking soda
          1 package (15 ounces) golden raisins
             (2-1/2 cups)

In a mixing bowl, cream butter and sugar. Add lemon juice and eggs. Combine dry ingredients; gradually add to creamed mixture. Stir in raisins. Roll into 1-in. balls. Place on greased baking sheets; flatten with a floured fork. Bake at 400° for 8-10 minutes or until lightly browned. **Yield:** about 6 dozen.

SOUR CREAM BISCOTTI

(Pictured at right)

I received this recipe from my uncle's mother. These crisp traditional cookies are perfect for dunking in milk, coffee or hot chocolate.
—Anna Ciraco, Hawthorne, New York

          1 cup butter, softened
          1 cup sugar
          2 eggs
        1/2 cup sour cream
     1-1/2 teaspoons almond *or* vanilla extract
     3-1/2 cups all-purpose flour
     1-1/2 teaspoons baking powder
          1 teaspoon baking soda

In a mixing bowl, cream butter and sugar. Add the eggs, one at a time, beating well after each addition. Stir in sour cream and extract. Combine dry ingredients; add to creamed mixture.

Line two baking sheets with foil; grease the foil. Divide the dough into thirds. On a floured surface, shape the dough into three 8-in. x 2-1/2-in. x 3/4-in. loaves; place loaves on foil. Bake at 350° for 25 minutes or until golden. Remove from the oven. Lift the loaves with foil onto a wire rack; cool for 15 minutes.

Place loaves on a cutting board; using a serrated knife, slice diagonally 3/4 in. thick. Place slices, cut side down, on ungreased baking sheets. Bake at 350° for 8-10 minutes or until golden. Turn cookies over; bake 10 minutes longer. Cool on wire racks. Store in an airtight container. **Yield:** about 2-1/2 dozen.

General Recipe Index

This handy index lists every recipe by food category, major ingredient and/or cooking method, so you can easily locate recipes to suit your needs.

Alphabetical Index

This handy index lists every recipe in alphabetical order so you can easily find your favorite recipes.

Metric Equivalents

VOLUME

IMPERIAL	METRIC
⅛ teaspoon	0.5 milliliter
¼ teaspoon	1 milliliter
½ teaspoon	2 milliliters
1 teaspoon	5 milliliters
1 tablespoon (½ fluid ounce)	1 tablespoon (15 milliliters)*
¼ cup (2 fluid ounces)	2 tablespoons (50 milliliters)
⅓ cup (3 fluid ounces)	¼ cup (75 milliliters)
½ cup (4 fluid ounces)	⅓ cup (125 milliliters)
¾ cup (6 fluid ounces)	¾ cup (200 milliliters)
1 cup (8 fluid ounces)	1 cup (250 milliliters)
1 pint (16 fluid ounces)	500 milliliters
1 quart (32 fluid ounces)	1 liter minus 3 tablespoons

*The Australian tablespoon is 20 milliliters,
but the difference is negligible in most recipes.*

TEMPERATURE

IMPERIAL	METRIC
0°F (freezer temperature)	minus 18°C
32°F (temperature water freezes)	0°C
180°F (temperature water simmers)*	82°C
212°F (temperature water boils)*	100°C
250°F (low oven temperature)	120°C
350°F (moderate oven temperature)	180°C
425°F (hot oven temperature)	220°C
500°F (very hot oven temperature)	260°C

At sea level

WEIGHT

IMPERIAL	METRIC
¼ ounce	7 grams
½ ounce	15 grams
¾ ounce	20 grams
1 ounce	30 grams
6 ounces	170 grams
8 ounces (½ pound)	225 grams
12 ounces (¾ pound)	340 grams
16 ounces (1 pound)	450 grams
35 ounces (2 ¼ pounds)	1 kilogram

BAKING PAN SIZES

IMPERIAL	METRIC
8 x 1½-inch round cake pan	20 x 5-centimeter cake tin
9 x 1½-inch round cake pan	23 x 5-centimeter cake tin
11 x 7 x 1½-inch baking pan	28 x 18 x 4-centimeter baking tin
13 x 9 x 2-inch baking pan	30 x 20 x 3-centimeter baking tin
15 x 10 x 1-inch baking pan (jelly-roll pan)	38 x 25 x 2.5-centimeter baking tin (Swiss-roll tin)
9 x 5 x 3-inch loaf pan	25 x 7.5-centimeter loaf tin in Canada
	19 x 12 x 9-centimeter loaf tin in Australia
9-inch pie plate	23 x 3-centimeter pie plate
7- or 8-inch springform pan or loose-bottom tin	20-centimeter springform tin
10-inch tube or Bundt pan	26-centimeter (15-cup capacity) ring tin

NOTE: *Pan sizes vary between manufacturers, so use this list as an approximate guide only. Always use the nearest equivalent available.*

LENGTH

IMPERIAL	METRIC
½ inch	12 millimeters
1 inch	2.5 centimeters
6 inches	15 centimeters
12 inches (1 foot)	30 centimeters